George Victor Le Vaux

The Science and Art of Teaching

The Principles and Practice of Education

George Victor Le Vaux

The Science and Art of Teaching
The Principles and Practice of Education

ISBN/EAN: 9783337004972

Printed in Europe, USA, Canada, Australia, Japan

Cover: Foto ©Thomas Meinert / pixelio.de

More available books at **www.hansebooks.com**

THE SCIENCE AND ART

OF

TEACHING:

OR, THE

PRINCIPLES AND PRACTICE OF EDUCATION.

BY

GEORGE VICTOR LE VAUX,

*Member of the Royal College of Preceptors, London, England; Author of
"The Twin Records of Creation," &c., &c.*

WITH AN

INTRODUCTORY ETHNOLOGICAL ESSAY,

BY

THE REV. GEORGE BELL, LL.D.

Queen's University, Kingston.

TORONTO:

COPP, CLARK & CO., 47 FRONT STREET.

1875.

IN MEMORIAM

PREFACE.

Our design in preparing the following work was to furnish Student-Teachers, and others engaged in education, with a Manual containing a comprehensive resume, within a moderate compass, of all the more important principles and details of their Profession. In the execution of this task we have endeavoured to combine brevity with clearness, so that our mode of expression might be as simple and direct as was consistent with the nature of the subject.

Several of the succeeding chapters have appeared from time to time in the English and Irish Educational Papers, some in the *American Educational Monthly,* and some in the Ontario *Journal of Education.* Those published in the old country, having secured the kind commendations of the London press, were reproduced in the *Journal of Education* for the Province of Victoria (Australia) and received with much favour by our fellow-labourers in the antipodes. These chapters (with others which appear in print for the first time) are now presented in book form, with the hope that they may to some extent fill a place, hitherto void, in our native educational literature, and thereby help to promote the interests of the young by reflecting mental light and youthful happiness into some of the darker and less attractive shades of the school-room. In years to come we hope to see the prejudices and moral weaknesses of present educational systems supplanted by the reign of light, love, and intelligence; so that children, at home and abroad, may be emancipated from the thraldom of fear, and educated according to the teachings of Nature and the laws of their being.

Believing it to be the duty of all who write for others to ascertain what their predecessors have thought and said on the same or similar subjects, we have perused with interest, in this and other lands, such educational works as have stood the test of time and popular criticism; so that while advancing our own theories by the force of concurrent sentiments, we have been enabled to present our readers with radiant gems from many authors. In some cases we have adopted the thoughts of others, diverting them into more practical channels, but in no instance have we recommended anything not authorized by experience—personal or otherwise. If we have receded in any point from that which is generally received and believed, it has been done in a spirit of amendment and in accordance with the advancement of modern science—not for the purpose of novelty or change. We might therefore say, in the words of Lord Bacon, that "we could not be true or constant to the subject we handle were we not willing to go beyond others; but yet not more willing than to have others go beyond us again."

The intelligent practice of the Art of Teaching must be founded on, and inferred from, experimental science—mental and physical. Keeping this in view we have based our conclusions on the laws of mental development (as we understand them), endeavouring, so far as our limits would permit, to evolve guiding principles from the latest science. We are conscious that many generations must elapse ere the philosophy of mind is so thoroughly understood as to ensure a rich professional success to every teacher who seeks it; nevertheless, each of us can give more attention to the laws of psychology and the right interpretation of Nature, and thus help to introduce and make perfect such a scheme of culture as will hasten the advent of light, and finally establish the Profession on a broad, scientific, and ever enduring basis.

In conclusion, we respectfully beg to submit our views on these matters to the kind and courteous consideration of the Profession and general public, hoping that their publication may not be altogether fruitless nor profitless.

The Author avails himself of this opportunity of recording his grateful sense of the valuable aid given him, in the revision of this work, by his esteemed friend, Miss Jane S. Chadwick—a lady whose educational labours, extending over more than quarter of a century, have reflected honour and dignity on the profession, whilst affording such an example of zeal, skill, and ability, as justly to entitle her to rank as one of the premier teachers of the Province.

G. V. L.

CLIFTON, NIAGARA FALLS,
    20th October, 1875.

ANALYTICAL TABLE OF CONTENTS.

PART I.—FIRST PRINCIPLES.

INTRODUCTORY ETHNOLOGICAL ESSAY.

CHAPTER I.

PRELIMINARY OBSERVATIONS.

CHAPTER II.

RESPONSIBILITIES OF THE TEACHER.

CHAPTER V.

SCHOOL GOVERNMENT.

SECTION 1. THE MINOR PUNISHMENTS.

SECTION 2. CORPORAL PUNISHMENT.

SECTION 3. MUTUAL DUTIES AND RECIPROCAL RELATIONS OF TEACHERS.

PART III.—METHODS OF TEACHING.

PART IV.

APPENDIX.

INTRODUCTORY ETHNOLOGICAL ESSAY.

To appreciate the real significance of questions of education, attention must be turned to the material to be acted upon—namely, the human being. To educate a human being is to draw out or develop all his powers or faculties. To ascertain what these are in our own race of the human species, we require to make a comparison between it and other races. As man is found in races differing so much in bodily peculiarities and mental powers, many questions have arisen both as to his origin and his history. Into the question of unity or plurality of origin I do not enter; but to another question, whether man's history, in civilization, has been an ascent or a descent, we must give a passing notice. All nations have certain traditions as to their early condition, and scientific inquiry brings out many important suggestions. Two pictures of primeval man are drawn, differing very materially. One is of a being pure, happy, simple in his tastes, but free from the degradations usually found in savage life. By many this is regarded only as a dream of poetry, or a beautiful myth, or, it may be, the mere yearning of the human soul for something better than is already possessed, reflected back into the dim mythical region of pre-historic time. The other is of a coarse and filthy savage, gross in tastes and habits, warring with the wild animals, tearing their flesh and cracking their bones, dwelling in caves, and little advanced above the lower animals, except in the superiority which the possession of hands gave him. While the superior weight of evidence, at present, is certainly on the side of man's descent to barbarism, much may be urged on the other side, and doubtless some portions of both pictures are true. Scripture, tradition and

2

science all point to the origin of man at a central part of the land of the eastern hemisphere, whence successive waves of population have been continually flowing towards the distant portions of the earth, the more debased races occupying the positions more distant from the centre, and the debased races being gradually and continuously exterminated before the succeeding waves of a superior race.

Without noticing minutely the many subdivisions of races, we may observe that there are three great divisions plainly distinguishable, popularly known as the white, yellow, and black races. The black or negro race, comprising the Negroes proper, the Bushmen, the Hottentots, and the Papuans, differ among themselves, but in their native countries have always remained barbarous, displaying little tendency to improvement, and very little educational capacity. Wanting in energy and perseverance, they show great sensitiveness. Below the white race in intellect, they are superior in imagination, and, when brought into contact with elevating influences, they will doubtless awake to a life of superior sentimental and imaginative power.

The yellow or Mongolian race has shown peculiar powers in the way of overrunning the territories of other peoples, founding great empires, developing an early civilization which reaches a medium stage and then becomes stationary. The names of Attila, Tamerlane, and Genghis Khan, will at once suggest their warlike roving habits, while the condition of Japan, China, Siam and the American Indians will indicate their unprogressive nature. This race, although so capable of conquest, and of founding mighty empires, is singularly devoid of inventive genius and improvement. They have depopulated fair and flourishing lands, but have not re-peopled them. They have servilely copied the architecture of their forefathers, or of the people they have conquered. The history of their progress has been ever the same; the Scythian invasion recorded by Herodotus, or the march of Tamerlane, alike leaves traces of bloodshed and devastation in a desert, without any great work of any kind as a monument of their power or skill. Were the Mongolian race swept from the face of the earth, they would leave but faint traces of their former existence, having no laws, no literature, no art to which, particularly, their name has been attached.

As they are in civilization, so are they in educational peculiarities. China well illustrates this similarity. At a very early period this country appears to have risen to a certain stage in education, and then to have remained stationary in the use of an artificial and stereotyped system. The regulations, not originally devised by Confucius twenty-four centuries ago, but, as he himself states, only revised from ancient ages, and formally reduced to system, were admirable for the age in which he lived, but they are unsuitable for the present time; yet they are rigidly adhered to. The education obtained has a great many grades, the higher grades opening the way to the possession of the civil offices of the Government. Throughout, the instruction in schools and colleges consists, to a large extent, of reading, writing, a little arithmetic, and a great deal of memorising of lists of names and events, and recitation and chanting of long passages from text books, the sense of which is little understood by the student.

The Caucasian or white race is that in which the highest development has taken place, both intellectually and educationally. The name Caucasian not being considered distinctive enough, that of Iranian has been applied to it, as Turanian to the Mongolian race. The Caucasian race occupies the central part of the old world, Western Asia extending as far as Hindostan, Northern Africa, the whole of Europe, and a considerable portion of America. The complexion is fair in the temperate and cold regions, becoming brown in those which are hot; and the cheeks are tinged with red; while greater variety of features prevails in this race than in any other. This race embraces many subdivisions, differing materially from each other. These may primarily be divided into two groups, separated by marked peculiarities, known as the Shemitic and Indo-European races. The name Syro-Arabian has been suggested as an improvement on Shemitic, and the name Aryan is now very properly applied as the designation of those branches of the Caucasian race formerly called Indo-European, or Indo-Germanic.

The Syro-Arabian or Shemitic race of men are distinguished for brilliant imagination, ready conception of idea, and repugnance to any constraint, whether of intellect or of person. They possess imagination in the highest degree. They have an intuitive conception of the beautiful, whether in idea or in material form, but have no idea of natural beauty being subjected to constraining rules. Their poetry is distinguished by spontaneous, beautiful figures; and in their mechanical works they naturally produce the most beautiful forms. The poor and ignorant Arab, who never heard of a rule or standard of beauty, moulds an earthenware jar for a drinking vessel in a form in which may be traced the most elegant vases of Greece and Rome, and identical with that sculptured by his refined and luxurious ancestors on the monuments of Nineveh three thousand years ago; and his speech consists of glowing words, expressing fanciful but appropriate figures. These qualities are innate, and not the result of cultivation.

The Aryan race do not possess the power in a high degree of *conceiving* beautiful forms, but they readily *perceive* the beauty of that which is presented to them. They readily adopt from others those beauties which they have never themselves invented. They investigate the cause of the idea of beauty, and by analysis and reasoning reduce it to first principles, on which they found rules. Then by the application of these rules, they modify and improve what they have borrowed from others. Deficient in imagination as compared with the Shemitic race, they are vastly superior in reasoning powers; hence their superiority both in a national point of view and in the advancement of art. One of the Shemitic race invents, or rather intuitively conceives, a beautiful architectural ornament, and there stops. The Greek takes up the ornament so furnished, and which he would not have invented; he investigates the reason why it is beautiful; and stops not until he has developed a system of beauty in architectural structure and ornament, which, commending itself to the æsthetic sense of mankind, must continue for ever to be pleasing.

From the peculiar characteristics of the Shemitic branches of the human family, we may naturally infer that they would be earnestly desirous of education, not perhaps for the highest intellectual development, but for the culture of imagination and the development of a taste for the fine arts, in a somewhat rude and primitive form. Such, as history informs us, was actually the case. On the fertile plains watered by the Tigris, the Euphrates and the Nile, the very dawn of history shows us wealthy and prosperous empires in the full possession of a written language, a class of men devoted to the cultivation and advancement of literature and science, and already an extensive knowledge of astronomy, geometry, chemistry, medicine, architecture, painting, sculpture and other decorative arts, music, the working of metals, gems and ivory, and the application of many of these arts to the uses of public and domestic life. Commerce and navigation soon followed the development of home art. In later days, especially in the times of the Ptolemies, Egypt was renowned for its schools of science, philosophy and literature, and for the formation of vast libraries.

The Hebrew nation, although comparatively small as a branch of the Shemitic race, has filled a very large place in history. Under special favouring circumstances of Divine Providence they attained to a high place in literature and science. No literature of any age or nation can compare, for beauty and grandeur, with the book of Psalms, and many parts of the books of the Prophets. Solomon, apparently without the addition to his education of foreign travel, was yet a prodigy of learning. Science and the useful arts flourished in a high degree during the time of the Hebrew monarchy; the æsthetic and moral, however, being preferred to the intellectual in their training. For the higher training of those who were to fill the important civil and ecclesiastical offices, collegiate schools were provided, under the name of "Schools of the Prophets." At a later period the Rabbinical schools, in both east and west, exerted a powerful influence on the world during several centuries after the Christian era.

Among the Arabs, in early days, education of an intellectual kind had made little progress, but poetry was highly cultivated; and their history was embalmed in a rude but highly picturesque poetry, which was chanted by their bards. From the days of Mohammed a new impulse was given to the Arab mind, which made it for the next six centuries the leading intellect of the world, and which exerted powerful influences of an educational kind both on that people and also on many other peoples, especially the western nations of Europe. No sooner had the first warlike fervour of the Saracens passed by, and Arabia, Palestine, Persia, part of India, Egypt and Northern Africa been subjected to the faith of Islam, than attention was turned to education. Thousands of schools were opened for elementary instruction, that the Koran might be read by all; and higher schools were instituted for the critical study of the sacred book. Greek and Oriental learning was called in and extensively cultivated, and magnificent libraries were collected at Bagdad, Damascus and other cities. In mathematics—especially algebra and arithmetic—astronomy, grammar, poetry, philosophy, medicine, jurisprudence and natural science, they attained an eminence probably never before reached. During the seven centuries of Moslem power under the Moors of Spain, along with the display of beautiful art in architecture, schools and universities, with rich endowments, able professors, and large and valuable libraries, had sprung up. It is noted that in the reign of Ab-der-rahman III., in the tenth century, there were in Spain seventeen universities and sixty-six public libraries, the celebrated university of Cordova having a library of 600,000 volumes.

In the Oriental colonists of America we find the same peculiarities which are distinctive of the Shemitic race in the old world. Without entering on the disputed question whether the ancient Mexicans were of Phœnician, Hebrew or other origin, there is no doubt of their belonging to the Shemitic race, and, as such, quite distinct from the wandering Indians of Mongolian origin. America had been known to China and Japan, as Fu-sang, thirteen centuries ago; the Atlantis of Plato, the Saturnian continent of Plutarch, and the Meropia of Elian, were not pure myths; there is probably some truth in the accounts of the commerce and colonizing of the Northmen in early times, and of the Welsh colony under Prince Madog, who either originated the Tuscarora tribe or became incorporated with it ; but, after all, the western world was practically unknown to the eastern until the time of Columbus. Then, as a new and unknown people, the Mexicans were found in the use of a written hieroglyphic language, with high attainments in mathematics, architecture, &c., and a superior mental culture. With revolting religious rites there co-existed much refinement of manners, sublimity in the forms of worship, and a strict system of morals. An extraordinary institution among them was a tribunal, called the *Council of Music*, which had jurisdiction over all matters of science and art, and under whose supervision the whole education of the country appears to have been placed. The Peruvians resembled the Mexicans in many respects, but were not so far advanced in education.

The Aryan race (called also Indo-European and Indo-Germanic) is widely diffused in different parts of the world. It established itself in Hindostan three thousand years ago ; very early occupied Persia and Europe, and is in modern times planting itself by colonization in all parts of the world. If we compare the national peculiarities, the religion and the poetry of the ancient Greeks and Romans, the ancient and modern

Teutonic and Celtic nations, the Hindoos and Persians, they may, to a superficial observer, present no similarities, or even very close analogies.   But the profound researches of the last few years, especially in the field of comparative philology and ethnology, have clearly shown their identity of origin and close relation in distinctive characteristics.   Not only do they all possess, in common, the mental and physical peculiarities which distinguish them from the Shemitic race, but their traditions all spring from the same root.   There is a grand parallelism in the myths of all, and the epic poems of India, Persia, Greece, Rome, Germany, England and Norseland, with their variety of life, heroes, wars and conquests, are in reality different versions of the same story ; and varied as these versions are by differences of climate and individual national circumstances, the origin of this story is to be found in the natural phenomena of the world, the course of the seasons of the year, and the alternations of darkness, dawn, light and twilight of the day. The mythology of the Vedic and Homeric poems contains the germs of the stories of Teutonic, Celtic, and Scandinavian folk-lore.   Among the infinite variety of shapes into which this material has been moulded by the poets and story-tellers of Greeks and Latins, Persians and Englishmen, Hindoos, Germans and Norwegians, Icelanders and Danes, Frenchmen and Spaniards, the same common stock may be traced, even to the subtle distinctions of feature and character in the actors and scenes of the great drama of the powers of Nature, which is the theme of all Aryan national poetry.   Distinguished for intellectual power and enterprise, this race are the great builders, manufacturers and merchants of the world.   Their educational characteristics are in accordance with the natural.   Less imaginative than the Shemitic race, their education has less of the æsthetic and poetic, and more of the intellectual development and solid acquirement.

In ancient Greece considerable attention was paid to education, but generally it was more in the way of physical development than intellectual culture. At Athens more attention was paid to intellectual and scientific attainments than at other places. In later days æsthetic and philosophic education became very popular; while under the influence of Socrates, Plato and Aristotle, a great advance was made in rhetoric, logic, ethics and mathematics. In these the schools of Athens and Alexandria became pre-eminent.

In ancient Rome the education, so far as it went, was principally moral and physical, until it came under the influence of the Greek system, which then prevailed, but not so generally as in Greece itself.

As the several nations of Europe emerged from the chaos of the ruins of the Western Empire, schools and colleges began to be founded, and attention was paid to the scholastic philosophy, but there was such profound, general ignorance spread like a dark cloud over society, that little progress was made for some ages. But years rolled on. The awaking time of the Crusades had come and gone, leaving a thirst for new developments of society. There were Oriental visions and longings which increased the vitality of the already awakened spirit of commerce and enterprise. The people of Europe were waking up from the night of the dark ages. The revival of learning was in progress, to which an immense impetus was given by the invention of printing from movable types, and thence proceeded what may be called the modern epoch of progress and development. To the awakening of Europe succeeded the founding of an English-speaking nation in America. There could not have been a better time for such an event than that in which it took place. The seventeenth century was exceedingly rich in moral and intellectual power in England. The Puritan founders of New England were men of gigantic intellect, great learning, deep religious fervour, inflexible moral principle, and quenchless love of liberty, and the deep impress of these elements of national life were inwrought into the early life of the young nation. Hence, freed from many hinderances in the way of progress which were inevitable in Old England, education speedily blossomed and bore abundant fruit in the new. Before the early colonists had comfortable homes to shelter themselves, they reared the church and school-house in each town, that provision for the wants of their spiritual and intellectual life might be in advance of that for their physical life. With extraordinary munificence, in their circumstances, support was provided for free common schools, grammar schools and higher seminaries of learning.

Scotland was the first country in Europe to establish a complete system of parish schools for general instruction, on the principle of the property of all being liable to taxation for the erection of a school-house and teacher's dwelling. It has ample provision for obtaining a superior education, but not for carrying it on to such an extent as can be done in the universities of England. In *England*, at the present time, the means are ample in the universities and great endowed schools, for acquiring the highest grade of education. Owing to ecclesiastical difficulties, England is far behind some other countries in Europe in provision for the education of the masses; but its prospects are improving. *Ireland* is rapidly progressing under the influence of its national system of education, which has outlived the violent opposition of extreme men among both Protestants and Roman Catholics. Established in 1831, it has had the honour of being the basis of our Ontario Public School system, and of furnishing us with masters and other officers for our Provincial Normal School.* Under its influence, the people of Ireland have made rapid progress in education and general intelligence. In *France*, ample provision is made for superior education. If inferior to Germany in classical knowledge, it is superior in mathematical and physical science. Primary education was much neglected until about half a century ago. The efforts of Louis Philippe and Guizot, followed by those of succeeding rulers, have recently

---

* T. J. Robertson, Esq., First Head Master, Provincial Normal School, Toronto; J. G. Hodgins, Esq,. LL. D., Dep. Superint. of Education for Province of Ontario, &c.

developed a very thorough and efficient system of public schools connected with the municipal organization of the country. In *Spain* and *Portugal*, harassed by internal discord, the glory of ancient universities has passed away, and there is no system of public schools of any practical value in existence. In *Italy*, the former States of the Church have ample means of superior education, but are deficient in the elementary department. The former kingdom of Naples is at a low ebb. Sardinia has been since 1848 rapidly advancing so as to occupy a very respectable position. The whole of Italy is likely now to advance with rapid strides in education. *Greece* has, since its independence, made zealous efforts to improve, and has provided a university, superior and primary schools. *Denmark* has for many years maintained a high standard of education. All grades of schools are provided, and the people are well educated. In *Sweden* and *Norway* the sparseness of the population presents a serious difficulty; yet education is general and well conducted. *Germany* in all its States occupies a high educational position, although there is a great difference among them. *Prussia, Saxony* and *Wurtemberg* are celebrated for the thorough organization and general practical usefulness of their systems. *Austria* is somewhat behind Prussia, but is making advancement. *Bavaria, Mecklenburg* and some of the smaller States are not so far advanced.

In the *United States* of America a great difference exists between the Northern and Southern portions, the latter being much inferior to the former. Ample provision has been made for superior education, but as yet it has not reached the high standard of that of Europe. In common and grammar schools the Eastern, Middle and Western States occupy a distinguished position, both in the wide diffusion of elementary education, and in the development of intellectual activity. In *Canada*, we have in Ontario an organization, of which an American writer says that " it is unsurpassed in its results, for attendance

and intellectual progress, by any in the world." The other
Provinces are behind Ontario, but are rapidly improving.

We cannot particularize further, and must turn to some
general considerations. Among all the various branches of
the Aryan race, there is much mingling of sub-varieties. The
result of this is often the production of a character highly conducive to improvement and advancement. For example, the
British race, at home, in the colonies, and in the United
States of America, mingles the patient enduring spirit of the
Saxon, the refined moral perception, grace and politeness of the
Norman, and the fortitude, perseverance and impulsiveness of
the Celt, together with many other peculiarities derived from the
smaller intermingling of Phœnician, Roman, Danish and other
elements. Such a race is pre-eminently fitted for overcoming
difficulties, advancing enterprise, commerce and agriculture,
making improvements, cultivating art and science, and attain-
ing the highest intellectual position which education can aid
in producing.

Closely connected with education are questions of language
and religion. Tracing back language to its earliest records, we
find in the vast drifting desert of human speech, three oases
which have been early formed, and in which, before history
began, language assumed a more stable form. These were the
Turanian, Shemitic and Aryan. In these, language was arrested
and became solid and petrified. In the first it assumed a form
mono-syllabic and agglutinate; in the second, radical; and
in the third, inflectional. And concomitantly with this fixing
of language was the fixing of three independent settlements
of religion. In China, where we have the earliest record of
Turanian speech, we find an ancient, colourless and unpoetical
religion, which may be called mono-syllabic, consisting of the
worship of single spirits, representing the sky, the sun, storms
and lightnings, mountains and rivers, standing side by side, with
nothing to bind them together; also the worship of ancestral
spirits: while above all there towers a lofty range of half reli-

gious, half philosophical faith, a belief in two powers, variously applied, but originally meaning heaven and earth. In the ancient worship of the Shemitic races we find names of God, which appear in the polytheistic religions of the Babylonians, Phœnicians, and Carthaginians, as well as in the mono-theistic creeds of Jews, Christians and Mohammedans. The worship of these nations is a worship of *God in history*—that is, as wielding the destinies of men, races and nations, rather than of the powers of nature. The names applied to God are generally expressive of moral qualities, such as Strong, Exalted, Lord, King. In the ancient worship of the Aryan race, carried to all parts of the earth by its adventurous sons, and which may be easily recognized in the classic remains of Greece and Rome, the valleys of India, or the forests of Germany, by the common names of the Divine Being, these names are expressive of the powers of nature. Their worship is, however, not a worship of nature, but of *God in nature*, as God hidden behind the veil of nature, rather than behind the veil of the human heart. As the races spread, and the true meaning of words was gradually lost, errors crept in; figurative language came to be understood literally; the Divine powers were transferred into many objects of worship; and widespread systems of idolatry gradually became developed. The early worshippers of India, who worshipped the Great Father in heaven, and the supreme power in nature, and even the writers of the Rig-Veda, who were beginning to lose their hold on the Divine, by the multiplication of epithets and names, would be astounded were they to witness the horrors of the durga pujah, the great festival of the goddess Kali, or contemplate the gigantic system of mythology of modern India, the most gorgeously developed and elaborated which the world has seen, with its 330,000,000 idols.

Christianity, by birth a Shemitic religion, has spread most widely among the Aryan race. In Christianity, therefore, we have now the highest blossoming, or rather fruitage, of the whole religious idea or life of both of the great branches of the

Caucasian stock, and the mightiest power on earth for the development of the highest faculties of man. The human mind held by such a power, anchored to communion with its Father in heaven, and thoroughly awakened to research, will speedily overturn and sweep away old superstitions, and build up a solid and enduring structure of religion and learning. Effete creeds, whether religious, scientific or educational, must pass away; and nothing will stand which cannot bear the fullest blaze of light. Our branch of the human race is destined to higher and higher developments, to mightier achievements than the world has yet witnessed, and the highest developing power of education is required that we may fill our destined place on the arena of the world.

The following work has been prepared by an experienced and successful Teacher, and as such, its conclusions are not to be regarded as merely theoretical, but as the results of actual experiment and practice. Mr. Le Vaux has made education, both theoretical and practical, the great study of his life. He has devoted to it the resources of a mind thoroughly trained in a wide range of general scientific knowledge, and a rich acquaintance with human life, derived from extensive travel and observation; to all which he has added the practice of his theories in the actual organization and government of various grades of schools. I can with much pleasure, as well as with much confidence in the soundness of the principles and practice laid down in the book, cordially commend it to the reading public as a valuable addition to the educational literature of the day.

GEORGE BELL, LL.D.

THE SCIENCE AND ART OF TEACHING.

PART I.—FIRST PRINCIPLES.

CHAPTER I.
PRELIMINARY OBSERVATIONS.

Napoleon Bonaparte, while in exile at Elba, was asked Anecdotes of Napoleon and Lincoln. by one of the ladies of his miniature Court if he would be pleased to favour her with his opinion as to "What France needed most?" Placing one hand in his bosom and the other behind his back, the Emperor reflected for a moment, and then, looking earnestly at his fair companion, he replied—in his usual grave and emphatic style—"*Mothers.*" Abraham Lincoln's answer to a similar question, though not so laconic, was equally suggestive. An English friend who had an interview with Mr. Lincoln the day preceding his assassination, after congratulating him on the apparent advent of peace, took the liberty of asking "What he conceived to be the best prescription for restoring order and prosperity in the prostrate South?" No threatening words or angry reproaches escaped the lips of the venerable President. The loving parent of a disobedient family, he was ever ready "to kill the fatted calf" and to receive "the penitent prodigal" to his bosom. While the question was being proposed, he approached one of the windows : feelings of sorrow seemed to agitate his heart ; but after looking out on the clear blue sky for a moment, his mind was cheered with more pleasant ideas, and a smile of benevolence lighted up his countenance. "Mr. B——," said he, "the query you propose is natural under the circumstances. It has engrossed my attention for some time. We must proclaim a liberal amnesty and establish good schools, and then *the best prescription we can offer the South will be efficient teachers.*"

Good mothers and efficient teachers.

Both Napoleon and Lincoln were right. Their conclusion, judged by the light of after events, proves that they thoroughly understood "the situation," and were fully conscious of the great wants of their respective countries. But what was true of France and the Southern States is, to some extent, true of the whole world. Every race and nation need *good mothers*, and every people, whether civilized or barbarous, require *efficient teachers*. Upon these benefactors—mothers and teachers—depend the temporal and spiritual welfare of the present and all future generations. History tells us that all the great nations of antiquity had great mothers and great teachers. Every student knows that those States which had the best mothers and most efficient teachers, always subdued or annexed their less intelligent or less worthy rivals. Recent events in Europe and America point to the same fact. The North overcame the South, because it had more excellent teachers than its rival; or, rather, the South over-indulged its selfish propensities, and rushed into a fratricidal contest, because its people were not sufficiently educated to know their own interests. Then, again, Germany has dismembered France, because the women of "Vaterland" were more excellent wives and mothers than those of Gaul. We feel assured, moreover, that there would have been no war in either case had the mothers and teachers on both sides been equally worthy.

First lessons.

A child's education commences when it first smiles in response to its mother's caresses. It unconsciously receives many lessons from those who listen to or applaud its first efforts to speak.　Children acquire a knowledge of men's character and disposition by indulgence in a natural impulse which impels them to study the human face.　They shrink from the clouded brow, but experience much delight when they perceive by the countenance that they have succeeded in exciting expressions of pleasure in the hearts of their friends.　Feelings of kindness, and perhaps self-satisfaction, induce them to repeat what they believe to have given pleasure.　Though this desire to please is an amiable and praiseworthy quality, it is, nevertheless, liable to many abuses, and should therefore be guided by reason and cultivated with caution.　While giving the child its due meed of praise or approval, we should occasionally direct attention to his errors, and be careful to check egotistical displays.

During the days of infancy, the mother, by her " teachings and influence," instils into the heart or incites in the mind of the child the germs of those characteristics which, in time to come, will distinguish him (or her) from all the world besides.　In after years it becomes the teacher's peculiar province to invigorate those characteristics, and so develop the mental, moral and physical powers as to fix indelibly the noble impressions first made by the dearest and kindest of earthly friends.　It is from mothers alone that children will learn as if by instinct, and in early childhood they are therefore the best of all teachers.　But as time rolls on, and the child merges into the boy, or the boy into the man, the nature of our institutions (in conjunction with domestic or public duties and the want of special teaching skill) compel the parent to delegate his (or her) educational powers and privileges to another.　That other—the teacher, tutor or preceptor—is thus constituted the *locum tenens* of the parent, and becomes forthwith his representative in all scholastic matters ; not the representative of one particular parent, but of *all the parents* whose children are committed to his charge.

Mothers the first teachers.

3

The parental substitute.

It will be seen that the teacher, by reason of his special training and experience, must be far more skilful as an educator than each individual parent could possibly be. In the division of labour of his little community, the educational interests have been committed to his care. He is, for the time being, the common parent of his pupils, and will treat them as if they were really his own children. To be successful in his calling, he must perfectly understand the nature of the materials on which he is to act; he must be acquainted with all the best and most approved methods of teaching, and be expert and skilful in using them; he must sympathize with humanity, and enthusiastically devote himself to his work. His responsibility is much greater than that of any individual parent, inasmuch as his "collective family" is much larger than that of any particular "home circle."

Mutual duties.

The authority of the parent and teacher are patriarchal, and to some extent inseparable. It is the bounden duty of the one to uphold and extend the influence of the other. Their interests are mutual and their hopes similar, if not identical. Children are easily managed when they feel that their parents and teachers understand each other, and work together in harmony and unity for their individual welfare. There should be no "clashing of authority;" parents and teachers must support each other. Anything like antagonism, or doubts and fears, would nullify the labours of both, and engender a tendency to rebellion and obstinacy. This would injure the pupils for time—perhaps for eternity—and prevent them from becoming amiable men and women, good and worthy citizens. Amongst the Greeks and Romans there was no profession so highly honoured as that of the educators of youth; and we understand that the modern Dutch and Germans exhibit a similar appreciation of that useful calling. It will soon be so in every civilized community. Parents are becoming conscious of the fact that if they wish their children to make "the largest amount of progress in the shortest space of time," they must teach them by example to love education and revere educators. "The great mind of the people," says Canning, "is becoming impressed with the idea that no office can compare in dignity, solemnity and public importance with that of the trainer and educator of youth; that skill to fashion the intellects of the young, and ability to lead them in the paths of truth and virtue are worth more than the knowledge of all other arts and sciences together, and that the encouragement of accomplished teachers is therefore the first and noblest duty of every intelligent community." The teacher is the life of the school. Its value, its efficiency, its success, depends on his personal character and professional qualifications. Commissioners and School Corporations may erect beautiful and commodious schools, furnishing them in the most approved style, but such labours will be comparatively fruitless unless the teachers employed be worthy of their vocation. Many of our Public Schools possess well stocked libraries, museums and philosophical apparatus, but these are lifeless and comparatively useless unless made effectual through the living agency of mind; the direct intervention of men, apt to teach, skilful in illustrations and happy in application. A few teachers, eminent in professional knowledge, skilful to understand, quicken, and direct the pupils' minds, are worth more than a whole army of unskilled and inexperienced men, even though favoured with every desirable extraneous aid.

The banker, the merchant, the farmer and the mechanic work on earthly and perishable materials, and by fair means or foul, endeavour to secure a competency, if not to accumulate wealth. How different is the work of the teacher? He works upon the living principle—the immortal mind, and his wealth is seldom of this world. It is his province and privilege to excite, draw out, cherish, develop and build

Education, a noble work.

up the divine fabric of the intellect; to cultivate the finer
feelings of the heart; to influence the morals of his generation;
to promote peace and proclaim the rights of man. His profession is connected with time and eternity—with the present,
past and future; its results are everlasting, its effects indelible. Teaching is a noble work, worthy of the holiest character, of the highest intellect, and of the greatest skill. Ever
foremost in wisdom, piety, and virtue, the literary and other
qualifications of the educator should always be in advance
of the age in which he lives, for great indeed are his responsibilities. He who spake as man never spake, even the Prince
of Life, lived and died as a teacher, and His last words,
"Go and teach all nations," are still ringing in our ears.
The soul, the mind, the materials on which the teacher
labours are everlasting, and said to be the express image of
the Creator. His work is therefore the noblest in which
man can be engaged. Much is required of teachers, but in
the midst of their trials and annoyances let them consider
the dignity and public utility of their calling, and remember
that, unlike the generality of men, they can lift up their
heads at any time and say, "We follow the profession of
the Great Teacher. We also are apostles and co-labourers
with Him who said, 'Suffer little children to come unto
Me and forbid them not, for of such is the kingdom of
God.'"

CHAPTER II.
RESPONSIBILITIES OF THE TEACHER.

Teachers
form the
characters
of their
generation.
Teachers form the character of each succeeding generation.
They cannot fail to transmit their characteristics. They are
sure to leave their impression on the plastic minds of their
pupils. The teacher can move the hearts of the young for
good or evil, just as the evening zephyrs move the leaves of

the forest trees. His acts and words, ideas and precepts are imprinted on their little hearts, as faithfully as the impression of a seal on softened wax. Neither time nor eternity can ever efface these mental impressions. Once made, they remain a blessing or a curse for ever. According as these impressions are good or evil, the pupils in after years emblazon or dim their country's fame, causing it to shine with the brightness of the mid-day sun, or to hide its head in a gloom blacker than Egyptian darkness. The influence of such youthful impressions is experienced at home and abroad in all the events of existence, and—after inciting, encouraging or restraining the child, the youth and the man, through all the varied and transitory scenes of life—they probably accompany the enfranchised spirit into the world beyond the grave, clothing it with peculiar characteristics through all the countless ages of eternity.

In all the avocations of life, there is probably no position in which the responsibilities are so great, nor is there any in which so much real permanent good, or enduring evil, can be done, as in that of the teacher. It is an old and true saying that "example is better than precept." They labour in vain who teach by precept and not by example. As a rule, example should always precede, or accompany precept. The precept should be the expression of the example, as the rule in mathematics is the expression of the principle. The person who does not teach by example is not an educator, and does not deserve success. "Do as I say but not as I do," should never be the motto of the teacher, for of all the powers at his command, that of example (or of setting examples) is the most influential.

Responsibilities.

The habits acquired in school are those which generally characterize the pupils in after life. These characteristics, taken collectively, indicate what the prestige of the nation will be in years to come. In the public school we may see the character of the future nation in embryo, and send it

The habits of pupils an index of their future life.

down to posterity stamped with our imprimatur. How anxiously should we endeavour to fashion it so that it may be admired of man and commended by God. The germs of some characteristics are born with the child; others are instilled into his mind during the days of infancy. When he is transferred to the care of the public teacher they are still in a crude state—ready for training, ripe for extensive development, and it becomes the bounden duty of the educator to cultivate them to their utmost capacity, eliminating the evil, strengthening the good, and faithfully performing every duty to the best of his ability. Successful teaching, like successful preaching, is always accompanied by example. If desirous of success the teacher, like the early preachers of the Gospel, must be a living model of the doctrines he inculcates. There must be no hypocrisy about him—he must be thoroughly in earnest. Every word, deed, and even the expression of his face have their effect for good or evil on the imitative beings committed to his charge.

Power of example, and of youthful impressions.

Example is infectious. It reigns supreme in early youth and childhood, as the imitative powers are then far stronger than reason or judgment. Benjamin West declared that a kiss from his mother had made him a painter; an approving smile from Madame Bonaparte made her illustrious son a soldier and an emperor; a story related by his teacher made Livingston a traveller. So is it in every stage of life; a look, a word, an act, a smile, or a frown, from those we love—from teacher, parent, or friend—may influence our destiny for time and eternity. "A pebble or a few grains of sand often decide whether the rain-drops falling on the crest of the Rocky Mountains shall flow westward to the Pacific Ocean or eastward to the Atlantic."* So is it in life; the most insignificant circumstance affects individual character, and often originates events which decide whether the innocent child is to be a patriotic hero or a "worthless sot"—an angel

---

* Rev. George Bell, LL.D.

or a demon. The influence of youthful impressions being immortal and indelible, it is impossible to calculate the result of their prospective or immediate effects. It is the teacher's peculiar province to make such enduring impressions. Next to parents, no other human being possesses such power for good or evil over the youthful mind. How extremely careful should he be therefore that they may be such as shall be conducive to the welfare of the immortal beings entrusted to his care. "Life is such as we take it and make it, or rather, as it is taken hold of and made for us by those to whom the care of our youthful days is entrusted."* The children of the present will be the fathers, mothers, teachers, authors, lawgivers and rulers of the future. Their character depends on their education, and that depends on our modern educators. Let our teachers then "be up and doing," remembering that they labour for posterity. Recognizing "no standard of superior worth but wisdom, truth, and nobleness of soul," let them commence the exercise of their influence over the young by looking well to their personal example, manner, and general temper—by becoming the right kind of men themselves; not indolent, cold, selfish, cruel or irreverent, but brave, faithful, gentle and self-sacrificing: all the powers of their intellect, all the energies of their hearts and souls being consecrated to their work. Under the light and influence of these aspirations the teacher's enthusiasm will be caught up by his pupils. It is sure to impel them to make such efforts as will deserve, even if they do not ensure, success. Having chosen his sphere, and engendered this laudable spirit amongst his pupils, let him pursue a straightforward course, not deviating therefrom to the right hand or the left, and ere many years elapse he will be sure to discover that there are grander objects of ambition than worldly prosperity or individual wealth. Though his road be dark and slippery at first, it will gradually brighten, and

How to make right impressions.

---

* Nathaniel Sands.

at the further end he shall be met by One who (when his race is run) will welcome him and say—"Well done, thou good and faithful servant. Enter thou into the joy of thy Lord."

To sympa-
thize with
the pupils,
and to seek
their love.
When a teacher takes charge of a school, his first object should be to win the affectionate co-operation of the respective pupils. Should he understand his work and be a good judge of human nature, he will doubtless succeed in doing so at once—otherwise, time will be necessary. In some exceptional cases time will always be requisite. Unless he possess the natural tact or ability to gain their esteem, confidence and affectionate regard, his success, if at all possible, will be very uncertain. If he really loves the children, and be desirous of deserving and winning their confidence and friendship, they will soon reciprocate his feelings. But, as a rule, he must love them ere they love him. They will become conscious of the affectionate interest he takes in their welfare by the kindness of his actions, the urbanity, suavity and earnestness of his manner, the brightness of his looks and the geniality of his disposition towards them in school and out of school. Self-sustaining patience, cheerful perseverance, dignified self-control, warm sympathy and a *real earnest abiding* love for children are essentially necessary in acquiring the love of youthful hearts. When the teacher has won his pupils' love, his ascendancy is established on a sure and lasting foundation. They will feel honoured in receiving his commands, and obey while he is yet speaking. Disobedience will be regarded as a "heinous" offence, and a prompt, cheerful compliance with the teacher's instructions or commands will be considered a high honour—a distinction which each and all will endeavour to acquire. Under such circumstances the work of education is no longer irksome to the teacher or the taught. Teaching becomes a god-like exercise when the pupils of a class, like little birds in a nest, aroused to a just sense of their wants, stretch out

their necks, bend forward their heads, and open wide their mouths to receive what their good friend has provided; when the skilful teacher like a parent bird stands over his little flock, sympathizing with their weakness, carefully dividing his provisions, and feeding them with the same until all their wants are supplied. Win the hearts of your pupils, and you win their prompt and cheerful obedience to all your commands, and their enthusiastic co-operation with all your designs; your rule over their minds will be absolute. You can then say to this one, "Go, and he goeth; to that one, come, and he cometh; and to another, do this, and he doeth it."

It has been well said that "a teacher who would com- Teachers. love your mand success must be an enthusiast in his profession;" and pupils. we would say in addition that he must love his pupils and, in turn, be loved by them. The teacher and the taught must be bound together in bonds of mutual affection. Man is a creature desirous of love and esteem, and therefore finds the greatest charm of existence in the affectionate regard of those around him, whom he has reason to admire for their possession of ordinary and extraordinary qualities, such as gentleness, kindness, honour, truth, sincerity, devotion, prudence, heroism, or forgetfulness of self for the good of others. Be a friend and protector, not a tyrant or task-master, and remember that "No empire is safe, unless it has affection for its basis."* As anger begets anger, so love begets love, and the hearts of the young never fail to reciprocate this god-like feeling. It is not necessary, nor indeed would it be prudent, on the part of the teacher to announce in words the existence of this affection—instinct will inform them of the fact. Teacher, they will read it in your face, and have the assurance of it in the tone of your voice, in your smile, in your manner and in your actions—all of which speak "louder than words." Let your pupils feel

* Racine.

that you *really* care for them, that you take a lively interest in all that concerns them, that you are their sincere and unselfish friend, that you sympathize with them in all their little sorrows, and would gladly share all their little joys; then you will have found the true key to their hearts. Frowns chill the sensitive little hearts of the young, and are frequently reflected back on their source. Those who smile on the innocent face of a child are sure to receive back an "answering smile;" the happy response being an enlarged and improved reflection of the original beaming glance. Smiles are like happy voices in a wooded vale. Their merry musical tones are sure to be reflected back with increased sweetness on those who uttered them. Let us always try to promote the present happiness, as well as the future interests, of our youthful friends.

To teach by example as well as precept. Before concluding this chapter we will take the liberty once more of alluding to the influence of example as an auxiliary in training pupils to act well their parts in the respective spheres of life, so that at last they may become worthy citizens of that bright world beyond the grave.

Educators should always remember that it is imperatively incumbent on them to teach by example. Precept without example has no more effect on the heart of the young than evening zephyrs on the tall grass of the prairie. They may bend their heads for a moment before it, but when the breeze has passed—when the living voice has ceased to speak—its influence is sure to vanish. Example should be the forerunner of precept, and, as a rule, the latter should be deduced from the former. This important principle should be engraven on the hearts of teachers, as their success in a great measure depends on its observance. If, for instance, the teacher be desirous that his pupils should attend to their business in school or elsewhere, he must set them the example by attending to *his*. And here we may remark, that as a public officer he is bound to devote his school hours exclusively to school work. Never should he forget himself so far as to transact extraneous business during those hours which are supposed to be occupied in the discharge of his official duties. Any personal indulgence in this respect is a direct violation of the principles of right and wrong which he, of all others, should never forget or infringe.

CHAPTER III.

THE SPIRIT AND HABITS OF THE TEACHER.

It is the teacher's province to train the finer feelings of the human heart, to develop the latent faculties of immortal beings, to strengthen their weakness, to remove their ignorance; being always careful to equip them with the armour of knowledge and sword of intelligence, that they may be able to hold their own in the great battle of life. It requires time, talent, energy, considerable skill and much experience to make a really good and skilful teacher. Nor are these sufficient. In addition, he must be "a man after God's own heart," kind and affectionate. He must be meek as Moses, patient as Job, zealous as Paul, *slow to anger and apt to teach*. He must have a spirit in him worthy of his noble and useful vocation. In every child, in every human being, he should recognize the handiwork and image of Jehovah. Always alive to the responsibilities of his position, he should possess a soul to which wisdom and science are as the sun and moon. Happen what may, he must cleave to what is right, and abhor everything low, mean, or selfish. In the nature of things, he will be an angel of light, elevating immortal beings to heaven, or an angel of darkness, sinking them to hell. He is a "light set on a hill and cannot be hid." He that would be a good teacher must aim high in his profession.

Things necessary to make a good teacher.

To have a
right per-
ception of
his work.

The great object of the teacher should be to engrave such impressions on the youthful minds of his pupils as will ensure them a happy and useful life. He should have a correct perception of his calling and of the various duties it entails. He must have a thorough knowledge of the logical ability and other requirements necessary for the skilful execution of its obligations, and be duly impressed by its capabilities for good. Otherwise he cannot have a clear conscience nor be possessed of the right teaching spirit. The faithful teacher will always endeavour to adapt his teachings to the nature and disposition of the innocent creatures committed to his charge—having an eye to their temporal welfare and eternal happiness. Of course he cannot absolutely command success; but much will depend on his judgment and personal skill in fashioning their "opening minds"—much also on the quality of the tools employed for that purpose, and the intelligent persistency with which he wields them. Mind is the subject of the teacher. His business is to *educate*. That he may do so effectually he should be perfectly acquainted with the disposition, nature and "surroundings" of his "subject." As a "mental physician," he must have a right conception of the object to be attained in education, and of the best means to be employed to effect his purpose. He must study man before he can teach him—he must thoroughly understand and wholly sympathise with children before he can *educate* them. Bonds of paternal love and brotherly affection should rule in school and out of school, so that, if necessary, every pupil will glory in sacrificing himself to serve his companions.

Candidates
for "Teach-
erships" to
look well to
their mo-
tives.

Teaching being one of the most important of the professions, no one should enter it lightly or without due preparation. Candidates for admission should look well to their motives. *No one is justified in adopting it as a chance vocation—as a mere temporary calling.* Let those who would enter it with a view to making it a stepping stone to something else, halt while yet on the threshhold, and not imitate Balaam of old by persevering in a course they know to be wrong. Let them ponder well over the awful responsibilities they would undertake, remembering that every word passing their lips, and every act performed in school may influence their pupils, individually or collectively, for better or worse, for time and eternity. Let them bear in mind that a time will come when they must "give an account of their stewardship," and not forget that the school is heaven's nursery as well as the world's cradle, and that the teacher's soul—like Jacob's ladder, while resting on the earth and piercing the skies—should lead the minds of the young to comprehend the things of this world and, if possible, guide their hearts to contemplate the glories of the next.

The teacher, being fully impressed with the almost overwhelming importance of his work, should thoroughly understand how his respective duties ought to be performed. His mistakes, be they ever so simple or insignificant, may injure his pupils individually and collectively for all time to come. Ignorance would be no palliation of his blunders. Such a plea would only add to his crime. The mental and moral faculties of "even little children" are too sacred and too precious to be "tampered with" by ignorant persons. Who would accept a plea of ignorance from a physician who, through incompetency or carelessness, had poisoned one of his patients? If such a medical man escaped capital punishment, he would be expelled from society, and no one would ever engage his services again. There are "mental and moral quacks" as well as medical ones. From year to year these gentry continue to murder their pupils' intellects, yet the public do not interfere: *miserly* school trustees engage their services, and illiterate people "believe in cheap teachers." Such 'instructors" may of course do infinitely more mischief than the unskilled or careless physician, inasmuch as the

Ignorance no excuse for professional mistakes.

heart and soul, to which they administer, are of far more value than the body which must ultimately perish. The errors of the physician affect his patients in this world only, but the errors of the blundering teacher will continue to affect his pupils for all eternity. It is the duty of every civilized government to pass a law prohibiting untrained, uncertificated, and unqualified men from practising the profession of teaching, and restraining public school trustees from employing them. This would have been done long ago were it not that such teachers' blunders and shortcomings—unlike those of the physician—seldom produce immediate effects. It is true they may not be visible—they may slumber, or like seed cast into the ground by the sower, they may require time to grow and ripen—but a day will come, in the far distant future perhaps, when the results of unskilful teaching will be clearly manifest. The effects of such teaching are the more pernicious because of uncertain or slow development; and this is why far-seeing people are often more careful in selecting a family teacher than in appointing a family physician.

Physical education. On the teacher, to a great extent, devolves the responsibility of promoting the physical development and of preserving the health of those little ones who are the joy of the present and the hope of the future. It has been said that more than half the deaths occurring between the ages of seven and twenty-one arise from transgressions of the natural laws of health. The seeds of many a lingering disease have certainly been sown at school, and if the teacher would have his pupils enjoy through life "Sound minds in sound bodies," he must see that their physical education is not neglected.

Science of national and self-government. One of the great objects of education is to prepare the rising generation to be good and patriotic citizens. They should, therefore, be instructed in the science of national as well as self-government. The youth of the country should not be left in total ignorance of the duties which will devolve on them when they come to man's estate. They should, at least, be well acquainted with the provision made by their nation for the election of its legislative, judicial and executive officers, and be ever willing cordially to submit to lawful authority. Submission to the laws is one of the primary attributes of good citizenship. Both parents and teachers should carefully "initiate the child into the mysteries of obedience."

The teacher, desirous of being successful in the practice of his profession, must be sure to begin each day aright. He must remember that there is no personal characteristic so attractive as an open countenance, and no quality so amiable as good humour or evenness of disposition. Before entering the school-room he should so regulate his temper and spirit as to be proof against whatever disturbing or disagreeable influences may greet his arrival or come under his notice during the day. Having control over himself he can the more easily control his pupils. Firm in command, strong in will, and pleasant in disposition, he can smile upon his pupils and enter cheerfully on his important work. He will *lead* "the little labourers" instead of driving them, and unconsciously induce them to feel that their work is a pleasant duty and not a disagreeable task. Under the influences of a genial nature, he will thus "allure them" to pursue their studies with profit, and bring them to sympathize with himself and with each other. Under such circumstances they will prefer the society of the class-room to that of the drawing-room; the school will be surrounded with hallowed associations, and "learning lessons" will become a pleasant, if not a delightful duty. Let them be encouraged to grasp the living present with all its energies, fulness and development, and be made familiar with the idea that labour is not only the source of subsistence but the fountain of comfort, wealth and happiness.

After reading this chapter some may ask perhaps, whether the public can honestly expect so much from men in return

To begin each day aright.

An important query.

for a salary of a few hundred dollars a year?—whether we
can hope to find such rare moral and intellectual qualifications in parties who (as the world goes) have to live on
"starvation wages?" We will revert to the subject of remuneration in another place, but in the meantime may be
permitted to say that, the teacher is a mind-builder or a mind-
destroyer whether paid five thousand a year or only five
hundred. If he does not understand the science and art of
his calling he is no more capable of educating one child than
he would be to educate one hundred or more. Of course
there would be a difference in the amount of labour, but
the moral and intellectual qualifications would be the same.
A physician has to spend years in studying his art before
receiving his diploma. This he must do even though he
were afterwards to extend his services to only one patient.
The mental and moral qualifications of teachers should be
equal to, or rather in advance of, those of other professional
men, and they should be paid in proportion to their responsibility, competency, and skill.

Who can be
a teacher?
Others may ask, perhaps, "If these things be so, and that
the responsibilities are so great as you point out, who then
can be a teacher?" Very few indeed can be really good and
great teachers. Nevertheless if a man feel that he has the
right spirit within him, if he be desirous of being instrumental in promoting in the highest degree the welfare of
the rising generation—by elevating and enlarging the capabilities of the human soul, by moulding the feeblest and most
innocent of God's creatures into intelligent and benevolent
"sovereigns of creation"—then, his motives being pure, let
him assume the duties of the office, and enthusiastically
devote his sole attention to his chosen profession. It is
necessary that at all times and seasons he should be in
sympathy with his work, and all that pertains to it. For
without devotion, enthusiasm, and professional sympathy,
though he may be a "school keeper," and be called a "school

teacher," yet he never can be a successful educator—at best he will be but a mere machine. If a man enter the profession, and finds after due trial that he does not possess the qualifications essentially necessary—that in fact he has mistaken his vocation—then for his own sake, and the interests of those committed to his charge, he should immediately "get out of harness" and seek some other calling. If, on the contrary, he have reason to believe that he possesses the essential mental and professional qualifications, then let him persevere unto the end. Let him steer a straightforward course, and having put his hands to the plough, never look back. His devotion will be acceptable to his Creator and his country, and in days to come his reward will be more valuable than any which silver and gold can purchase. Even in this world, he shall have his reward. Superior worth—especially superior knowledge—is always honoured. People cannot long withhold their love and affectionate appreciation from those faithful citizens who devote themselves to the service of humanity, and are ever willing to sacrifice their worldly prospects on the high altar of education.

CHAPTER IV.

CHARACTERISTICS OF THE GOOD TEACHER.

Any person desirous of becoming a successful teacher must possess an extensive knowledge of human nature, more especially that branch of it which relates to children. Cautious and sensible, he must know when to censure and when to praise ; when to rule their passions ; when to guide their affections ; when to repress their animal spirits ; when to direct their attention, and when to govern their ambition. Courtesy of manner, kindness of disposition, and sympathy in feeling, will enable him to rule with almost despotic authority through the influence of mutual esteem and affec-

To be a judge of human nature.

4

tion.   Let him therefore be careful to cultivate these noble
and pleasant characteristics.   If not endowed with the power
of building "a royal road to the temples of learning," (and
few ever were,) he ought, at least, to be able to strew the
way with flowers, and competent to relate the history of
every scene along the route.   His mind should abound with
apt illustrations.   He should be able to awaken the young
idea to a full consciousness of its wants, capabilities and
responsibilities, so that he may stir up or incite to activity
every worthy feeling of the human heart.   To do so effectually
he must be a good judge of child nature, have a thorough
knowledge of the workings of mind under different influences,
and of its expansion and growth under different systems of
training.   An acquaintance with the writings of ancient
philosophers, and with the most approved modern works on
education, will assist him materially in this respect; but, as
a rule, he must rely for success on his own observation and
professional genius or aptitude.

Aptitude for   From what has been said, it will be seen that it is a very
teaching.   difficult thing to be a good teacher; and we have the highest
authority for stating that without being *apt to teach*, it is
impossible to be a successful one.   Integrity of character
and literary or intellectual attainments, though essential,
are as nothing without this divine quality.   Of course these
accomplishments add to the worth of the individual possessing them, but without being *apt to teach*, he cannot efficiently
or effectually transfer them to others—he cannot develop
the mental capacity of pupils, nor impart to them the knowledge accumulated in his mind.   In some persons this *aptness
to teach* is the gift of nature; but in the majority of cases
it is an acquired power—the result of a careful study of
humanity, and of the young heart in particular.

Pupils   We may here remark that a good teacher will never
should be
led to do   decline to lend a helping hand to his pupils when such
everything   assistance *is necessary;* but, on the other hand, he should
for them-
selves.

carefully avoid doing *too much* for them. It is said that young teachers have a tendency to do this from feelings of mistaken kindness, or through ignorance of the child's capacity. A teacher should be careful also not to say more than is necessary on any subject, for, as Kossuth observes, "an unnecessary word is a word too much." Too much may be done *for*, and too much may be said to, the pupil. Both must be avoided. Milk is fit food for babes, and beef for older people. The former are fed with the spoon, but who would attempt to feed the latter in the same way? What man, enjoying the use of his hands, would accept such infantile civilities? None. So is it with the teacher and the taught. There should be no unnecessary nursing—no literary dandling—in the public school or private study. Too much aid is as bad as too little. Pupils should be taught to exercise their own faculties—to depend on their own resources; and, as a rule, the *teacher should never do anything for them that they themselves could do without his assistance.* His great object should be to *lead* them to do everything for themselves. By such practice their intellect will be expanded, their various faculties strengthened, and their self-reliance increased, and they shall grow up to be men and women in the true sense of the word—"sturdy trees," defying the battle and the breeze of life. They will thus learn at an early age that "whatsoever is worth having can only be had by climbing;" that knowledge can only be acquired through honest, well sustained, well directed, personal efforts.

Real courtesy should be a leading characteristic of every teacher—we mean true politeness—that genuine solicitude and earnest attention which spring from benevolence and the well-meaning kindness of a noble heart. This is indispensably necessary to his success. Being cheerful in disposition, kind and courteous towards friends and enemies, he cannot possibly fail in due time to obtain and retain the

Courtesy of manner and other characteristics of the teacher.

esteem and good-will of all—both intelligent and ignorant. In his walks abroad should he meet his pupils (or any of them), he should recognize them courteously—with smiles, not with frowns; with kind and affectionate looks, not with a cold, stern countenance. He should take the earliest opportunity to make the acquaintance of their parents. He cannot cultivate the friendship of all, but he should be sure to greet them cordially whenever he meets them. In public or in private, he should be careful to act so as to merit their esteem. He will thus obtain "a good name," which "is more desirable than great riches." At all events the experiment will cost him nothing; let him give it a trial. It is his duty to teach his pupils politeness by example as well as by precept.

Youth to honour age.

Whilst impressing on their minds the respective claims of superior worth, and pointing out the duties they owe to humanity in general, he should never forget to claim their filial reverence for old age in particular. Let it be a point of etiquette with them—nay, let it be the rule of their daily life—to "rise up before the hoary head and honour the face of the old man."

An anecdote —a Grecian legend.

We may be excused if we digress for a moment to relate an anecdote which will illustrate the spirit of the foregoing quotation—an anecdote exhibiting clearly what we mean by *true* politeness, whilst it affords an example worthy of imitation by the youth of all generations. On a certain memorable occasion, in days gone by, a number of Greeks assembled at an Athenian theatre to see the performance of "a star"—a primitive Shakspeare doubtless. The actor was popular and "drew a crowded house." The Spartan ambassador and his suite happened to be present. They occupied seats opposite those allotted to, or engaged by, the Athenian aristocracy. Before the play commenced, or during one of the intermissions, it happened that an old man— a citizen of Athens—came in. He surveyed the audience for a moment, but though his head was white with the snows of age, and a staff supported his feeble form, yet no one offered him a seat—in truth, there seemed to be no seats vacant. However, the young Athenian aristocrats, seeing his position, resolved to have a joke at his expense. They therefore pretended to make place for him, and made signs inviting him to come amongst them and be seated. He bowed in reply, and walked to the place indicated, but when about to sit down, "the wags" closed on either side and re-occupied the vacant space. They then winked at each other and laughed at the chagrin of the old man. The cheeks of the gallant young Spartans burned with shame and indignation as they observed this rude and insolent "performance," For a moment they gazed at each other in amazement, and *Spartan courtesy.* then, as if moved by one will, every man of them rose and remained standing whilst one of their number went over to the old gentleman, and, bowing reverently, begged permission to conduct him to a seat. The old man complied, and, leaning on the arm of the noble youth, crossed to the other side of the house, where he was cordially received by the ambassador and requested to take *the most honourable* seat. The comfort of the old patriarch being thus secured, the Spartans quietly resumed their seats and turned their attention to the stage.

After a moment's silence, a mighty cheer shook the foundation of the theatre. The audience "were struck by the *Courtesy recognized.* little adventure," and took this method of showing their appreciation of such noble conduct. The gallant Spartans smiled with inward satisfaction, but the rude Athenians, now blushing at their own behaviour, held down their heads with shame. Both parties had received their reward—remorse was the lot of the one, and an approving conscience the glory of the other.

When the cheers had died away, the worthy old gentleman arose and, after thanking the kind "foreigners" for their attention and example, expressed his regret that his fellow-citizens *knowing what was right, did what was wrong;* but that nevertheless, he was glad to find "the Spartans practised what the Athenians knew." Thenceforth Lacedæmonian courtesy was praised in the patriot homes of Greece, and every citizen felt proud of his Spartan countrymen. By that one act these young Spartans set a worthy example to the youth of every generation, and made the world their debtors for time and eternity. Young friends do you approve of their conduct? If so, "Go, and do likewise." Macaulay, referring to this anecdote, writes as follows :

* In Athens, ere its sun of fame had set,
'Midst pomp and show the gazing crowds were met,
Intent for ever upon something new—
The mimic wonders of the stage to view,
The seats were filled, but ere the show began,
A stranger entered—'twas an aged man.
Awhile he sought a place with aspect mild,—
The young Athenians sat and smiled.
How poor the produce of fair learning's tree,
That bears no fruit of sweet humility.
The Spartan youths had their appointed place
Apart from Athen's more distinguished race,
And rose with one accord, intent to prove
To honoured age their duty and their love ;
Nor did a Spartan youth his seat resume
Till the old man found due and fitting room.
Then came the sentence of reproof and praise,
Stamped with the sternness of ancient days ;
For, standing full amidst the assembled crowd,
The venerable stranger cried aloud ;
" The Athenians learn their duty well ; but lo !
The Spartans practise what the Athenians know."
The words were good, and in a virtuous cause—
They quickly earned a nation's glad applause
But *we* have surer words of precept given
In God's own Book—the words that came from Heaven:
" Be kind, be courteous, be all honour shown—
Seek others' welfare rather than thine own."

Amiability of disposition. The teacher's face, like the full moon in an azure sky, should, if possible, be always bright and pleasant-looking. Smiles, like sunbeams, should light up his countenance so

---

* Condensed from original.

that all with whom he comes in contact may, for the time
being at least, be made to feel comfortable and happy.   His
aim should be to "Attract all and repel none."   He must
remember that to teach self-control by example, it is necessary that he should not allow the trials incident to life, and
to his profession, to ruffle his countenance or influence his
actions.   An amiable disposition, a smiling countenance, and
an engaging manner, never fail to warm into life the generous
affections of the human heart, whilst they dispel the moonless
gloom which so frequently besets the paths of both young
and old.   For these reasons, and others too numerous to mention, we should carefully cultivate those agreeable personal
characteristics.

Teachers should be particularly careful never to upbraid
a pupil with his (or her) mental or physical defects.   It is
not consistent with refined feeling or Christian principle to
do so.   On the contrary, his interest *in* and kindness *towards*
such parties should be the more marked in consequence of
these defects.   Children, naturally irritable, selfish or obstinate, like those who are blind and deformed, are objects of
pity and compassion.   They are unfortunate in being subject
to infirmities and misfortunes which can only be overcome
by peculiar management, aided by sympathy and encouragement.   Mental or physical deformities are heavy burdens,
and perpetual censure (besides being useless in itself) only
adds to the crushing weight of these afflictions.   Let children
be assisted in overcoming unpleasant natural peculiarities,
and not abused for the misfortune of having inherited them.
They are naturally weak, and should be treated with extreme
tenderness.   Mental defects and the singularities of manner
peculiar to any pupil should be mentioned to him in private,
and they never should be alluded to in the presence of his
companions.   When addressing a pupil the teacher should
not gaze on, or appear to notice, any physical defects with
which he may be afflicted.   To do so would be inconsistent

Not to up-
braid pupils
with their
mental or
physical
defects.

with gentlemanly feeling, and might be the cause of unnecessary pain. No vulgar jests, no coarseness of language, no disagreeable epithets, and no profanity should ever stain the lips of the teacher. His language should always be pure, accurate and chaste—a model worthy of adoption and imitation by the innocent beings committed to his charge.

Absence of personal kindness.

It has been well said that "Children's happiness depends on the attitude assumed towards them by their comrades more than on anything else in the school, and a great part of the misery which they have to endure is what they inflict on each other. . . . . The chief violations of the spirit of kindness which will come under the teacher's notice are these: a selfish want of sympathy in the misfortunes that befal others; a disobliging spirit, which churlishly refuses to accommodate others . . . want of courtesy in speech and manner; nick-naming, which wounds the feelings of others; the playing of practical jokes to their detriment or inconvenience; tyranny on the part of the strong towards the weak; ridicule of the poor or deformed; and cruelty to animals. Much apparent unkindness amongst children arises from thoughtlessness; they do not consider the consequences of their words or actions, or they have not imagination enough to realize them. . . . The training to kindness consists in the training to considerateness."* The teacher should gradually seek to foster in them the disposition to do good to others independent of its direct consequence to themselves—to do good for the love of doing it; and though he cannot force the development of kindness, he can and should restrain oppression. Pupils should be led to see that the duties of life are mutual, that they should bear with each other's infirmities, and be guided in all things by the word of Him who said: "Whatsoever ye would that men should do unto you even so do unto them."

---

* Currie.

Aristides "the Just," and "Honest" Old Abe of the West, To be honest, just and true. have become household names.   The former title speaks to us of Grecian worth and gratitude ; the latter quaint cognomen expresses the affectionate regard of a great nation for one of her noblest sons.   These are two of the most noble titles that can designate a human being—two of which every teacher should endeavour to be worthy.   Every man and woman should cultivate, and endeavour to unite in themselves, these two characteristics ; but in no person is their combination so necessary as in the teacher.   Strictly just and honest in all his dealings, he should always use the words of truth and soberness ; for if honour, truth and justice were banished from all the world besides, they should find refuge in the heart of the teacher.   It has been said that people gradually grow into the likeness of that upon which they constantly gaze—mental or physical.   For this reason, if for no other, they should carefully foster all the nobler sentiments of the heart by the daily practice of benevolent deeds.   Following the higher instincts of their nature they should surround themselves, so far as possible, with objects calculated to cultivate the taste, elevate the mind, and excite good and pleasurable emotions.   If there be any truth in the foregoing statements (and there is) it follows that the constant "worship" of honesty and justice will secure our happiness in early youth, and crown our old age with wreaths of purity and peace.

"There is (says a learned writer) something very admoni Regularity and punctuality. tory and awe-inspiring in the punctuality of God in His universe and in His providence.   The laughing stars know their courses and rejoice to run them.   The moon, ever true to her seasons, duly observes her time to wax and her time to wane.   The great sun himself never forgets his time to rise, nor his time to set."   Onwards for ever roll the heavenly orbs on high, never a moment late in fulfilling their appointed courses.   Teachers, parents, pupils, friends, let us take a lesson from the works of Nature, and make "Punctuality and Regularity" the rule of our lives. It has been well said that "the standard of a school depends sensitively on the regularity and punctuality of every person in it—but more especially on the regularity and punctuality of its teachers."* A teacher should be regular and punctual in all his dealings and undertakings, no matter what others may be. It behoves him to be a bright example of these virtues not for his own sake alone, but for the sake of those imitative beings committed to his charge. Unless his actions exemplify his precepts, he cannot with propriety insist on their observance by others. He who neglects to practice what he teaches or preaches is, at best, but a recruiting agent for the already numerous army of hypocrites. His tongue says one thing and his actions say another of opposite or different import, so that he is divided against himself, and therefore his teaching "cannot stand." The rules a teacher makes, and the precepts he utters, are as binding on himself as they are on the pupils. The teacher, as well as the taught, must be subject to the common law of the school. If possible he should never be late in his attendance. As a rule, he should arrive at least ten minutes before the time fixed for the commencement of business, and he should dismiss the pupils punctually "when *their* time is up." If he be not regular and punctual himself, how can he insist on others being so? especially when these others are little children. "Method is the hinge of business," and there can be no method without punctuality, and no progress without regularity and continuity of application.

Lord Palmerston's opinion.

The late Viscount Palmerston stated on one occasion to a deputation, comprising some members of the Royal College of Preceptors, that "if there were any class of men who could or should know everything, that class were teachers; for (continued he) they can never know too much." No

* Rev. Dr. Ryerson.

man has known, or ever can know, all the branches of knowledge—at least not in this world. A teacher must be ever on the *qui vive*, always learning, always studying—he can never know enough; or as Palmerston said, "he can never know too much." The first-class teacher should know, or endeavour to know, the whole circle of knowledge; but more especially those branches which are of daily use in his vocation. In the grand march of intellect and science, he should lead instead of being led. Fixing his eye on the star of his country, his great and paramount object should be to train up the youth of his fold, so that they may be good and worthy citizens—an honour to him and a credit to themselves during the long years to come. Such a teacher will be affectionately remembered when lying in his grave. The teacher should always recollect that if he be acquainted with all the branches of knowledge except *one which he should know*, he may be said to be an ignorant man. In order that an edifice may be substantial, the foundation must be sound. A teacher's knowledge of the higher and more advanced subjects may, in many cases, be regarded as an accomplishment; but, in all cases, a thorough knowledge of the elementary branches is absolutely necessary. However, learning alone will not make an efficient teacher, nor enable him to overcome the many difficulties peculiar to his position. As already pointed out, there are sundry other requisites of a personal nature, which, if he does not naturally possess, he must endeavour to acquire—amongst these we must give a prominent place to good sound common sense; a quality which implies the power of looking at things in their ordinary nature and relations, irrespective of their connections or associations with ourselves or our interests.

Teachers to lead in the march of intellect.

Sir Isaac Newton was one of the greatest scholars ever England or any other country produced, yet, during the evening of his life, he repeatedly stated that he appeared to himself as a little child picking pebbles on the shore, whilst

To beware of pride and vanity.

the great and boundless ocean of knowledge and truth spread out unexplored before him. These were the sentiments of a philosopher—of a true christian—of a great and noble, yet a meek and humble, man. Sir Isaac, notwithstanding all his learning, was a mere child in his own eyes—ever ready and anxious to learn more. This should be the spirit of the *true* teacher, and with the false ones we would have no communication. The teacher should avoid self-sufficiency and false pride as he would avoid Satan, and, like Sir Isaac, be ever ready to learn something new—something useful. The wisest man that ever lived—even Solomon himself—was but a mere cadet in knowledge. How therefore can any sensible man be a pedant? too proud to learn more—too vain to profit by the experience of others. Teachers, as a class, should certainly be the best scholars of the age; but if, in consequence of their superior knowledge, they (or any of them) be puffed up with vanity, pedantry, false pride and self-conceit, they are unfit for their calling—unworthy of the name of educators. We cannot see how any human being, not the victim of a diseased imagination, can be guilty of such follies. A teacher should possess a sound mind and a sound body, and by practising such vanities, or pursuing such bubbles, he unintentionally indicates that he is personally conscious of the existence of a defect or imperfection in one or both—whilst he, unconsciously perhaps, degrades himself in the estimation of his fellow-men, and thereby brings contempt on his profession. Learning always endows those who possess it with a certain superiority above their fellows—a superiority which will be duly acknowledged by people in every rank in life, provided it be accompanied with no absurd pretensions or ridiculous airs. Modesty seldom fails to charm. We should never allow self-deception to swamp the faculties of reason and judgment. Be we ever so good or great, still there is ample space for improvement. There is no real or genuine comfort in considering ourselves better than we really are. Let us be blind to our own merits, and leave the perception and appreciation of them to others. All men, at best, are but dust and ashes. In one sense, all had the same beginning, and all will have the same end. It has been well said that "the greatest and best men mentioned in history were the most humble"—the most forgetful of self, and the least given to foolish parade. So it has been, and will be in every age. Humility and personal worth are inseparable.

CHAPTER V.
KNOWLEDGE TO BE REPLENISHED.

The Falls of Niagara would soon cease to exist were the immense lakes above them not regularly replenished by the snows of winter and the surplus waters of the various fountains, streams and rivers of the adjoining countries. Were these supplies suspended, or directed into another channel, ere many years would elapse boys might explore the empty caves of Niagara's tide, and reptiles gambol in the pulverized dust on the bed of the once mighty river. Not a drop of water would remain even in the great lakes—all would disappear from the effects of evaporation. So is it with the teacher's mind. He must study continually—he must keep adding to his stock of knowledge. He must pursue a regular plan of study. In the nature of things his learning will increase or decrease—there is nothing stationary in this world. In knowledge, as in everything else, we must either advance or retrograde. It behoves us not only to perform some good work every day, but also to learn something new. If we do not draw a regular supply of information from the fountains of knowledge, they will (so far as concerns us) gradually dry up, and our learning will evaporate or become uncertain and indistinct, like the faint remembrance of the dreams of childhood. If we do not keep on the *qui vive*, and endeavour to expand and

Teachers to study continually.

strengthen our minds by continual acquisition and reflection, our faculties will certainly stagnate to a greater or less degree, according to the quality and extent of our previous education. Every man, and the teacher especially, should occasionally refresh his memory by taking a tour through the various fields of knowledge. He should add something to the furniture of his mind—to his mental accomplishments— every day. Necessity will compel him regularly to replenish his "capital in trade;" reflection will suggest the propriety of systematically exploring the sources of knowledge, so that he may sip freely of their crystal waters. By so doing his mind will become a well stocked treasury from which he can draw as he has need. In this respect, as in others, a little forgetfulness or neglect will be sure to breed more or less mischief. Intelligent teachers periodically pursue a course of professional study, and diligently labour to cultivate their various faculties. Teachers should be as hard students as any of their pupils. They are expected to be *educators*, and should not content themselves with being mere "lesson hearers." Considering the public utility of their work, and having higher and holier aims than the accumulation of money, "let them exalt the dignity of their profession by adding daily to their mental accomplishments and by indivi- dual growth in personal worth."* They will thus keep ahead of the age in which they live, and grow in grace with God and man. Let it be remembered, however, that though reading may sow the seed of knowledge, reflection alone can ripen the fruit.

Temptations incident to the profes- sion.
It has often been observed of individual teachers on both sides of the Atlantic, that the schools they first taught were their best—that in after life they retrograde in efficiency instead of advancing. Indeed it is a matter of notoriety that many young persons practice the profession for years, and in the end are more backward in intellectual ability and more deficient in the science of teaching than when they

---

* Rev. E. Ryerson, D.D.

commenced. These effects are the results of many causes (too numerous to mention here); but when they prevail to any great extent, it is evident the delinquents are *unfit for*, and have *mistaken*, their calling. It must be borne in mind, however, that there are many peculiar temptations incidental to the profession which tend to make the teacher a backslider. For instance, few men do (or can do) more than one thing at one and the same time. Still, in the nature of things, this is just what the teacher has to do. He is compelled to do two things—to teach and to govern—at one and the same moment. This double duty—requiring the concentration of all his faculties—continues not for a day. or two, but week after week, term after term, and year after year; so that after his daily work is over he is completely fatigued, and therefore, instead of devoting his spare hours to his own private studies or mental accomplishments, he is tempted to rush away to the nearest and most convenient place of recreation.* This feeling of weariness is strengthened, and not unfrequently produced, by a press of business, by the inconsideration or thoughtlessness of pupils, by want of fresh air, by the insufficiency of his remuneration, and the legion of other anxieties incident to his position. However, if the teacher can only strive resolutely against these things, he will triumph in the end. If he resist these anxieties they will flee from him. Remembering that spare moments are "the gold dust of time," let him not fritter away his precious moments on insignificant matters, nor yield to depression of spirit; and then, indolence—consequent on fatigue—will keep at a respectful distance. Hope, energy and perseverance conquer all difficulties. Let him, at least, devote *one* hour out of the twenty-four to sweet communion with the educators and philosophers of other ages. From their writings and his own observation he will be sure to acquire the instruction and experience, if not the peculiar tact, necessary to his professional success.

Doing two things at the same time.

To turn spare moments to good account.

* David Page.

The culture of the intellect will improve the natural disposition, enlighten the conscience, feed the flame of generous sentiment, enhance our perceptions of the dignity, utility, and obligations of life, whilst making us fountains of happiness and centres of holy influence in our respective spheres of usefulness.

Sir W. Raleigh's advice. Before concluding this chapter we would beg to direct the attention of pupils and younger teachers to the following words of Sir Walter Raleigh : " Bestow thy youth (says he) so that thou mayest have comfort to remember it when it has forsaken thee—so that when old thou mayest not have cause to sigh and grieve at the account thereof. Whilst young thou wilt think thy youth will never have an end ; but behold the longest day hath an evening—thou wilt enjoy it but once and it will never return. Use it therefore as the spring time, which soon departeth, and wherein thou oughtest to plant and sow all provisions necessary for a long and happy life."

Precepts by Pythagoras. Before retiring to rest we should carefully review the various transactions of the past day. The great teacher Pythagoras made a rule to this effect for his own personal guidance. His modern admirers should follow so worthy an example. How desirable that young and old before resigning themselves to sleep should take stock of the day's doings and, in the words of the Grecian sage, exclaim : "The day is past ; where have I turned aside from my rectitude? what have I been doing? what have I left undone which I ought to have done? . . . . Begin thus from the first act and proceed to the last (says the philosopher), and, in conclusion, be troubled at the ill thou hast done and rejoice for the good."

> " Still in the paths of honour persevere,
> And not from past or present ills despair ;
> For blessings ever wait on virtuous deeds,
> And, though a late, a sure reward succeeds."[*]

---

[*] Congreve.

CHAPTER VI.

MUTUAL DUTIES OF THE PROFESSION AND THE PUBLIC.

It has been well said that "every man owes a debt to his profession." This observation is specially applicable to the teacher and his vocation. How are teachers to discharge the debt, admitting its existence? In many ways, but chiefly by arousing the public to a just sense of duty in respect to education—by doing all in their power to magnify the real importance of their profession—by making it more and more honourable as a result of their profound learning, intelligence, character, and general merit.

We are all indebted to our profession.

Skilful teachers can only be formed by several concurrent qualifications, such as a natural love for the work, natural impulse, and individual fitness or professional aptness; but these must be efficiently seconded by *adequate remuneration.* If education be worth having, it is worth paying for. The teachers' salary should bear some proportion to his responsibilities, qualifications and success. "The labourer is worthy of his hire;" and no people should be so mean, or so forgetful of their children's interests, as to only half pay for their teacher's services. So useful, so important is the faithful teacher's work that he can never be fully paid for it in this world. What are the paltry few hundred dollars which he annually receives, compared with the value of the services rendered? An intelligent community should blush at the idea of paying teachers starvation wages—in fact an intelligent community won't do it—they will have a better appreciation of their own and their children's interest. Besides, intelligent people have too much honour and discrimination to offer half a year's pay for a full year's work. "Every member of society (says Goldsmith) should be paid in proportion as he is necessary; and I will be bold enough to say

Adequate remuneration.

that schoolmasters in a state are more necessary than clergy-men, as children are in more need of instruction than their parents. . . . Of all professions in society, I do not know a more useful or a more honourable one than that of a schoolmaster, at the same time I do not see any . . . whose talents are so ill-rewarded. . . . I would make the business of a schoolmaster every way more respectable by increasing teachers' salaries, and admitting only men (or women) of proper abilities. . . . Masters and teachers, when they are men of learning, reputation, and assiduity, cannot be sufficiently prized in a state."

Good ser-vices, good pay.

It is pleasant to know that at the present moment the public, in all civilized lands, are awakening from their political lethargy and indifference about educational matters. The rostrum, the pulpit, and the press, are astir in favour of education and educators. The public press—the angel flying in the midst of heaven—has done much for the teacher, and will doubtless continue its favours. The people may rest assured that his efficiency and devotion will increase in pro-portion to the increase of his remuneration. The great mass of the people are of opinion that the time is at hand when the pay and position of the teacher must be improved; for all feel that "good hands should receive good hire." High accomplishments secure esteem, and better services command better pay. The liberality of employers will never fail to stimulate the faithful teacher to still greater exertions in discharge of his duties, and still higher attainments in the various departments of knowledge. Hence, the action of the profession and the public should be mutual. The former must equal, if not surpass, the other learned professions in knowledge and "business tact," and the latter (the public) must duly appreciate the labours of the teacher, and, in addition, pay well for his services. In fact, they will have to do so, whether they will or not, ere many years elapse.

Test of civilization.

If we look abroad upon the modern history of the world, we will observe that wherever education is prized above wealth, and the educator preferred to the money maker, there, and there only, are the people truly refined, happy and enlightened—there are those who lead the world in the march of civilization—there the golden rule is observed, and men "do unto others as they would have others do unto them." In such a country every man follows some useful calling—there are no fops, no idlers, no "place hunters" or "hangers on," and but few cases on the criminal calendar. Good and learned teachers are the cause and consequence of a learned national character. It is therefore generally con- *A cause and consequence.* ceded that the esteem in which they are held is a measure of the intelligence and civilization of the people. The recent victories of Prussia and the United States may be directly traced to the superiority of these nations over their opponents in the matter of education. In no other countries of the world (except Holland) are teachers so highly respected, and in none are they so well paid as in gallant Prussia and free America. Great and enlightened nations appreciate their teachers, and the teachers in such nations— considering the obligations mutual—render themselves more and more worthy of public regard, as scholars, patriots, citizens— "doing whatsoever they find to do with all their might." When teachers, as a class, duly honour and appreciate their profession, and the law of the land prevents parties entering it who are not thoroughly qualified, the people will, and must, liberally remunerate and properly esteem those who are qualified and in successful practice. When the teachers and the laws work together to this end, the emoluments and public appreciation of the educational profession will be equal to its importance, and its most successful sons will be no more attracted from its ranks by the more lucrative inducements of other callings.

The low estimation of our ancestors for the profession of *The rich fool's argument considered.* teaching arose decidedly from their personal ignorance and the little value they placed on education itself. Some amongst

us who received little or no education in their early days
may still inherit this spirit, and be induced thereby to
undervalue the advantages of learning and the merits of the
teacher.   These people, or any of them, may perhaps speak
on this wise—"Oh! I have got along pretty well in the
world—made an independent fortune—and yet I have had
very little book knowledge. I spent only six months at
school. ` Many of my acquaintances who received a college
education could never succeed at anything. I wish my
children to follow my example in all things."   By entrench-
ing themselves behind such arguments these anti-education
people only exhibit their inherent folly, vanity, and utter
ignorance.   If they got on so well in the world with so little
"book knowledge," how much better would they have got
on had they been favoured with a good, sound, liberal education ?   Might not their educated (?) acquaintances have been
equally unsuccessful even though they had never entered a
college ? In that case perhaps their fate would be worse
than mere failure in business.   Was extensive learning and
profound knowledge the real cause of their want of success
in life ? Are you sure, dear parent, should your children
grow up uneducated, that they (like you) will be successful
in amassing a fortune, or even a mere competency ? Was
not your success as an uneducated man an exception, rather
than a general rule ? Does ignorance really elevate a man,
enabling him to become a better individual and a more useful citizen ? In your intercourse with the world did not
you yourself acquire an education before you acquired a
fortune ? Answer these queries honestly, and abide by the
result; but remember always that God and your country
expect you to do your duty.   Why should men, otherwise
respectable, be advocates of darkness and enemies of progress ? Without education and without teachers to impart
it, man, in the course of a few generations, would, in all
probability, retrograde into a state of barbarism.   We

earnestly hope that the time is at hand when none of our citizens will be so ignorant as to exhibit such ignorance, and when every man will gladly aid in promoting the intellectual, moral and physical welfare of his fellow-men.

In some of the foregoing pages we have taken the liberty *An international association of teachers.* of impressing on teachers that they should embrace every opportunity of doing good and of acquiring knowledge, so that while improving the faculties of others, their own may not remain stationary or decay. We would now say that their personal welfare and the interests of education materially suffer from the want of a more extensive and effective professional union than any which has hitherto existed. Without combination, teachers are like little stars scattered over the firmanent—united, they would be as the mid-day sun. Isolated or divided, teachers are comparatively powerless, but united they would feel their strength and could use it too, to their own advantage and the nation's welfare. Let the teachers of every county or district unite and form local associations, based on the principles of mutual instruction, mutual aid, mutual sympathy, and mutual interest. Let these county "unions" unite and form provincial or national associations. Let these again unite and form an international association. Then will teachers be "a power" in their respective states—they will receive sufficient remuneration for their services, and education will be honoured as it ought. Teachers, awake from your lethargy. A moment's reflection will convince you that mutual welfare and common interests require you to form a universal brotherhood, embracing teachers of all denominations, climes and nationalities. Arise then in the interests of posterity. "Be up and doing"—lose no time in organizing these unions and "the union of unions"—a Teacher's International Institute.

CHAPTER VII.

RIGHT CONCEPTIONS OF EDUCATION.

The kinder-
garten
system.

The teacher's duties towards his pupils are somewhat analagous to those which characterize a gardener skilful in the management of "little nurslings." "Indeed," as a learned teacher remarks, "the public school may be regarded as a garden or 'nursery,' in which children are the plants and the teacher the gardener."* We will become more impressed with the resemblance if we remember that, in addition to the elimination or amputation of diseased or unfruitful members, both have to remove hindrances and strengthen favouring circumstances; so that their little "flock" may have sufficient room and opportunities for development in their respective spheres, according to the laws of their organization. It must have been some such ideas as these which induced the Germans to found their *Kindergartens*. The term Kindergarten means "garden of children," and may be regarded as a school in which the "little plants of humanity" are trained and developed in accordance with the laws of their being and "the teachings" or promptings of child-nature. Like Pestalozzi, Frœbel, the founder of the system, was the most eminent teacher of his time—his special province being "the culture of the young." After spending more than forty years in studying the science and in practising the art of teaching, he proclaimed "the Kindergarten;" and, if we mistake not, the system will make his name immortal. It has been introduced (though in a modified form) into many of our best schools, and has been received with much favour. In philosophy of method it may be justly regarded as the most scientific of our educational systems. As might be

---

* Frœbel.

expected, it is peculiarly successful in primary schools; but the principles on which it is founded are common to all children, and applicable to all "learners;" so that, with a few judicious alterations or additions, the system may be adapted to schools of all grades. The essential characteristics of the system *are*, that instead of repressing the pupil's spirit with the view of "making him good," and instead of attempting to paralyze his natural activity with the view of "keeping him quiet," it encourages the development of these things by organizing play itself into educating media. This is so literally true of the system, that children under its influence gradually come to regard play as work, and study as recreation. Such a system begins at "the right end." It does not encourage the indolent practice of looking at things through the eye-glasses of others. On the contrary, it induces the pupils to make the most of their precious time, and, by encouraging personal investigation, it impels them to exercise their respective faculties. But to practice this, or any other system successfully, the teacher must carefully study the peculiar propensities or natural characteristics of children, and be sure to make child-nature his ally in the pursuit of knowledge.

Mere knowledge is not education, but education includes knowledge. To teach is not to educate, but education implies the intervention of teaching. To *teach* means to "cram in," and to *educate* means to "draw out," or lead forth. It is obvious, therefore, that the two terms are far from being synonymous. The term education is derived from *e* or *ex* (out), and *duco* (I lead), and, in the sense in which we use it, signifies the expansion, unfolding, training and strengthening of all the human powers—of the entire man: not of the mind alone or of the body alone, but of both together. An educated mind in a well-trained body, subject to the direction of superior moral sentiments, is the surest guarantee of present and future happiness. Educa-

Meaning of education.

tion excites the mind to thirst after knowledge, whilst it endows our faculties with strength to acquire sufficient supplies of mental food. It enlarges the intellectual capacities, whilst it cultivates, elevates and refines all the feelings of the human heart. It may, in fact, be regarded as an absorption of surrounding elements into the mind and body—an assimilation of the substances, qualities, and relations of things, whereby they become a part of our being, mental or physical—a new supply of faculty upon which we can draw as we have need. Education enables us to acquire and use knowledge. Hence, in a civilized community the Art of Teaching may be justly regarded as the most important of all arts, as well as the basis of all the sciences.

The best teacher.

The best educator is not the man who can "cram in" the most information, but he who can most successfully stir up or inspire the human mind to think, observe, reflect, analyze, combine, and execute, *without doing any or either of these things for it.* The best teacher is not he who can pack into the pupils' minds the greatest number of facts, but he who can thoroughly discipline the mental faculties, and thereby enable his pupils to educate themselves. The efficient discipline of the mind and proper training of the heart are things to be desired far more than the mere acquisition of information. It is, however, a reliable axiom that knowledge is the twin sister, if not the offspring, of education—no human being can really educate his heart or mind without acquiring knowledge. The latter always accompanies the former; but unfortunately the former does not always go hand in hand with the latter.

Special preparation necessary.

To be successful in any of the callings of life men must be educated in that particular business by long study, labour and apprenticeship—no matter how great may be their aptitude or natural tact. This is specially true of the teacher. Without study and due preparation no man can possibly be an educator. Moreover, if careful preparation and continued study be necessary for success in other professions, they are doubly so in the case of the teacher, inasmuch as his responsibilities are much greater than those which devolve on the members of other callings—seeing that he has to work on the minds of immortal beings, whereas they, for the most part, have to do with earthly and transitory things. He has to work on heavenly subjects—on the everlasting materials of mind and spirit. Why should he, therefore, through blunders arising from ignorance or inexperience, maim or mar what was intended to be blessed, and the source of blessings to others? He has to educate vital and immortal principles, to train the human body, to fashion the human soul, and, unlike the productions of other workmen, his work, be it good or bad, will endure forever. If good, it shall be his delight in future ages; if bad, it will be a source of shame to him for all generations. How important therefore that he should fully understand the mysteries of his profession, and be duly impressed with its responsibilities! How absolutely necessary that, like the *To have a* skilful artist, he should have a *beau idéal* before him in all *beau idéal.* his labours? Every word he speaks should be fraught with meaning, and every sentence he utters should more clearly develop the *idéal* of his mind. The skilful teacher is a "mind artist," whose works will influence the world for good, and leave their impression on the history of our race. The unskilful teacher is just the reverse—he may influence the world *for evil* more or less in proportion to his mental calibre. He may be likened to the novice who would attempt to chisel an Apollo or a Venus from a marble block. His highest efforts would be at best but a series of failures or painful blunders—blunders that probably could never be remedied so far as that block of marble may be concerned. How much more irreparable would be the errors of the blundering teacher? How many blocks of marble would be worth one good citizen—one immortal soul? Other labourers may blunder, and perhaps destroy the materials on which they labour, but the teacher cannot afford to do so. A thousand diamonds, each the size of the world, could not buy one of the little souls entrusted to his care. How absolutely necessary is it, therefore, that before commencing his professional duties he should have *correct ideas* of his work, and be fully posted in *the best and most approved methods* of performing it? The teacher who possesses these qualifications, and avails himself of every opportunity of turning them to good account in the interest of the public, will surely command success, and in days to come " many

Future reward.

shall rise up and call him blessed." It has been well said that "he who labours for others, forgetful of selfish interests, is sure of immortality."

A perfect man—unison of culture.

Man was designed to be "perfect after his kind "—in his physical as well as in his mental and moral natures : not in one only, but in the whole three together. No man can be perfect after his kind who does not possess a benevolent heart, a vigorous mind, and a healthy body. It is the due development and "proportional combination" of these characteristics which constitute a "whole man." It is a well-known fact that persons friendly to education have often affirmed that during the early years of childhood the physical powers should be allowed to develop themselves, unchecked by the tempering restraints involved in the exercise of the other two. Others again have held that the mental faculties of children should engross all attention to the exclusion of the physical and moral powers, whilst a third party (equally earnest) make a similar affirmation with respect to the moral feelings. These three views are equally erroneous. Nature and experience inform us that the true course consists of a due combination of the whole three. All of them are equally important, so that none of them should be placed "afore or after the other" in the order of culture. Their development should be contemporaneous. From infancy up, the respective mental faculties, physical powers and moral feelings, should be carefully attended to, so that, being called forth into harmonious action, none may flourish at the expense of the other. It will be seen from the foregoing that those who consider education to be the mere art of carrying children through a certain programme of intellectual studies, are grievously in error as to the right meaning of that science, whose object is to develop, "perfect men and women" out of the crude material so characteristic of childhood and youth.

If we were to watch an icicle from the commencement of *The forma-tion of character.* its formation until it has attained its full growth (or length), we would notice that it froze one drop at a time. "Should the water be clean, the icicle will be clear and radiant in the sunlight; but should the water be muddy, the icicle will also be muddy and deficient in 'sparkling' beauty. It is thus human character is formed—one little thought or feeling at a time. If every thought be pure and right, the soul will be bright and lovely, and will sparkle with happiness! But if the thoughts or feelings be evil or impure, the mind will be soiled or darkened, the character depraved, and the heart miserable and wretched." The first principle of all *First princi-ples of education.* good sound education *is* that more attention should be paid to the *formation of character* than to mere expertness in the respective branches of learning; and the second is like unto it, namely—that far more emphasis should be laid on the right cultivation of the feelings of the heart, and development of the faculties of the mind, than on the mere acquisition of knowledge. Every act of the teacher should tend to develop and strengthen these eternal principles, and the exercise of all the means at his disposal for that purpose is not only legal and right, but obligatory. Strict attention to these matters must be reckoned amongst his most important duties. How important that the educators of youth should keep constant watch over the development of the characters of the immortal and imitative beings committed to their charge, constantly impressing on them the necessity of being always on their guard against the idle allurements and impulsive propensities peculiar to their age.

CHAPTER VIII.

PUBLIC AND PRIVATE EDUCATION CONTRASTED.

Pupils of studious habits will "gain more book knowledge " from a private tutor, in the same space of time, than they could possibly acquire in a public school. But on the other hand they gain experience of the world and its customs at public schools, such as they could never obtain in their own homes. As Goldsmith says, "Boys will learn more true wisdom in a public school in a year, than by a private education in five." If privately educated they generally reach the age of discretion before they become acquainted with the vices or extravagancies of life ; and as their reason and judgment are then well developed, they are better prepared to resist the temptations or enticements of the world than they could possibly be at an earlier age. On the other hand, if kept in ignorance of the allurements of life during their early days, they are the more likely to be carried away by them when they escape from the restraints of home— when they enter the universities or go into business. If boys be kept in ignorance of the allurements of the world, and subject to rigid restraints, while at home, they generally (or at least frequently) go beyond all due bounds when they leave the parental roof, "for the novelty of vice may then have irresistible charms."* It is unwise to raise children in this rigid puritanical manner. Nature will have its way sooner or later. Too much restriction in youth is often suc-

---

* Goldsmith.

ceeded by licentiousness in after life. In fact it seems to be a law of our being, that unrestricted liberty suddenly or unseasonably obtained is almost sure to be abused : and as a rule, the succeeding licentiousness is in direct proportion to the indulgence or antecedent harshness of the ruling authority. In this respect, as in all others, let us follow nature. Let children be raised to know the world as it really is; let a spirit be implanted in them which will enable them to steer their course free from the danger of shipwreck on the rocks and quicksands of life. Let them be raised to know themselves and taught to understand humanity as it is, and we need not fear the result. They will then be almost sure to feel and act as becomes worthy citizens, and will prove by their deeds that the discovery of truth and the practice of courtesy, kindness, and benevolence are the noblest objects of life.

Private instruction may perhaps be best adapted to the training of youth to habits of virtue and piety; but the emulations, trials, and triumphs of the public school form the best preparation for the battle of life. If the affections and passions of human nature be not properly directed and duly restrained by a firm hand during childhood days, manhood is apt to be barren—totally devoid of those qualifications and accomplishments

A public school course the best preparation for the duties of life.

> " Which adorn youth and cheer with brilliant rays
> The fading spirit of winter's gloomy days."

Parental affection frequently nullifies parental authority. As a necessary consequence the child is indulged intemperately, and all the evil propensities of human nature develop themselves unchecked. It is seldom so in the public school or collegiate institute. In those institutions the various powers of the mind are called into activity by the noble influence of example. Emulation is excited, and every pupil knows and feels that shame and disgrace are sure to follow idleness. In those national institutions the

obstinate heart is induced to yield a willing obedience;
friendships are formed which will endure for ever; equality
is felt, and no superiority acknowledged but that of merit;
the diffident and shy become confident and bold; the rude
learn politeness, and literary improvement is pursued by
all with more or less zeal and success. Some learn from
their companions, others from their books and teachers, but
the fires of emulation gradually seize upon all—upon even
the most indolent. Here, as the mind of the child or youth
expands, and as he wends his way to the temple of learning,
he will have the sweet companionship of co-labourers and
fellow-travellers. He will learn to esteem the noble qualities, usually known as generosity, gratitude, and courage,
and, by the example of companions, be led to despise perfidy,
sloth, and selfishness. He will thus (insensibly, as it were)
be taught to cherish in his heart the nobler feelings of
humanity, whilst he learns to avoid the baser instincts of
our fallen nature, as if they entailed instant death. Finding that his reputation in a public school depends on his
own conduct, and being constantly impelled to act with
decision, his mind must gradually expand, and he will
attain a certain firmness and manliness of character otherwise unattainable. He will thus learn to feel that patience,
perseverance, energy, fortitude, and industry, are the true
elements of success, whilst he becomes convinced that real
merit, like the water of a river, is silent in proportion to
its depth.

Elements of
success.   The future success in life of each individual child depends,
in a great measure, on the right cultivation of its talents by
appropriate studies—on the proper training or development
of its intellect—on the vitality, energy, and amiability of its
disposition, and on the morality of its early youth. "Public
schools are the best arenas in which to prepare for the
duties of after life."* No person can receive a thorough

* Prince Von Bismarck.

practical education without availing himself of their advantages. Awkwardness, timidity, doubt, and uncertainty, are the accompanying characteristics of pupils "educated" by private tutors at their own residences. Such parties seldom fail to contract the habit of looking upon the world through narrow or bigoted channels, as their judgment is formed or rather deformed by their own limited experience of men and things.

It is true the advantages of the public school may be Self-deception. within their reach, but (as in Europe) the foolish pride of parents, the culpable vanity of caste—antequated ideas of a dark and barbarous age—clinging to the skirts of their garments, often prevent them from availing themselves of their educational opportunities. They then seek to appease their conscience by abusing the public school system. The children of such parents, not having the opportunity of coming in contact with enlightened or intelligent minds, often imagine themselves to be beings of gigantic intellect—of "angelic mould"—by birth, position, and education worthy of the worship they would fain claim from their fellowmen. Puffed up with self-conceit and imaginary importance, they are unconscious of being victims to the vice of self-deception. Instructed without being educated, they would fain have us believe the scream of the crow to be the voice of the eagle. Ignorance and inexperience may be regarded as an excuse for such erratic pretensions if not a palliation for such selfish stupidity; but we can scarcely regard any system of education with favour, which tends to make men unconscious of their personal deficiencies. As a learned teacher well observes, "There are some things which a boy learns from none so well as his parents, but there are others which are better taught him by men who have made education the study and business of their lives. And though it may seem rash and cruel to drive a boy out (to college or public school) from the sanctuary of a quiet home into a scene where the darts of Satan are flying thick, yet it is really wise and kind. That fight must be fought by all; and if a man learn not in youth to face the noise and the dangers of the battle, he can scarcely be firm and fearless in manhood. To have never met danger is not courage, nor is it innocence to be ignorant of evil." *

Union of the public and private systems. In the education of our children, if we are to have a choice between the public school and private tutorial system, by all means let us have the former with all its faults, rather than the latter with its "alleged advantages;" but, if possible, let us have both together. While children are very young, mothers are their best teachers, and governesses are the mother's best substitutes. They should be sent to school at an early age; and thenceforth, until they emerge from the University, private tuition (if it can be procured) should go hand in hand with public education—the former being secondary to the latter. Parties availing themselves of the advantages of both systems, will have reason to be pleased with the result.

Necessity of national provision for education. It is a matter of the greatest importance, if not of absolute and imperative necessity, that "Every child should be educated—and this is specially true of those destined to occupy prominent or important positions in society."† One of the greatest duties we (citizens and legislators) owe to posterity is, to make a liberal provision for the efficient education of the rising generation. Should we not do so, we may be sure that our sins of omission will be visited on our posterity "to the third and fourth generation." This provision should be national in character, and subject to central administration—each city, town, or district being compelled by law to provide school accommodation, with an efficient staff of teachers, for all the resident children within the legal school ages; and entitled, as a necessary conse-

---

* Ascott R. Hope.
† Earl Dufferin, Governor-General of Canada.

quence, to a share of the national school fund in proportion to the amount raised for school purposes by the local Board of Education. Every parent, rich or poor, should be com- Compulsory education. pelled to send his children, for a certain length of time, to some public school—that is, a school taught by a teacher (or teachers) licensed by Government. Each child in a country is as much the child of the nation as it is the child of the parent, and the nation, therefore, should provide for its future welfare so far as educational matters are concerned. Parents should not be allowed to raise their children in ignorance, when facilities are at hand for their right instruction. Every nation, making a national or public provision for education, should have a clause in its legal code compelling all children between certain ages, enjoying good health, to attend some school, public or private, a certain prescribed number of days per annum. A Government which neglects to make, or declines to enforce, such a law, has no moral right to impose (or levy) a school tax on its citizens. The Chief Superintendent of Education for the Province of Ontario, taking this view of the matter, had a clause inserted in the recent Canadian School Act making attendance at school compulsory within certain limits. Toronto, and some other cities, have given effect to the Act by appointing "Truant Officers," whose duty it is to see that the law is obeyed within their respective jurisdictions.

6

Fundamental principles.

Education may be defined as the art of developing, in due order and proportion, the respective mental, moral, and physical powers. It behoves the teacher to ascertain the order of sequence in which nature develops the respective faculties; so that he may be able to supply each with suitable mental nourishment during the process of evolution. If we would command success, our arrangement of matter and mode of instruction must conform to the natural order of mental development. No one can be a skilful teacher unless he knows not only how to impart information with facility, but also the order in which the various branches of knowledge should be presented to the understanding. These principles form the basis of Nature's method of instruction—

Development of the faculties.

the great archetype of all methods. The same faculties are not always ready to germinate at the same age in different individuals ; nor does the order of sequence remain invariable. Both time and sequence are subject to slight fluctuations arising from certain inherited or associated causes ; but the skilled teacher will discover these variations, and "govern himself accordingly." In the generality of cases the order of development follows the order of sequence observed in this chapter.

Order of sequence.

Observation is one of the first—if not the very first—of the mental faculties which awakes to consciousness. Then come memory, faith, reflection, imagination, reason, and judgment. The mental faculties which should be particularly attended to in childhood are those which bud, blossom, and bear fruit during that period—namely, observation, reflection, memory, and faith. By faith, in this instance, we mean that faculty which impels people to receive as true those things which are told them by others. As children advance in years, and ascend into higher classes at school, the other faculties should be gradually cultivated—the first lessons in the cultivation of each being of a simple kind, partaking more of the nature of direct intuition than of formal propositions. One of the chief objects of education is to enable pupils rightly to instruct themselves, and unless we take Nature for our guide, this object can never be achieved. The great secret involved in the right cultivation of the respective faculties is, that the order of sequence indicated by Nature should be observed in their development.

SECTION 1. ATTENTION.

Observation and reflection are often regarded as sub-divisions of what some call *the faculty of attention.* By the word attention, as here used, we mean that elective affinity or faculty of the mind which enables us to fix on (or select for consideration) one particular object, of the many which may present themselves to the mental vision—to the exclusion, for the time being, of all others. It is a well known fact that when we thus direct our attention to any individual object, all extraneous ideas—or thoughts foreign to the subject—naturally retire from the mind. The ability to single out or fix on one particular idea, to the total exclusion of all others, is of course a very important, useful, and necessary mental power. The power of continued attention is, in fact, one of the most important elements of success. Without it, natural talent will remain dormant or undeveloped, and even genius itself will fail to command professional success. Observation and reflection may be regarded as the parents of all human ideas. Without their aid there would be little or no knowledge. It is a matter of fact that the strength and utility of our ideas are in proportion to the degree or intensity of the attention

Continuity of attention essential.

devoted to the subjects concerning which conceptions are generated or conceived. The majority of our ideas perish at their birth. None permanently remain except those produced by accurate attention—direct or indirect. By direct attention we mean perception or observation, and by indirect attention we mean reflection. The former refers, of course, to impressions engendered by external objects received through the media of the senses; and the latter refers to thoughts or sensations produced by mental analysis, synthesis, or comparison,—or by the recurrence and consideration of former ideas. The recalling, or summoning back, of such ideas is sometimes spontaneous and sometimes the result of a direct effort of the will.

Cultivate habits of observation and reflection. One of the principal duties of a primary teacher is the training of pupils to habits of accurate observation. The development of the reflective powers should be the special duty of the teachers in charge of intermediate departments, whilst the development of judgment, and its kindred faculties, should be the province of those in charge of the higher departments—the principal teacher being careful to review, revise, and overlook the work done in all classes. The order of development may be fixed, but the age at which the reflective faculties of the child should be aroused, called orth, and educated, is very variable. In this respect, as in others, let the teacher follow Nature. But to return: Conceptions of qualities, such as taste, smell, etc., are comprised under the head of reflection. They are difficult of comprehension to the youthful mind, and cannot be recalled or compared with much accuracy or clearness; but the reverse is the case as regards conceptions of visible objects. The latter are generally definite and precise, and can almost always be recalled without dimness or uncertainty. This circumstance proves the superiority of sight as a medium of intelligence. It is an axiom with teachers that knowledge acquired through the eye is always the most accurate, the most durable, and the most easily learned. For these reasons, all knowledge, so far as practicable, should be communicated through the medium of that organ. If the subject of a lesson be not of a spiritual or "intangible" nature, it will probably belong to "the physical world;" and if the object itself, or a model of it, cannot be presented to the class, they should, at least, be shown a picture of it. If a picture or chart of it cannot be obtained, then a drawing of it should be made on the black board. This plan will not only enable them to understand the lesson, but will quicken and cultivate the habit of attention, without which there can be no permanent acquisition of knowledge—no improvement in mental capacity. As Archbishop Fenelon well observes, "There is no pleasure equal to that of diffusing happiness and exciting attention."

The happiness of life depends chiefly on the right use of moderate enjoyments—on the continued succession of small but agreeable sensations. The happiness of childhood depends in a great measure on the continual supply of little pleasures—on its opportunities of observation and experiment—the true sources of early enjoyment. The child is ignorant; everything is new to it, and Nature impels it to seek for knowledge. Hence its continued activity, its love of variety, and its craving for sympathy—essential elements of its happiness. Success in securing attention depends on the teacher's ability to understand and satisfy these longings; and his personal experience will prompt him to avail himself of their combined influence in imparting instruction. Reciprocal regard is the surest index of successful teaching— the best evidence of good education. The cultivation of a generous affection, on the basis of mutual confidence and mutual esteem, seldom, if ever, fails to refine the heart and ennoble the understanding. Such an attachment sweetens the fountains of knowledge, and awakens every chivalric feeling dormant in the human heart.

A child's happiness.

Mutual affection.

How to
secure
attention.

To secure attention, on ordinary occasions, the matter must be interesting, and the manner of treating it gracious and attractive; the terms or words must be selected with care, defined with accuracy, and adhered to with firmness. If the language used be beyond the pupil's comprehension, the words will convey no ideas, the attention will be lost, and the children will yawn and exhibit symptoms of weariness, or mental repulsion. Every method of instruction which fatigues attention, and every effort made to convey information after the attention is fatigued, must be injurious to the pupil. For this reason it is not wise to attempt too much at once. We should, at first, exercise attention only during comparatively short periods. We should advance but few ideas that are new, in our early lessons on any subject. Novelty and variety when concurrent and continuous, always fatigue the mind. The acquisition of one distinct idea brings the pupil more knowledge and real pleasure than the recollection of a dozen hazy and confused notions. The actual information gained in a lesson is of little account in comparison with the desire of further progress engendered thereby.

Not to
discourage.

When a subject is new, an unnecessary amount of labour is often expended on the acquisition of terms and ideas. Under such circumstances children are often fatigued by overstrained and misplaced efforts. They should, therefore, be relieved from any apprehensions of the teacher's displeasure; for undue anxiety will be sure to weary and weaken their attention. While sympathizing with the pupil in his difficulties, the teacher should not exhibit or express any doubts of the pupil's ability to master them. On the contrary, he should intimate that though success may not smile on the child's present efforts, yet time and perseverance will give him the victory. Such judicious encouragement will prevent children from contracting an antipathy towards any branch of knowledge, by failure in first attempts.

A learned writer justly observes that, "when we experi- Cause and
ence any disagreeable sensations, mental or physical, we try certain
to procure temporary relief by certain motions of the limbs ties.
and muscles most habitually obedient to the will." * Great
thinkers often unconsciously endeavour to relieve the pain of
intense thought by indulging in certain awkward gestures.
By frequent repetition these gestures become habitual, and
hence the eccentricities and peculiarities so characteristic of
thoughtful men. The same fact holds good in the case of
children. They wrinkle their brows to mitigate the mental
pain caused by close attention; or, when application becomes irksome, the body becomes restless, and assumes
strange attitudes; and thus Nature declares it time to
change employment. These eccentricities are voluntary at
first, but, from frequent association with certain states of
the mind, they recur involuntarily whenever the ideas or
sentiments with which they were associated are recalled—
particularly when the soul is absorbed in the solution of
some difficulty. Judicious oversight may break these absurd motions, and prevent them from becoming habitual;
otherwise, when the pupil comes to man's estate, thoughts
are sure to be governed by external circumstances, and his
manners will, therefore, appear crude and awkward. To
effect a permanent cure, the hours of study should be short-
ened and agreeably intermixed with bodily exercise; so
that the pain arising from close attention may be alleviated
and assuaged.

Incentives or excitements need not be very numerous to Concentra-
produce attention; a judicious variation will sometimes be attention.
more agreeable and effective. Children become conscious
at a very early age of the pleasure arising from successful
application, as well as from the performance of good and
kind actions. In many cases this alone will be sufficient

---

* Darwin.

inducement to continued exertion. Those who are not idle, stupid, or obstinate, sometimes exhibit an indisposition or incapability to concentrate the attention on the subject of a lesson, chiefly because the exertion required is too great for their patience, or because the language employed is inaccurate or of vague signification, or because they despair of understanding the explanations given or the ideas intended to be conveyed. In either case they can not attend, and the fault lies with the teacher or the text book.

Natural disposition.

In forming an opinion of the degree of a child's attention, the teacher must not forget to consider the natural disposition of himself and pupil. If the one be slow and the other quick—one phlegmatic and the other vivacious—mutual sympathy may be wanting, and there will be a possibility of mutual misunderstandings and misconceptions. Vivacious children are very susceptible to censure or commendation. They are quite as honorable, and perhaps more sensitive and affectionate, than other children. Hence the desirability of regarding them with feelings of attachment, and of rewarding them with our approbation when they give proofs of long continued exertion and attention. Children of this disposition are often enthusiastic admirers of what is good and great, hence the feasibility of creating or fostering the desire to excel. Let them once feel the necessity of persevering industry, and with the rapidity of genius they will conclude that attention is the primary source of success, and that they must act accordingly.

How to sweeten labour and ensure progress.

When we have a friend whom we admire, esteem, and love, his approbation becomes necessary to our happiness. His affection sweetens labour, and the smile of his approval throws a flood of sunshine round the heart. Work in the service of such a friend is always pleasant, always attractive —never wearisome, never fatiguing. When associated with the pleasant sensations of affection, liberty, and enthusiasm, labour often becomes the medium by which we express our attachment, and we therefore consider no exertions too great, provided they give pleasure to the object of our affections. Is it not possible to cultivate the affections of pupils to such an extent, and in such a manner, as will ensure their attention to their respective duties, not alone because of the personal benefits arising therefrom, but because of the pleasure which such a line of conduct would afford their teacher and other friends? It is possible, and we believe that it behoves every teacher who aspires to anything more than an ordinary successful career, to acquire the power of exciting young people to great mental and physical exertion. For this reason, human nature and the philosophy of mind must be his constant studies.

The degree of children's timidity, or personal confidence, *Self-reliance to be encouraged.* depends in a great measure on the quality and quantity of their first instruction, and the mode of its conveyance. If many things be forced on their attention, which they can not understand or recollect, they lose confidence in their own mental capacity, and will often feel diffident to undertake exercises which they can easily perform. For this reason, whatever is attempted should be within their comprehension. Success in small things will encourage them to attempt the performance of greater. If we would endue the timid with confidence, we must expect little from each effort, and award to each triumph its full meed of praise. With some people, to will is to conquer. Hence the advisability of occasionally leading timid children to observe that attention, patience, and resolution are equivalent, and sometimes superior, to quickness of intellect, and that under such circumstances, the length of the period of application is the only difference between the quick and slow. When a succession of small triumphs has given them confidence in themselves, they may then be pressed a little as to velocity—the time allowed being gradually curtailed. Long continued efforts of attention fatigue the mind, exhaust the physical strength, and cause the pupils to appear sluggish and torpid. In this case, the pupils should be allowed rest, or the subject of study changed. Quick transition of thought cannot be reasonably expected unless the child be mentally active, and partially, if not perfectly, conversant with each idea expressed on the subject; otherwise it would only weaken the understanding, confuse the intellect, and destroy the ambition of the timid. Children are often timid from an anxiety to please, and often unduly fatigued from the same cause. We should therefore seldom, if ever, act towards them so as to promote terror. On the contrary, we should use all suitable means in our power to allay their anxiety, dissipate their fears, and strengthen their affectionate reliance on our sympathy and esteem. We can never command the intelligent attention of the timid until we have diffused their fears. Habits of observation and reflection are always more enduring when associated with pleasure, and where there is fear there can be no pleasure.

Abstraction, or the power of withdrawing the mental gaze from surrounding objects, or extraneous subjects, and of concentrating it upon some particular idea or series of ideas, is one of the most useful forms of attention, and perhaps the most difficult of acquisition. It is necessary to the successful operation of the understanding, and essentially characteristic of genius, heroism, and presence of mind. Without this faculty, no one can be a great or successful thinker—there can be no concentration of thought; the powers of the mind will be diffused like mist; continued application will be impossible, and, if possible, it will be unfruitful, and therefore unremunerative and of no effect. By the aid of this faculty, the industrious student will continue his labours in "the midst of alarms," and heed them not; the soldier will be unconscious of the roar and smoke of battle, and the hero will be blind to personal danger—

one idea, and one alone, will absorb every power of the heart and soul. In such moments, the personal is lost in the general, self retires from the field, sympathy subdues fear, and humanity is ennobled by a rich success or a devoted sacrifice.

Section 2. MEMORY.

Memory, the secretary of the senses, is closely allied to attention, and may be defined as that faculty of the mind which enables us to recal past impressions. Information is received through the media of the senses or by the exercise of the mental faculties. But it is not enough to receive it passively, as if our intellectual powers were composed of sponge. The faculty of attention must be aroused, interested, and fascinated ere the mind will ardently grasp, receive, or appropriate the knowledge placed before it. Merchants often say that "it is more difficult to keep money than to make it." However this may be, it is certainly less difficult to infuse knowledge into the mind than to retain it there after its reception. Its retention is the duty of the memory. From want of sufficient strength (arising from defective development), this faculty is often unequal to the task—unable to discharge the important duties of its office. Such a state of things indicates a sickly condition of the intellectual system, and should therefore receive the earnest and immediate attention of "the mental physician." The teacher must take steps to improve and duly develop the weakened faculty. *Memory and Retention.*

It has been well said that "memory is the store-house of the understanding." But it should be remembered that the value of things stored depends, in a great measure, on the order and system of their arrangement. Everything (even in mercantile establishments) should be stowed away in its appropriate place, so that it can be readily and promptly found when required. So of mental accumulations. Know- *Mental store-house.*

ledge should be arranged under its proper heading. Intellectual wealth, like other riches, will be the source of much embarrassment, should confusion prevail in the mental store-house. For these reasons, the teacher's ideas must be arranged in regular sequence, and, if possible, be presented to the pupils in logical and coherent order. Love and veneration may be regarded as the parents of memory. Hence, wise and skilful teachers always lead their pupils to contract a fondness for that which is to be learned or remembered. We ourselves may• possibly recollect some subject which, at one time of life, we may have regarded as repulsive and difficult to learn, yet, how easily did we master it in after years, when time and experience had led us to discover its worth and to admire its beauties? Looking at the matter in this light, we would say that, reverence for our teachers and love for the subjects of instruction, are two of the most powerful aids in the cultivation of memory and education of the young.

Visible Illustrations. Knowledge acquired when the mind is apathetic, evaporates instantaneously, hence the importance of exciting a lively interest in the subjects of study--the necessity of mutual sympathy between the teacher and the taught. Knowledge is never learned so quickly, nor retained so firmly, as when taught through the eye. This is why visible illustrations are so popular and effective, and so easily remembered in after years. When information is imparted under such conditions, memory will always be vigorous and retentive.

Two varieties of memory. There are two kinds of memory—the retentive and recollective. The former accumulates and retains facts, with little or no reference to their further identity, whilst the latter selects and reproduces, when necessary, such as may be considered useful, desirable, or important. Both of these varieties of memory have their advantages and advocates. The selective variety, usually called recollection, is, however, the higher and more intellectual branch of the faculty. People who can guide their memory by natural selection, or inherent taste, will improve their understanding and acquire the same amount of facts with far less fatigue than those who are satisfied with mere acquisition by rote. Memory is one of the faculties first developed; but its growth continues as we advance in life, and its cultivation in the higher stages is materially assisted by judgment, taste, and kindred powers.

Memory furnishes the materials on which invention exer- *Invention.* cises its ingenuity. The two faculties are closely allied. The development of the latter under proper guidance should therefore receive careful attention. In proportion to their knowledge and experience, children can judge quite as well, and perhaps invent much better, than adults. This circumstance arises from the fact that they are comparatively free from prejudice, and can, therefore, judiciously analyze, compare, and combine the few ideas they possess—those ideas being accurate, clear, and distinct.

A good memory is all-important to a public speaker—in *Utility to the public speaker.* fact, he cannot succeed without it, as no other quality can compensate for its absence. It endows him with personal confidence, command of language, and capability to arrange the ideas he is about to express, while engaged in giving utterance to others.

The efficiency of memory depends (1) on its *fidelity,* by *Conditions of efficiency.* which it reproduces faithful impressions; (2) *tenacity,* by which it retains what is committed to it, irrespective of the lapse of time; (3) *readiness,* or rapid reproduction of former conceptions when required; (4) *facility,* or rapidity of acquisition.

The memory is strong or weak in proportion to its power of analysis and generalization. The principles of association by which we analyze or combine, for the purposes of memory, may be regarded as the instruments of method.

They are three in number, namely, (1) *natural contiguity*, by which objects or incidents, impressing the mind in conjunction, recur to it in the same connection ever after; (2) *resemblance* or *analogy*, by which objects or incidents resembling each other are retained together in the mind by the fact of their resemblance; (3) *cause* and *effect*, by which facts that are at first conceived as casually related to each other, recur to the mind ever after by mutual suggestion.

SECTION 3. IMAGINATION.

Imagination —what it is.

Imagination is that faculty of the mind which forms conceptions, ideas, or mental images of things temporal or spiritual; so that whether far or near, past or future, their ideal presence is, for the time being, a living reality—distinct, clear, and tangible. It comprises two branches— the conceptive and creative. Besides assisting in the work of education, the right use of this faculty increases our enjoyments, and adds materially to the happiness of life, by enabling us to group, analyze, and combine objects as well as create them. Mental exercises and intellectual amusements are the best antidotes or preventatives of weariness and dissipation, and may, therefore, be regarded as essential to the right existence of intelligent and responsible beings.

When recollection recals former ideas, imagination presents them in vivid pictures before the mind; and then, by rearrangement and new combinations, it creates characteristic pictures of its own. The imagination often rambles through "scenes sublime," in search of mental enjoyment. Obscurity and terror may be regarded as the parents of sublimity. The natural fears arising from a consciousness of their presence, when uncontrolled by reason, tend to enervate the mind, whereas a right conception of the grand and beautiful always tends to elevate it. But there are branches of the sublime free from associations of the obscure and terrible, and there

Connection with the sublime.

are many branches of study and thought connected with them which have no connection with gloom or violence—such works of art, for instance, and scenes in nature as excite ideas of infinity with respect to power, space, and duration. These are praiseworthy media for the exercise of the imagination. Being founded on observation and conception, they are also the most simple sources of the sublime, and, therefore, the most suitable for children as well as the most attractive for the generality of adults. They are, perhaps, "the first fields" in which the young imagination delights to ramble, as well as the last which it will explore. Some children are slow in comparing, deliberating, or associating ideas, and others seem to have little inclination for mental exertions of any kind, whilst a large number of those who are naturally vivacious, prompt, and energetic, take more delight in strong feeling than in deep reflection. Hence, the sensations of pleasure or pain are intense or acute, torpid or sluggish, according to the mental capacity or natural inclination of the pupil—strong association of ideas being a characteristic of such as are over-sensitive or enthusiastic.

In cultivating the imagination so as to counteract the various defects peculiar to different natural dispositions, the teacher must have more than ordinary knowledge of child-nature. He must, in fact, be as well posted in "the anatomy of the mind" as a surgeon is expected to be in that of the body. He will then be able to read the mental through the physical, and can prescribe the necessary remedy according to his skill. The best and most approved regimen for the quick and slow—lively and dull, the worker and dreamer, observer and reflector—will be duly considered and faithfully administered in his plan of education.

Imagination counteracts defects.

SECTION 4. REFLECTION AND REASON.

Reflection—
a creative
faculty.

Memory endows man with the power to recal any, or all, impressions once strongly, vividly, and accurately conceived. Reflection then enables him to compare their respective properties, estimate their concurrent or divergent influence, and ascertain their mutual or relative connections. It is this faculty which enables us to associate old conceptions so as to produce new ideas on which to base the inferences or conclusions of reason. Reflection may, in fact, be regarded as a creative faculty; since, by its aid, we analyze, compare, and combine old ideas so as to generate new ones. It does not directly impart the vital energies of conception; but it nevertheless develops and enlarges the capacity of thought. Its agency is chiefly directed to a consideration of the positive qualities of objects; and, by leading us to form just ideas of their relations, it enables judgment to give fair and impartial decisions, in accordance with the sober realities of life and the plain dictates of unadorned truth.

Reason—its
utility and
importance.

Reason and reflection are faculties of the highest order; and though their presence may be discovered in children at a very early age, yet they do not attain perfection until late in life. Their development is essentially progressive, and may be referred chiefly to habits of accurate observation, arising from mental and moral culture. Reason is an exercise of the will which controls thought and regulates the mind, and may be defined as the art of drawing inferences from the association of facts or ideas. Having collected certain data, it abstracts the attention from external objects, analyzes its perceptions, associates its ideas, estimates their general bearing and relative importance, recals previously acquired knowledge, reviews former and present ideas as with a kaleidescope, and finally, with the aid of conscience, it arrives at conclusions which may be regarded as the fountains of justice and "stepping stones" of judgment. Reason is one of those rays of Divinity in man, which ennobles human nature, and brings us nearer the Creator, while shining in on our hearts, calmly and placidly, like moonbeams on a silvery sea. The greater the development of this principle, the greater our knowledge of humanity—the more we understand ourselves and others, and the wider and more efficient our sphere of usefulness. The existence of this God-like principle in the human soul proves that man was not created to be a slave, mentally, spiritually, or physically—that he was originally endowed with free will, and all inherent or collateral privileges implied by that term, and that he is expected to use every faculty with which he was favored to the fullest extent of his ability. Reason impels us to receive truth, however painful to our feelings of pride or self-esteem, and it continually commands us to do every man justice, however inimical such action may be to our personal interests. "Its still, small voice," aided and directed by the kindred voice of Conscience, tells us that the art of being happy implies the dispensation of happiness to others—that natural kindness and fraternal affection ensure the happiness of society, collectively and individually, and that the interests of all are secure in the hands of God. Though the understanding may be regarded as the principal working power of the mind, yet all the inferior faculties must perform their respective duties ere reason can exercise her authority, or judgment make known his decision.

Formal reasoning scarcely falls within the province of elementary education, and is, therefore, professedly taught in but very few of our public schools. The art of reasoning, however, is not wholly ignored. It is practiced, more or less, though indirectly, in every school in the land. It is taught practically, however informally, wherever rules and principles are deduced from examples, or inferred as a result of comparison from simple questions—wherever the conclusions arising from personal discoveries in Grammar,

Art of reasoning considered.

7

Science, or Mathematics, are summarised and prepared for application in the solution of similar or more complex difficulties. The highest and purest forms of reasoning practiced in our public schools are imparted by the study of Euclid, Algebra, and Grammar. These subjects present exercises in reasoning (within certain definite limits) which are well-connected, conclusive, exhaustive, absolute, and therefore, complete, explicit, irrefragable, and free from fallacies. The study and acquisition of a liberal course of public school subjects (such as suggested or prescribed by the Council of Public Instruction for Ontario) develops and invigorates the reason, while intuitively and unconsciously imparting the art of reasoning. Such a course of instruction, when fully adopted and intelligently taught, gives each faculty of the mind its due share of attention, so that there is a successive, concurrent, and continuous development of the various powers in an order of sequence as near as possible to the order of Nature. In planning a system of education, or in projecting a mode of instruction, the teacher should carefully consider the peculiar talents and ever-varying tastes of children, so as to give each an opportunity of developing his specialty in accordance with the indications of his natural disposition.

To ascertain motives—How and why. Vivacious children, and others who feel quickly, should be encouraged to describe and compare their sensations in a deliberate manner. Their motives of action can be thus ascertained, while their minds are strengthened by the voluntary exertion entailed by such an exercise. By this means, and by careful attention to the circumstances which give birth to hope and fear, joy and grief, a good knowledge of a child's habitual mental associations, designs and aversions, may be obtained ; and the teacher will thus have gained such information as will enable him to modify, guide, or alter the child's character as he may think expedient, whilst fixing his own ascendancy and authority on an immovable basis. By a judicious preparation of his pupils' minds, he may increase the attraction and effect of his lessons so as to make their impressions indelible.

Some have laid it down as an axiom, and apparently with truth, that those who are favored with more than ordinary powers of imagination, are usually defective in judgment. In this case, the reason and judgment should be strengthened even at the expense of the imagination, as they are the more important faculties. A cultivated imagination, however, is not only a never failing source of pleasure and entertainment, but a positive necessity to those who expect to occupy a high sphere of usefulness. The different callings in life are indebted to imagination for the ardent professional enthusiasm which enables their votaries to overcome every obstacle in their path, and at last stand prominently forward as leaders and masters in their respective arts. Different professions require different degrees of enthusiasm, but its source is the same in all. Men of genius are generally characterized by an enthusiasm which is often mistaken for insanity by the uninitiated— the world has never exhibited much repugnance to the persecution or crucifixion of its great reformers. The enthusiasm arising from strong imagination makes military and political heroes—poets, patriots, and others—strike out in the direction best suited to their tastes and genius, hence the vast variety of callings. Should our enthusiasm fail during our apprenticeship in life, we ourselves will fail also from the want of energy and stamina. Enthusiasm is, in fact, the first, and perhaps the greatest, element of success. Hence the desirability of rightly cultivating, training, and guiding the imagination, without which there can be no enthusiasm. Enthusiasm increases the value of objects whilst it depreciates real difficulties. To be really advantageous and useful in the highest degree, imagination and enthusiasm must be subject to the control of the judgment.

Callings in life indebted to imagination.

SECTION 6. THE JUDGMENT.

"The key stone" of the intellectual arch.

Judgment being the highest of the faculties, Nature would seem to imply that its chief development should take place near the close of a school career. The faculty of judgment would be comparatively useless unless assisted by the minor faculties, just as the head would be if deprived of the services of the less important parts of the body. Memory, imagination, reflection, etc., must support judgment with facts or data, even as the inferior organs of the body nourish and support the brain. Judgment is a monarch, and cannot exist without subjects and servants. Before exercising judgment, we must necessarily have some experience of the world and of men. It is the key stone of the intellectual arch. To retain that position, every stone of the under structure must be sound and of due proportions, and, in addition, occupy its proper place. Every faculty must do its duty ere Judgment can do "his," just as the wheels and works of a clock must do, ere the hands indicate the hour on the dial plate.

A compound faculty.

Judgment expresses itself in propositions; ideas in terms. It therefore bears the same relation to a thought that observation bears to an idea. The exercise of judgment comes into partial operation in early life, and continues its growth through after years, and probably never reaches its full maturity in this world. It may be regarded as a compound faculty, comprising abstraction and generalization. By the process of abstraction we compare the whole of anything with its parts, or *vice versâ*; and by generalization we compare one entity with another. Judgment implies comparison, contrast, and analogy, or resemblance. The idea of resemblance suggests that of dissimilarity. Comparison deals with the resemblance of objects; analogy with the resemblance of qualities or functions.,

Inference.

The dependence of cause and effect will gradually lead to inference, which, in itself, is the creature of reflection, as it has no *sensible* or tangible existence. Inference comprises two divisions—the inductive and deductive. Induction infers the general from the particular—the law which governs facts from the facts themselves—the cause from the effect. Deduction enables us to draw the particular from the general—the facts from the laws which govern them— the effects from the cause. As Currie observes, "Both are necessary parts of that completed reason by which scientific knowledge is established." In the order of logical development, time, and effort, induction precedes deduction. "Induction comes first and lays down the plan or outline, and then deduction reduces the contents to order within that outline."

Section 6. INTEGRITY.

The consciousness of having deserved well of our friends, and the certainty that we enjoy their confidence and esteem, are sources of continual happiness. The pleasure of being trusted and esteemed by those we love is, perhaps, one of the most delicious experiences of early life. Children will do much to earn such rewards. They should, however, be led to look impartially on their own merits, so that while gratefully accepting well earned praise, they may have sufficient sense to regard flattery with contempt. Confidence is the reward of integrity and intrinsic worth. Children feel proud of being trusted, and, when they learn that their character depends on their conduct, and that to secure respect they must deserve it, they will strive to maintain a good reputation, and the generous enthusiasm of their nature (if not habit and reason) will win them to the side of honour and virtue. They may then be led to understand that truth is the reflection of God in the heart of man—the light of heaven revealed on earth. *Pleasure of being trusted.*

We have often noticed during our school experience—as visitor or pupil—that many teachers wear masks while on *Not to wear masks.*

duty. They are radiant, cheerful, and happy (and apparently desirous of bestowing happiness) in their ordinary intercourse with society, but in the school-room they seem to be totally different personages. Cold, stern, and severe—the light of a smile never relaxes their iron features. Grave and solemn, as if the school was the tomb of their affections, a word of sympathy or encouragement never escapes their indomitable lips. Teachers, if you feel kindly, don't fear to let the little ones know it—they will appreciate and reciprocate. If you cannot sympathize with child-nature, yourself and pupils will not understand each other—your school associations will lose half their attractions, and more than half their real happiness. Try, therefore, to be natural: throw off the mask; let the warmth of your affections and the radiance of your face be as sunlight to your pupils. Be happy, and the fountain of happiness to your little friends; then will the school-room be a haven of rest to you and them. Reveal your real nature. We should not act a falsehood even to win an erring child to the truth. It would be wrong to do so, and, besides, children would see through such an artifice, and gradually, if not immediately, withdraw their confidence and esteem.

Courtesy to children. We should listen with pleasure and attention to such narratives of children as relate to their personal experiences, and as Rousseau well observes, " We should not doubt, nor appear to doubt, their veracity ; nor should we question them too minutely on any matters concerning which it might be their interest to deceive us." Suspicion would be injurious, and unbelief imprudent.

Praise in proportion to merit. If teachers flatter indifferent pupils, then the more worthy will gradually lose their desire to deserve or receive praise. Praise increases personal confidence, and is a strong stimulus to industry if it be judiciously managed ; but in awarding it we must not give false ideas of merit—the degree of approbation must be in proportion to the value of the action. The pleasures of praise should be associated with what commands our approval, and, as the stimulus is of a powerful nature, we should administer it in small quantities—the smallest calculated to produce the desired effect.

Section 7. PRUDENCE.

Judgment, resolution, and benevolence are the essential elements of prudence. We require judgment to calmly review the objects of happiness; resolution to put our convictions in execution; benevolence to enable us to prefer the greatest amount of felicity; so that, if necessary, we may cheerfully sacrifice ourselves for others. Prudence also implies tact, or what some call intuitive analogy—a system of " short-hand reasoning," by which we arrive at immediate conclusions without going through the steps of actual demonstrations. It may justly be said that sensible people possess tact, prudent people use it, and imprudent people lack it or abuse it. *Elements of prudence.*

Objects appear differently to different people, and each person, while strictly following his own conviction according to the light of his understanding, may, nevertheless, be the victim of false associations or false appearances. Personal feeling may make them oblivious of past experience, and negligent as regards future calculation. If so, wisdom will not inspire their minds, nor prudence guide their conduct. Reason and friendly counsel may even fail to recal them to a right sense of their position—more especially if they happen to be victims of false impressions. In the latter case, false ideas must be removed, and wrong ones rectified, before we attempt to improve the judgment or inculcate prudence. *Certain impressions to be rectified.*

Should children entertain false ideas on any subject, we must change their manner of viewing it before we can alter their feelings. In fact, we must induce them to change *How to correct false habits and ideas.*

their habits of thought. In doing this, their age and experience should be taken into account. Habits of action and modes of thought may be easily broken, or formed, in young children; but, before attempting to produce similar results in the larger pupils, we must first rectify the principles which guide, or regulate, their conduct. The habits of larger children are based on principles—true or false—as they generally exercise reflection, more or less, before they act. Hence, to change their mode of action, we must correct and purify the source of action by changing their manner of thinking.

CHAPTER X.
POWER AND EFFECTS OF SYMPATHY.

Sympathy and its effects.

Sympathy may be regarded as the essence of sensibility. It is the primary source of compassion, courtesy, kindness, ambition, friendship, love—the genuine language of Nature, the fountain of moral sentiment and social virtue—the most pleasing peculiarity of childhood—the most charming and attractive characteristic of riper years. Yet, strange to say, there is no necessary connection between sympathy and virtue. If misdirected, or injudiciously guided, it may be productive of evil. To be useful to the individual and to society, it must be governed by the light of reason. Children long for the sympathy of their companions—they wish their friends to admire their efforts—to be proud of their success— to take pleasure in their superiority. Their hearts yearn for our sympathy and approbation. Let us be generous, and make them happy while we may. Beaming glances of affection will repay our efforts. Children can feel and reciprocate sympathy long before they can exercise reason or judgment.

To this feeling may be traced the desire to excel—the ambition to dare and do—the motives of good and great deeds. Involuntary imitation is its natural expression at an early age. Children with strong sympathies are, therefore, the most liable to be injured or improved by example, habit, or other external circumstances. For this reason, young children should never be exposed to the influence of bad example. This restriction will not be so necessary as they approach the years of discretion, for their habits will then have attained greater strength, and they will probably have acquired sufficient sense to choose for themselves, and sufficient fortitude to abide by their decisions. Kindness and benevolence seldom fail to inspire emotions of gratitude and love. It will be difficult, perhaps impossible, to transform sympathy into virtue, should the faces of teachers and relatives frequently exhibit the stern and vile expressions of anger, malice, or other malevolent passions.

If a teacher's intercourse with his pupils be honorable, candid, and straightforward, and if he treat them with habitual kindness, courtesy, and generosity, and should he be so fortunate as to be always able to cheer them with the light of sympathy and love, then will they always feel happy in his presence; for, work under his auspices will be a pleasure, and even continued attention will become agreeable. In fancy they will often see him surrounded with a halo of light, and will gradually come to regard him as a kind of sacred personage who delights in removing doubts and difficulties, and in dispensing knowledge and pleasure. His presence will recal the remembrance of triumphs won by his aid. Their recollection will excite associated affection, and revive instinctive love whilst renewing former pleasures—pleasures arising from a sense of duty done. *Effects of associated affection.*

Children naturally expect a gratification from the society of strangers similar to that derived from a friendly intercourse with teachers and relatives. The curiosity and *Fellowship with companions.*

sympathy arising from this source impels them to wish for society and friendship. The present and future happiness of the child requires the judicious indulgence of this propensity. Its lonely little heart yearns for companionship, sympathy, and love. Shall it crave for these things in vain? The best way to supply these blessings is to grant children free intercourse with their peers in years and station. They will relish this privilege with a keenness unknown amongst adults.

Manage-
ment of
sensibility.

Nothing wounds the feelings of children more than to despise their friendship, or doubt the genuine character of their expressions of regard. In fact, we often alienate their affection, and perhaps change it to antipathy by undue suspicion or cold reserve. If, on the contrary, we receive their expressions of kindness and gratitude with feelings of thankfulness, they will feel delighted with the idea that their sentiments are reciprocated, and that they can give as well as receive pleasure. The desire to give pleasure will probably lead them to repeat these demonstrations from time to time; but, for fear of fostering a spirit of affectation, such repetition must not be unduly encouraged. In such cases it will require no little skill and delicacy to preserve a proper medium between the indulgence and repression of youthful sensibility. As Marmontel truly observes, "People seldom feel a desire to be cured of any defect which makes them agreeable." Hence, if possible, the cure should be effected in youth. As children advance in years, the enthusiasm arising from fine feeling should be gradually and cautiously repressed by the greater cultivation of the reasoning faculties; so that the heart, if possible, may be made impervious to disappointment—the seat of abiding pleasure instead of fluctuating felicity.

Principles of
happiness.

Children should be treated with such courtesy, kindness, and consideration as may be necessary to transform childhood into a possible state of uniform happiness. They

should not, it is true, be indulged inordinately or impru-
dently, but they should be invariably given the largest
amount of present pleasure consistent with future advantage. Our happiness, like that of children, in every stage
of life depends, to a great extent, on the genuine heart-felt
sympathy of our fellow creatures. We cannot command
lasting sympathy or enduring friendship unless we ourselves
possess some useful and agreeable qualities, or social virtues,
which will endear us to our companions. Mutual intercourse, under such circumstances, will develop mutual
thought, and thus enable us to derive pleasure and profit
from the sweet influences of society and friendship.

PART II.—SCHOOL MANAGEMENT.

CHAPTER I.

CHARACTERISTICS OF THE SCHOOL.

Good order and system essential. Order has always been, and will ever be, the faithful handmaid of the Creator. We gaze with awe on her movements in the heavens, and with feelings of the deepest interest contemplate her doings on the earth during the dark ages of old. Without Order, chaos or confusion would run riot as at "the beginning;" nothing could be efficiently done; all our efforts would end in disappointment, and our labours be comparative failures, if not worse than useless. Order and system are essential to success in every calling. No railroad or steamboat company could possibly prosper if they neglected to make arrangements regulating the arrival and departure of their trains or steam boats. Nor is this sufficient—they must afterwards publish (or inform the public of) the rules they have made, and strictly adhere to the same. Order must be apparent in all the transactions of the company (and of its agents), otherwise they will lose the confidence of the public. The rules of the company once fixed, should, if possible, be invariable. The preliminary arrangements being made, and the time table drawn up for the guidance of the public, both parties will save time and money by being punctual and regular. **Necessity of time table.** This "Time Table" and its accompanying code of rules, being the agreement of the company with the public, forms the basis of a common understanding between the contracting parties, neither of whom can infringe the conditions with impunity and convenience. The time table is the plan of the company's work—an abstract of their agreement with the public. It is absolutely necessary on both sides. Without it, all would be confusion and dissatisfaction, and no efforts of the officers or employés could make the line pay. In fact, it would be a general nuisance instead of a public convenience.

Order and system are essential to success in any line of life. This is true of nations, of armies, of societies, of public meetings, and of individuals. No order; no progress. Such is the rule in the university, the college, and the school. Without order, without system, without a plan of work—without a well regulated time table—the best efforts of the teacher will be fruitless, and his establishment little better than an "incarnation" of chaos. The observance or enforcement of good order in schools, curbs the lawless propensities of youthful hearts. civilizes their animal tendencies, and, by obliging them to conform to its conditions—conditions naturally repugnant to their will—it day by day strengthens the power of mind over matter, facilitates all mental acquirements, and endows every individual with the graces of self control. By its aid, those accomplishments and qualities, which at first were foreign, become customary, and then habitual—that is, personal characteristics. Laxity of order will nullify the good intentions of both teachers and parents. Its tendency is to transform children into boisterous, riotous rowdies, instead of educating them to be good and useful citizens—ladies and gentlemen in the true sense of the words. Children will practice order in school if trained to habits of order at home. They naturally love order, and will observe it if it be made more convenient to them than disorder. Suitable and attractive occupation is the best guarantee of good order. Order and system, punctuality and regularity, are the sides of a "moral square," within which every true craftsman should duly exercise his skill for the benefit of himself and his fellows.

Effects of good order.

A time and place for everything.

"True order," as Miss Chadwick well observes, "is that which is maintained with the least apparent effort, just as the best ruler is he who governs without seeming to govern. The school should be a model of refined taste and good arrangement—every article of furniture should be in its proper place, and every exercise should have its appointed time, and *vice versâ*."

A plan of study.

The various duties of the day, arranged according to a pre-determined plan (as in the case of the railroad company), should be attended to in order. The plan of study or time table, drawn up by the teacher for the guidance of himself and pupils, should be hung up in a conspicuous place in the school-room, and each pupil should be instructed to take a copy of the same. This copy will direct the pupil in his studies, or in the preparation of his lessons at home, and will show the parents what he is doing while at school. By referring to it he will see at a glance what lessons he has to prepare for the current day, or for the morrow, as the case may be. This course will save much time and trouble, and, if hung up in the private study at home, will furnish parents with information which they are often anxious to possess.

Guidance of youthful activity.

Having classified his pupils and given them employment in accordance with the directions on the prescribed time table, he should insist on their earnest attention to their respective duties. By carefully attending to this matter, and taking up each subject according to its order of sequence, he will be dispensing an effective antidote to that law of nature which impels children to activity; or, rather, he will have discovered an effective means of directing it to other ends than the pursuits of indolence and pleasure. Neglect in this case, as in others, will give birth to much mischief, and make it almost impossible for the teacher to "resist the beginnings" of idleness, disobedience and self-indulgence. Change in the subjects of study, within short intervals, is not only favourable to good order, but also to good health and mental vigour. " Animal motions, or configurations of the organs of sense, constitute our ideas. The fatigue that follows a continued application of the mind to one object, is relieved by changing the subject of our thoughts, as the continued movement of one limb is relieved by moving another in its stead."* The truly wise educator," says Ascott Hope, " will take care to let the latent energy of youth have some natural vent." In other words, physical recreation and mental labour should succeed each other alternately.

In our opinion, it is simply impossible for the best of teachers to maintain good order in a large school, under certain conditions—conditions for which parents and trustees are wholly responsible. It not unfrequently happens that teachers who are not appreciated in one locality become the idols of another. It is a fact of common occurrence that he who has failed to maintain order in one school becomes eminently successful in this respect when he removes to another sphere of labour. What is the cause of this apparent anomaly? Why is it that in one place his labours produce nothing but leaves, whilst in the other they bear abundant fruit? The efficient teacher of the one school is voted inefficient when he assumes a similar charge elsewhere, and why? Teachers, and other experienced persons, will give a variety of practical and suggestive answers to these queries. Many will ascribe the result to prejudice, factious opposition, difference of locality and in people; but, although all these answers may be true in certain cases, yet there is still another cause of local or temporary professional failure for which the trustees and parents are personally and collectively responsible. We allude to the absence of comfortable and attractive school accommodation. The school house should be large and airy, agreeably furnished, comfortably heated,

Unfortunate professional connections.

---

* Darwin.

A hint to parents and guardians.

and well supplied with school apparatus. The school should be well swept every evening, and properly dusted every morning. All its appendages should be a model of cleanliness, neatness, and comfort. The apartments should be properly ventilated, and sufficiently large to accommodate all the pupils in attendance. The various articles of furniture should be kept in their proper places, and each place should have its proper furniture. Pupils should be clean in person, neat in dress, smart in appearance, kind and courteous in disposition, dutiful and obedient—ever ready to "bear and forbear." But how can such habits of order and propriety be inculcated with success where external conditions are militant—where the school and everything connected therewith are suggestive of disorder, misery, and meanness? How can a teacher, however skilful, be expected to command success in such a place? How can children be expected to form habits of order and industry in over-crowded schools—the windows being broken, the desks "ricketty," the seats uncomfortable, the cold unbearable, or the heat oppressive? Where there is no pump, no washing apparatus, no playground or gymnasium, no cloak-room, no singing, no music—nothing whatsoever to render the school attractive. It is impossible. Such a school-room, with such surroundings, is a silent but powerful inculcator of disorder and discontent, and would counteract the precepts and example of the most eminent and worthy educator on earth. It is time that parents and trustees should become conscious of the fact that the best and most skilful teacher cannot *permanently* maintain good discipline in a miserable over-crowded class-room, where defective appliances and insufficient appointments ever tend to generate discomfort and produce disorder.

A Canadian village school.

Some years ago the writer was officially connected with a public school in one of our western settlements, in which the average attendance exceeded one hundred and sixty. In the junior division, many of the pupils had no desks;

in the primary division, more than one-half of the children had no seats, and were under the necessity of squatting themselves on the floor, so that their class-room resembled an infant "tailoring department." The few seats were densely crowded. There were no maps, no cards, no books, no decorations—absolutely nothing in the room but some old-fashioned desks, which apparently were old enough to have "come over in the *Mayflower*," a few ricketty benches, a table minus a leg, a stove, a poker, and an old drum. The senior division, on the first floor of the building, was tolerable, but devoid of any decorations or furniture calculated to cultivate the taste of the pupils. The intense noise which occasionally prevailed in the former divisions was favourable to the cause of disorder in the latter, and had a tendency to "drown" the voice of the teacher as there was no "deafening material" in the floors. Just fancy such a state of things, and the impossibility of any teachers (under these circumstances) to inculcate, with success, habits of order and propriety. For twelve months or more, the trustees "quarrelled" about the provision of desks and other requisites—half being in favour of supplying the necessary articles, and half against it—and during all that time the parents and guardians of the children looked on with calm indifference. The evils arising from the persistent meanness of trustees, and the culpable negligence of parents, are often imputed to the teacher. Finding that "things do not progress satisfactorily," they put themselves to no trouble to ascertain the real cause; and, if pointed out to them, their bigotry, selfishness and ignorance are so great as to prevent them seeing it: they think it more convenient to impute the cause of failure to want of skill in the teachers, and accordingly the latter are converted into a kind of scape goats, and sacrificed for the sins of others. How convenient for our educational guardians! You send the scape goat into the wilderness; still the greatest sufferers

8

are your own little children. Is it possible that men can be found who would see children die, or grow up deformed in mind or body, rather than call on the ratepayers to pay an additional tax of a cent on the dollar? We fear it is so in many places. The foregoing is not an isolated case—there are hundreds of similar ones in Europe and America. Teachers in such localities, though unfortunate in their professional connections, must make the most of their limited opportunities, and learn to cheer themselves with the idea that they labour for posterity. The poor children are more unfortunate than their teachers, seeing that they have such careless parents and unworthy educatioual trustees. Let them resolve to do better when they come to man's estate, and provide for *their* children *those* advantages which we would fain bestow on themselves.

Effects of exterior influences.

A large, airy, well-furnished, well-arranged, comfortable school, enlarges the perceptive faculties, captivates the heart, generates cheerful emotions, fosters taste, and has a special tendency to render the minds of children susceptible to the precepts of the teacher. Broken windows, broken desks, "lame" benches, wet walls, damp or uneven floors, and rooms too hot or too cold, have a contrary effect. No matter what "economical" trustees say to the contrary, the quality of the building and furniture have a most powerful effect on the minds and bodies of teachers and pupils. How can a sweet little child like to spend five or six hours every day in a building which has a cheerless exterior and a gloomy interior? It would be strange, indeed, if such sensitive and innocent little creatures did not look upon such schools as men look upon asylums and jails, or as sheep would look on the shambles, were they endowed with reason. Bright children love a school which is bright inside and bright outside. The building should be a handsome one—comfortably furnished, large, cheerful-looking, exhibiting artistic taste in all its arrangements—a model of neatness and convenience. Everything connected with the institution should bear evidence of refined taste.

While speaking of this subject, we will take the liberty of stating that personal neatness is one of the primary essentials in a good teacher. It is a necessary qualification, a cardinal virtue, which no educator can afford to neglect. He must insist on its practice by his pupils, and be careful to exhibit it in his own person. Success in teaching depends, in no small measure, on the observance of this rule. Next to cleanliness, there is scarcely any other personal characteristic so essential in the practice of education. Create an intellectual atmosphere in the school, so that honour, truth, and justice may "flourish like trees planted beside rivers of water." Then strive to make the class-rooms cheerful and attractive, and let the teachers endeavour to acquire similar characteristics. Success will then depend on the good sense of the community, and the generosity or justice of trustees. *Personal neatness.*

A quiet, gentlemanly (or ladylike) manner should be the leading characteristics of boys (and girls) in school. The behaviour of all should be gentle and unassuming. Each pupil should possess a business-like air, and during business hours a general calm should reign throughout the respective departments. The teacher should tolerate no conversation in the desks during school sessions, and, when "hearing a class," he should never allow one pupil to interrupt another, or two to speak at the same time. Then, a pleasing calm, a genial quietness, a salutary restraint, will pervade the whole school—thus increasing the comfort of the pupils and the efficiency of the teachers. *Manner of pupils in schools.*

While giving a lesson, a teacher should be all life and animation. We do not mean to imply that he should lecture—lecturing is not suited for the school-room; we do not mean that he should be a perpetual talker, as mentioned elsewhere; we do not mean that he should devote himself to *Teacher to be animated.*

continual repetition, and such like—for should he do so, his pupils will make comparatively little progress: but we mean that instead of defining, explaining, and repeating laws and principles, etc., to his pupils, he should *lead them* by a series of appropriate questions, *to define, explain, or repeat to him.* In this manner he will guide or lead them to discover the laws and principles of things for themselves. Knowledge acquired in this way becomes part of their being, and will never be forgotten, whereas that which is gained by the process of "telling" will evaporate like water, leaving not a trace behind.

Brevity a characteristic of a good school.

Brevity of expression should be one of the leading characteristics of the school. Ideas should never be covered with a multitude of words. Every thought should be expressed clearly and fully, but as laconically as possible. Useless verbiage obscures the sense and weakens the expression; but the effects of brevity are just the reverse. The teacher should thoroughly understand the particulars of each lesson, subject, or part of a subject, before introducing it to his pupils. In defining, explaining, or discussing its difficulties, uses, beauties, etc., he must be careful not to say himself, nor allow his pupils to say, more than is absolutely necessary.

Urbanity and suavity.

In school, as elsewhere, urbanity and suavity should be the motto of each pupil in his personal intercourse with those around him. Courtesy of manner, sincerity, truthfulness, unselfishness, and a careful regard for the feelings of others—love of God and nature—are, or should be, the guiding stars of every man or woman born into this world. Children, even from the earliest age, should be led to cultivate a genial manner and an amiable disposition, so that as they grow up, these endearing qualities may become personal characteristics.

Pupils to do their duty.

Each pupil should do his own work—the teacher should never do it for him, as many teachers do through feelings of mistaken kindness. Each and all should understand that their teachers and parents expect them to do their duty, and that they must do it. More assistance and attention should be given to the children of the lower divisions, or classes, than to those of the upper. The latter are generally able to help themselves, and require little which a few judicious questions will not lead them to discover, whereas the former may often really need assistance of a more minute and substantial kind. But, from the commencement, each pupil should be taught to rely chiefly on himself—babes or invalids are the only individuals fed with a spoon. So in literary matters. Self-reliance, perseverance, and industry, should be practised by all.

At home and abroad, pupils should be encouraged to love their own particular school, and to revere its teachers, preferring them to all others. Want of zeal in maintaining the honour of the school is a sure sign that a pupil does not stand very high in his respective classes, and (worse still) that he is deficient in that laudable ambition. Every pupil in a school should be ambitious of adding to its glory. Each should endeavour to make it superior to all others, always remembering that its prestige depends on individual efforts, and that they can command success by working earnestly, perseveringly, and harmoniously with their teachers. Should they do so faithfully and well, they can, in after years, look back with conscious pride and affection on the memory of their school days-—ever fondly and gratefully remembering the devoted teachers and school mates of their early youth. As a French writer (Thómãs) justly observes, "Gratitude is the sweetest as well as the holiest of duties." *To love their teachers, and be zealous of the honour of their school.*

The teacher should occasionally tell his pupils *how to study.* Calling their attention to some particular subject, or part of a subject, he should explain how he himself would study it were he to take it up for the first time—how he would examine, analyze, and combine the respective asser- *How to study aright.*

tions or statements, and revolve the whole matter in his mind as in a kaleidoscope, seizing or appropriating the leading ideas or "landmarks" as they presented themselves to his mental vision; how, by means of reflection, he would arrange these ideas in natural and logical order, and then lay them up for future use in the storehouse of his understanding. By these means, he will lead his pupils to study in a philosophical manner, and much valuable time will be saved which would otherwise be lost or wasted to no purpose. If a pupil, having a thirst for knowledge, *knows how to study aright, and has a clear idea of what he should study*, he is sure to become a learned man. If the habit of thinking justly, and strongly, be formed at an early age, the circumstances of future life will, of themselves, carry on the great work of personal improvement.

Quality and quantity.

One book studied well, and properly "digested," will be of more real service to him than would a hundred studied cursorily and without order or reflection. Quality will always tell against quantity. For these reasons, the *manner* and quality of study are far more important than the matter and quantity—far more essential to the right development of the faculties and the proper cultivation of literary taste.

Language to be pure and simple.

When the teacher undertakes to explain a subject, he should be careful to use language which will be intelligible to children. In fancy he must descend to the level of their mental capacity—standing beside them as one of themselves; and from that point, gaze in imagination on the cause or causes of their perplexity. He will then see the respective difficulties as children see them, and be able to explain each in its natural order, and in language both simple and expressive. This method of analyzing subjects, the logical order observed in explaining each component part, and the art of putting all together again—skilfully presenting it to the youthful mind as a complete whole—constitutes what may

be called *the science of teaching*, and will seldom fail to excite
an interest in study, or to create a desire for the acquisition
of knowledge. The teacher must remember that language
which would be plain and simple to him might be incomprehensible to children. He should, therefore, never use words
of foreign origin if he can express his ideas in pure Anglo-
Saxon. Should he do so, the explanatory language may
sometimes be more incomprehensible to his pupils than the
original difficulty, as it will only cover the pre-existing
"swamp" with a canopy of clouds or fogs.

We could cite many examples to show that the answer to
a question may be correct and yet be more incomprehensible
to the child than the query itself, but will mention only one
or two. Many years ago a certain little boy met with the
word "eclipse" in one of his books, and, feeling rather
puzzled about its meaning, he requested the principal of his
school to tell him what it was. The teacher graciously
smiled, and told him it was "a phenomenon." Some time
afterwards he requested another teacher to inform him "why
it was that a stone would sink in water, whereas a log of
wood always floated on the surface?" The teacher replied
that, "The cause should be attributed to the difference in
their specific gravity." Of course, the pupil *appeared* to be
satisfied with "these lucid explanations," but in reality they
had only increased his difficulties. "Phenomenon" and
"specific gravity"—"words of learned length"—were to him
as a "sounding brass or tinkling cymbal"—mud-banks over
which he might jump, but through which he dared not wade.

Prompt and accurate recitation of lessons saves much
time, strengthens praiseworthy habits, and will exercise no
small influence on the pupil's character in after life. For
these and other reasons, the teacher should always insist on
their observance. Should the interest in the subject grow
dull during recitation, he would do well to stop proceedings
until it is revived. The interest created by him in any sub-

(margin note) Lucid explanations

(margin note) Recitations of lessons to be prompt and accurate.

ject, and the amount of information imparted, are sure to be in proportion to the attention of the pupils. He should decline to proceed with the lesson without the attention of his class, or should the pupils be unable to recite without aid. By following this plan, each individual will have to stand on his own basis; the deficiency of the indolent will be exposed, and all will feel that disgrace will overtake those who fail to study the lessons thoroughly. It has been well said that "the teacher is the school;" but it is equally true that he should be the text book. He should be perfectly acquainted with all the authorized works in use in his sphere, and be able to catechize in the various subjects without reference to the book.

CHAPTER II.

HOW TO MAKE STUDY ATTRACTIVE.

Child-nature.

People who have been so unfortunate as never to have enjoyed the companionship or friendship of little children, are ignorant of some of the greatest pleasures in life. They have, perhaps, carelessly passed by the little flowers without investigation and without interest, not knowing or appreciating their value. What can be more beautiful than the radiant orbs which reflect our image as we look into the clear wells of light, so characteristic of youthful eyes? How earnestly they gaze at us! How merrily, affectionately, and gratefully they return our smiles! How full of love, hope, curiosity, and innocence are those windows of the soul! How fruitful! how interesting the study of those living, laughing, rolling, dancing gems! If patient, watchful, and sympathetic, we may perceive in the light of their reflection, the various thoughts and fancies which chase each other through the youthful mind, as well as the germs of those feelings which will some day stir up the heart and fire the imagination of the adult.

If the teacher acquires a fair knowledge of the child's mental organization, he will be the better able to adapt his instructions to the child's requirements. His professional success depends chiefly on his knowledge of Nature, and his ability to interpret her precepts aright. It behoves him to study her operations carefully, closely, perseveringly. Let him question her in all his difficulties. She is the great teacher of teachers, and the only one whose instructions are free from error. Her admonitions will direct him "in the way he should go." She will tell him that enjoyment must be combined with education, and that methods of instruction should produce a happy and healthful activity. "La tout est beau (says Rousseau) parceque tout est vrai." We naturally dislike such places and things as suggest painful reminiscences, and, in accordance with certain laws of mental association, we delight in those which recal former pleasures. The remembrance of painful lessons may make the acquisition of knowledge repulsive, and the remembrance of pleasureable ones will make it attractive. If the process of education be made pleasant and agreeable, it will not cease when school days come to an end—it will be progressive and continuous. Those therefore who would succeed as educators must study child-nature, and adjust their instructions to the laws of life. Pleasure and instruction go together in the teachings of Nature: they should not be divorced in the school-room. If feelings of pain be associated with words or ideas, the pain will invariably return to the mind whenever these words or ideas are recalled, and the child will soon contract a dislike for what he believes to be the cause of his sorrow.

Pleasure to be associated with instruction.

Education should be conducted on "the happiness principle." Pleasant feelings excite intellectual action whilst im-

The happiness principle.

proving the bodily health and natural disposition. Teachers
and pupils, according to the laws of their being, are at the
mercy of associated ideas. Their relations are friendly or
antagonistic in proportion to the happiness or misery produced by the prevailing mode of culture. A teacher will
be hated if he create no other than painful emotions; he will
be liked if he sympathize with his pupils, and can lead them
to daily conquests; he will be esteemed and admired if his
precepts be good, noble, and confirmed by practice; he will
be loved if he teaches in accordance with Nature's principles.
From these facts we infer that that system of education
which gives the most pleasure and least pain is the best and
most appropriate.

Guiding
principles.
When children are well taught in accordance with Nature's
plan, they will often prefer mental to physical exercise;
they will take delight in their studies, and generally prefer
school to home life. Our pupils deserve our warmest smiles
and deepest sympathies—let us give them promptly, generously, and cordially. Let us cheer them on to victory, let
us inspire them with the desire of mental conquests, and
show them how to "storm the fortifications" of doubt and
difficulty, ourselves leading the attack. Let us encourage
them in their attempts to concentrate attention, and, if possible, endow them with a desire to persevere through repeated
failures. Constant exercise will produce a constant appetite,
and a working mind will inhabit a working body. Such
efforts must educate the finer feelings of the heart whilst
creating mental enjoyment, and will thus increase the sum
total of man's happiness.

How to cul-
tivate the
love of
study.
Should children acquire a dislike to study, it would be
imprudent, and, perhaps, unjust, to force books and studies
upon them. It would be cruel to punish them for not loving what they consider uninteresting. Better far to associate pleasure with the cultivation of habits of attention and
application. Better to create or cultivate the desire for

knowledge by a series of interesting conversations on such subjects as are likely to be useful and attractive. When this desire is created, study will become pleasant and books cease to be repugnant. To preserve this desire in good working order, the attention when aroused must not be fatigued; there must be variety in the subjects of study, and periods of application must be regularly followed by intervals of rest. As Mons. Marcel observes, "Lessons should cease before the child evinces symptoms of weariness. . . . . His desire of variety should be indulged, and the gratification of his curiosity should be combined with his improvement." We believe that a lesson should cease while the child's attention is still on the *qui vive*— before the desire for further information begins to wane. "The various powers of children's minds stretch out like young tendrils to grasp the truths of the material world;"* but their yearning for knowledge should not be gratified so far as to destroy their desire for more.

When a lesson should cease.

Knowledge should be self-mastered, and is best acquired by a process of self-instruction, more or less modified. For this reason, the subjects in the programme of studies should be so arranged as to make it possible for the pupil to ascend the successive steps with little or no external help. To effect this object, the ascending steps must correspond with the successive stages of evolution in the ordinary development of the respective faculties. This concurrence will tend to make application pleasant, and thereby endow acquisition with intrinsic gratification. The mental vigour educed by self-evolution, "will guarantee (says Herbert Spencer) a vividness and permancy of impression which the ordinary methods can never produce." The concentration of thought, essential in the solution of difficulties, necessitates a continuous organization and classification of knowledge previously acquired, and, in connection with the pleasurable excite-

Self-instruction the best.

* Rev. Dr. Bell.

ment peculiar to success, it tends to make a permanent
record in the memory of all facts received.

Let children be allowed perfect freedom of action in the
play-grounds, so long as they recognize and respect each
other's rights and privileges; but insist on perfect discipline
in the school.   When taking fresh air and exercise, Nature
impels them to be lively and sportive, and, in our opinion,
the teacher or parent who would unnecessarily damp their
flowing spirits and joyous hilarity of heart, would be little
better than a tyrant.   During their younger years, and
under such circumstances, let the innocent little creatures
be free to run, leap, and romp just as they please.   Nature
prompts them to do so.   How can we be so forgetful of our
own young days as to curtail their happiness!   Let us make
Nature our guide and ally, and encourage the little ones to
"sing for joy."   She impels them to run, jump, and shout
with delight.   God's works smile on them from every side·
Why should man alone be frowning and stern?   Freedom
will promote health, and increase the delights of life.   After
due exercise in "Nature's sportive fields," a return to order
will be agreeable, and the labours of study attractive.   If
children dislike studies, it is chiefly because their teachers
oppose, neglect, or ignore Nature, and cannot, therefore,
make them attractive.   Dislike of study, or failure in acquisition or application, point to personal ignorance or professional incapacity on the part of the teacher, or to mental
debility on the part of the pupil, arising, perchance, from
imperfect instruction in the past, or a too rapid promotion
in the present.   "Experience," says Fallenberg, "has taught
me that indolence in young persons is so directly opposite
to their natural disposition to activity, that unless it be the
consequence of bad education, it is almost invariably connected with some constitutional defect."

Mons. Vernet justly observes that "the exercise of our
faculties is always attended with pleasure so long as the

exercise can be continued without fatigue." For this reason, lessons should not be too numerous, nor the term of application too long. It matters little how much is learned in a given time, provided the habits of attention be strengthened or acquired, the wish to improve excited, and a longing for more information created. Children regard their lessons as some grown people regard friends—they love them while they think them useful and pleasant; but contract a dislike for them when they imagine them to be troublesome or disagreeable. In teaching, we should point out the design and practical utility of the respective subjects of study, and then exercise all our ingenuity to make them attractive and agreeable.

If we watch a child studying under the guidance of Nature, we will notice that he earnestly examines the object of his attention. He feels it, tastes it, breaks it, weighs it, and makes it undergo the scrutiny of all his senses, committing his respective observations to memory, one by one. There is no distraction, no confusion, no interruption, no mental sleep in Nature's mode of culture. The attention is undivided, vigorous, and active; all the energies of the mind are concentrated upon one object, and only one, at a time. Hence, we infer that children should never be interrupted in their experiments on surrounding objects, or while engaged in work, play, or the solution of difficulties. Such interruption breaks the course of their ideas, and, besides giving them real annoyance, prevents them from acquiring knowledge by personal experience. Instead of thwarting or interrupting them, teachers or parents should direct their activity, furnish materials for additional combinations, and make such suggestions as will enable them to take fresh, and, if possible, more extensive observations. It is our duty to foster their love of play by directing it into useful and scientific channels; and, instead of finding fault with their physical restlessness and apparent mental idleness, we should

Nature's mode of culture.

hearken to the voice of Nature and arouse ourselves to the consciousness of the fact that it is our privilege to guide their energies in the pursuit of knowledge by giving proper direction to their natural curiosity and bodily vigour.

How Nature teaches. Nature teaches by means of tangible and familiar objects. She does not fatigue the mind with long lessons. Her instructions are practical, not theoretical or abstract. She calls for no painful exertion of mind or body. She proceeds gradually, from the known to the unknown—from the simple to the complex—one step at a time, taking due care that the foremost foot is firmly fixed before she moves the other; hence, her lessons are always received with real gratification and positive delight. She fills the minds of her pupils with ideas, but leaves the mode of expression to their judgment and choice. All her lessons are useful, and imparted to be used. She is, therefore, the best and most successful teacher Under her guidance, as Dr. Gall observes, "Every new lesson is a pleasure, and an additional step in advance. In every instance, the exercise of to-day revives and consolidates that of yesterday, while it smooths and prepares a way for that of to-morrow."

When Nature dismisses her school. Mental enquiry creates mental hunger; but after a certain length of application, a child's attention will necessarily wane. Having stored up for future use the ideas acquired, his desire for further investigation, or additional experiment, will cease for a time in obedience to Nature's promptings. His lesson has been learned, and the law of his being declares it is time to play, or change the subject. Any attempts to stimulate, or further force, the attention, would, under the circumstances, be injudicious and unjust—perhaps cruel. The mental appetite has been appeased, and time is required for rumination and mental digestion. Prolonged or compulsory efforts, in such a case, would probably excite feelings of dislike. Nature requires rest, variety, change. Let her have them.

CHAPTER III.

INCENTIVES TO STUDIOUS HABITS.

The desire to be useful and to do what is right, are the Noblest incentives of human action—the most praiseworthy principles of individual character. Being the offspring of a good conscience, they are the worthiest preceptors of personal conduct. United with the anxious desire of advancement and the earnest love of acquisition, they are the fundamental elements on which the teacher must repose his efforts whilst exciting and promoting studious habits amongst his pupils. Emulation is, perhaps, one of the most commendable aspirations which can stir up or influence the human mind. By emulation we mean the love of distinction, the earnest desire to advance in knowledge, to improve our condition in life, to excel others without wishing to depress them. Progress is imprinted on our nature—we were never created to retrograde or remain stationary. "Onward and upward" should be the motto of man in particular, as of Nature in general. Wholesome emulation will seldom fail to develop progress in youth or manhood, and should, therefore, be judiciously employed by every teacher. It tends to make men and boys better, wiser, or greater than they really are, and (as the saying runs) often "enables them to surpass themselves." It is, therefore, one of the noblest aspirations which can fire the heart of youth or guide the feelings of man.

Curiosity is the expression of a desire for knowledge— the earliest development of the young intelligence, and, since it is "the first motive of sentient, intelligent being," it may be regarded as the source and stimulus of attention. Curiosity often "runs wild," and is then the source of importunity, impertinence, inconstancy, and change. Its development, therefore, requires careful cultivation and guidance. Its energies should be concentrated on a few ob-

Noblest incentives of action.

Curiosity—its regulation and cultivation.

jects—objects of personal worth or public utility—and these should be pursued in accordance with Nature's mode of teaching.

The desire of acquisition.   The pleasures experienced in acquiring useful and interesting information more than repay the labours of study. This "delicious pleasure" varies in proportion to the age and mental development of the student.   Its influence is greatest in infancy, and least in old age.   A baby feels more delight in studying the philosophy of a drum, out of which it has just "knocked the bottom," or in contemplating the fragments of a China cup it has just broken, than the aged miser would experience in discovering a gold mine.   "The propensity in children to do mischief" is, in reality, a wholesome and commendable curiosity—an intense desire to acquire information.   Their mind is conscious of its ignorance and want of experience—it is awake to acquire knowledge of men and things.   They have been placed as strangers in a world of wonders, and in exercising their "destructive ingenuity," or in asking "peculiar questions," they are merely seeking to gratify their curiosity—they are fulfilling one of the conditions of Nature, and, in this respect, should be aided rather than discouraged.   In after years, he will be the most successful teacher who can most effectually excite and satisfy this curiosity or thirst for knowledge. This laudable propensity once properly aroused, the mind of the pupil shall thenceforth neither slumber nor sleep, and, instead of a task, learning will be a pleasure to the teacher and the taught.

The love of approbation.   The love of approbation is a very powerful incentive to study.   Many educators consider it to be a very commendable one ; others regard it as reprehensible.   We don't. Being a selfish propensity inherent in our nature, its application requires considerable caution, discrimination, and judgment.   It is commendable so long as it excites the child or the man to desire the admiration of the good, the pious, and the learned—so long as it incites him to seek the approval of his teacher, parents, and friends—so long as it impels him to increase his own merit without wishing to depreciate that of others. The skilful teacher will seldom appeal in vain to this propensity—the desire of distinction and approval. Indeed, it is the opinion of many old and experienced educators, that the teacher will frequently succeed by its means in governing his pupils, and in awakening a thirst for study, when he would fail to produce the same effects by an appeal to other motives. Should the skilful teacher appeal to all these incentives in vain, and that the pupil is really indifferent about the approbation of his friends, devoid of curiosity, and careless about being useful and of doing what is right, then indeed will we admit that there is little hope for the improvement of that child—but such a child we have never met, nor do we ever expect to meet with such a hardened specimen of humanity.

Whether it is commendable to offer prizes to be competed for in schools, and whether the incentive to study thus produced, does not more than counterbalance the envy and jealousy it may be supposed to engender, have, for many years, been questions of discussion between the great educationists of the age. On the whole, we believe that the balance of opinion is in favour of their introduction and use. It must be remembered, however, that *when the prizes offered are but few in number*, and the candidates numerous, it is often exceedingly difficult to do full justice to the several competitors. Men are not, and never will be, of one mind; the candidate who would be considered best by one judge, might be rated as second by another, and *vice versâ*: so that the examiners may be divided as to the relative merits of the youthful "rivals." Then again the facilities of the competitors in preparation and acquisition may be unequal. The facilities of some of the pupils may be more than sufficient, whilst those of the majority are inadequate.

The prize system considered.

9

Some may have all the assistance afforded by good text
books, kind parents, and intelligent friends, besides having
no extraneous matters to attend to after school hours,
whereas other children, equally anxious and equally industrious, may have none of these advantages. It is true,
moreover, that the prize is often the measure of success, not
of effort—of good luck, not of worth; and, in any case, every
experienced person will readily concede that success in such
a contest is a very unreliable test of a pupil's merit. The
most meritorious does not (but should) always wear the
crown. Nature and good fortune may have given one child
mental advantages superior to those of another who is far
more industrious, so that what the one can learn in a few
hours, may cost the others as many days or weeks of persevering toil.* If the *motive* and *effort* of the latter be taken
into account, the former must yield him the palm of merit,
and these are the only means by which we can justly measure the virtue and value of an action. Though the intention
and effect be the same in both cases, there is a vast difference
in the effort.

Some teachers regard prizes as a sort of "literary bribe,"
and affirm that they tend to make children seek their end
by fair means if convenient, and by ignoble means if necessary. It is true that ambition is seldom scrupulous about
the character of her servants. Her devotees are often willing
to stoop to anything that will ensure success. That "the
end will justify the means" is a positive falsehood, and the
root of much mischief. But if such ignoble means be used
to ensure success, the teachers or examiners may possibly
detect the fraud, and punish the guilty by public exposure
and forfeiture of privileges. However, it is not at all likely
that pupils will resort to such artifices, and, if they do, the
prudence and experience of the teacher will be more than a
match for them.

*Prizes by
ignoble
means.*

---

* Page.

A prize or two offered to the best and second best scholars When they stimulate only a few. in a class, stimulates only a few. The teacher—and even the pupils themselves—knowing by experience the capabilities of the respective candidates, can tell beforehand who will be the victors at the examinations—or, at least, who are likely to be. Those pupils who have no hope of obtaining a prize, and who feel confident of their inability to win one, will make little exertion, or perhaps be totally indifferent, seeing that persevering toil will bring them no immediate reward—despairing of success, they may in fact pretend to despise "the bauble."

It is obvious that unless the mind of each child in the Uniformity of mental capacity. respective classes be awakened—unless the individual will of all be influenced to increased efforts, to *honourable* rivalry with each other, by awarding prizes, then the system is a failure.* If the system fails to arouse the whole school to renewed activity—to increased exertion, to additional efforts, to a higher ambition—and that only two or three or half a dozen really contend for the prize, the remainder being indifferent, then it is a mere gift to this limited number— one of them being sure of it. If it be a gift, why call it a prize? The efficiency of the prize system depends on the uniformity of the competitors in mental capacity. Prizes are the most powerful, popular, and perhaps the best of all incentives when the members of the respective classes are of the same degree of mental standing, and when the facilities of acquisition are similar, and the services of skilful examiners can be secured.

We are inclined to believe that prizes or rewards should The reward system. be used in every school. The prize system, in its purity, is more suitable for colleges and universities than for common and middle class schools. Judging by our own experience, and the information gleaned from others, we have no hesitation in stating that, when "prizes" are offered in these

---

* Page.

schools as an incentive to study, they should partake of the nature of rewards, and be so numerous that every industrious, well-conducted child can receive some token in recognition of his efforts "to become good and great." The number of prizes offered to each class should be in proportion to its size. Prizes should be offered for efficiency in each *individual* subject, and also for proficiency in the *whole* programme of school studies. No pupil should be eligible to compete for the latter prizes unless his character and conduct were irreproachable; but every pupil having his name on the school register should have permission to compete for the prizes for individual subjects. There should also be "good conduct" and "regular attendance" prizes, or rewards, in addition to the foregoing. Unless these things be carefully attended to, the system of awarding prizes or rewards, will fall short of the object in view. If prizes or rewards be introduced at all, they should be awarded to good conduct, diligence, punctuality, amiability, and intrinsic worth, as well as to superior talent, or marked success in certain examinations; and, as aforesaid, they should be so numerous that every deserving pupil shall receive some tangible evidence of the appreciation of his efforts.

The merit card system. An accurate register of scholarship and individual deportment never fails to engender and promote healthy emulation; yet such a journal is seldom kept. If not attended to at the close of each lesson or recitation, it must be made from memory; and, in the latter case, perfect accuracy is impossible. The pupils will, therefore, have little confidence in the record, and its moral force will be nullified. Taking these things into consideration, many of our most experienced teachers recommend the use of merit cards. These "merits" act as a substitute for, whilst securing the good results of, accurate records—and they possess the advantage of occupying less of the teacher's time than would the record system. They also enable the pupil to take home with him every evening witnesses of his daily progress, and therefore command for him a lively paternal interest, whilst securing for the teacher the active co-operation of his pupil's natural guardians.

There are many ways for using the merit cards. We will mention one or two of those commonly used. In the morning each pupil may receive as many merits as will represent the perfect work of one day—the same, or a certain number of them, to be forfeited should the recipient fail in recitation, or infringe any of the rules of the school, with reference to conduct, diligence, or punctuality. Or, if preferred, the following plan may be adopted, provided the pupils "change places" in their classes. Give a merit to each pupil as often as he may happen to get a head mark in reciting his respective lessons—the recipient to go to the foot of the class each time he receives the same. The less advanced and " more bashful" will thus have "a chance," and the more clever will have an opportunity of winning their way up again. Each time a pupil gets head of his class he is to receive a "ticket" or "merit," and then retire to the foot as before—no pupil to receive a merit for giving correct answers to questions directly addressed to himself, unless pupils "above him" have failed to answer them. According to this plan, as in the former, the teacher may fine any pupil one or more merits should he be guilty of a misdemeanor during the day. It may be remarked that the smaller merits may be exchanged for " fives, tens, fifties, or hundreds." The merits should be " paid into the treasury" once a month, and a receipt for the same handed to the pupil.

A chart or roll of merit, containing the names of the pupils, and exhibiting the number of merits won by each during the respective months of the season, should be placed in some conspicuous part of the school-room.

It must not be forgotten, however, that the "merit card" system is liable to abuse unless it be supplemented or checked

How used.

The roll of merit.

Abuse possible.

by registration. It is possible that pupils may sell or give away some of their merits to others. Unless such transactions be discovered, the latter would, by such a species of dishonesty, attain a higher standing than that to which they were justly entitled; and the suspicion of foul play thus engendered in the minds of their more honourable companions, would destroy their confidence in the system, whilst paralyzing their efforts to excel.

The number of "merits" handed in by the pupil, and credited to him on the roll of merit, at the end of the month, or at the close of the school session, will show his individual and relative standing; so that, if premiums or prizes are given, there can be no difficulty or mistake in ascertaining or determining to whom they should be awarded. No suspicion of favouritism or foul play can possibly arise, for, by looking at the roll of merit, even the pupil himself can tell to whom the rewards belong—provided the number of merits given to each individual are duly checked or registered.

Power and effects of the system.
It is needless to discuss the value of prizes as incentives to study—no experienced educationist will deny their power. When mismanaged, the system has doubtless been the origin of some evil; but when skilfully conducted, it has been productive of much good. Rewards bestowed as indicated (or even prizes) can do no harm—they afford no food for misapprehension, envy, or jealousy, and no scope for deceit or hypocrisy. Every pupil will feel that if he deserves a memento of his benefactor's kindness, his teacher's love, or of his own honest, earnest efforts, he will be sure to receive it. Each, perchance, may reason with himself and say—" I have every chance of obtaining a prize or award. If I fail in talent or perfect recitation, I will acquire one for diligence, or for good conduct, or for regularity and punctuality, or for some other individual excellence, if not for general merit. I will persevere in my studies, and carefully avoid giving trouble or offence to my companions, or to my teachers. I

will infringe none of the rules of the school, and do everything I find to do 'with all my might,' so that, even should
I fail to win a prize, all will admit that my efforts deserved
success." It is evident that either reward or prize system,
conducted according to the foregoing principles, would secure
the due recognition of the merits of each individual pupil,
whilst it would prevent the larger pupils from appropriating
all the pearls, and incite the smaller ones to press forward to
the goal set before them.

CHAPTER IV.

ELEMENTS OF GENERAL ADMINISTRATION.

The teacher should always endeavour to be consistent in
his doings, and never forget to respect his own authority.
He should say what he means, and mean what he says, and
never issue an order unless he intends it to be obeyed ; nor
should he give a second command until the first has been
executed. All commands should be issued coolly and deliberately, in a voice clear and distinct—loud enough to be
heard by all, but not too loud—and when uttered, he should
permit no hesitation in their execution. "A low, decided
tone of voice accomplishes much more than a loud, bluster-
ing one ; the former attracts and fixes attention, the latter
divides and confuses it." The teacher should be possessed
of the faculties of decision and firmness of purpose, so that
he may determine quickly, and act promptly and justly in
accordance with his sense of duty. In teaching, as in everything else, decision of character is the first element of success. There should be no hesitation apparent in his manner
—no vacillation visible in his conduct, for "a courageous

Teachers should respect their own authority.

heart and a resolute mind are omnipotent." When he decides, he should be sure to decide justly. When he issues orders, he should, if necessary, compel obedience. "Unless in case of error," as Locke affirms, "his word should be irrevocable." He must convince the whole school, individually and collectively, that he is a man of energy and tenacity of purpose, and will exact prompt and implicit obedience to all his commands—that he will permit no half measures, and tolerate no habits of partial submission or indolent compliance. Then shall his pupils confide in his justice, and, as Milton observes, "None will question the equity of his decisions;" then (and not till then) will order, regularity, prompt obedience, persevering industry, and steady progress, become the characteristics of his school. It is far better, however, that these things should be the result of dutiful affection, than the effects of mere slavish submission.

Decision of character.

A sensitive pupil will obey with greater pleasure and alacrity when requested than when ordered; it is, therefore, better to request than to command. It is imprudent to foster or exhibit a love for commanding, and unwise to manifest any feeling which would indicate a want of personal confidence or a doubt of professional ability. Require only what is reasonable, just, and necessary; be sure that the pupil comprehends your meaning, and then enforce your orders to the letter. The teacher should do all things for the best— best for his pupils, for himself, and for the public. Revering justice, loving what is right, acting in accordance with religious and patriotic principles, professional failure will be impossible; success certain. Such a party will be a good, if not a great, teacher—a fellow-labourer with his Creator in the noble work of progress.

Requests v. Commands.

Courage, resolution, and tenacity of purpose are just as requisite in the principal of a school as in the commander of an army. The mode of discipline or manner of government should be kind and gentle, for the assurance conveyed there-

Force as an element of government.

by, that no harm is intended, will tend to secure a perfect and willing obedience ; but this obedience implies the existence of a power sufficient to enforce it if necessary. This power is the basis of that authority which commands and subdues the will. But power should always be united with kindness, so that children may obey the one while they love the other—so that they may yield submission affectionately, and as the result of affection. Authority and love form the basis of all good government, and these in turn may be referred to force—a force based on strength, power, or influence. Every child is more or less a reasoning creature, an intelligent being, and a loyal, loving individual, and hence a subject for compulsion, persuasion, or inducement, according to the prevailing peculiarities of his disposition. Government by force is the lowest order in the scale of discipline, and government by personal or moral influences is the highest, purest, and best. Government by supremacy of will is a mean between these extremes. But any of these methods, if used exclusively, would, doubtless, prove a failure, owing to difference in disposition and home associations. A mixed method, combining the advantages of all, will, therefore, be the most useful in the management of large numbers of children. In all cases, the teacher must possess the ability to command obedience when necessary, to control stubbornness, quicken diligence, and reform bad habits.

It will well repay the teacher to make himself thoroughly acquainted with the more approved systems of education and school government as practiced at present and in days gone by. He can then strike out a new and independent course for himself, and with the success which always follows well-directed efforts. His chances of success will, at all events, be materially increased by an acquaintance with the maxims and writings of the teachers and philosophers of other ages. Apropos of what we have been writing are the following maxims of Jacob Abbott :—"When you consent, _Abbott's maxims._

consent cordially; when you refuse, refuse finally; when you punish, punish good-naturedly: commend often—never scold."

Self-reliance.

Before undertaking the office of a teacher, the candidate should duly consider the duties to be performed, the difficulties to be overcome, and his personal qualifications for the position. He should not accept nor adopt such a responsible calling unless, after due consideration, he has reason to believe that he can teach and govern efficiently—unless he possesses self-reliance, and has perfect confidence in his ability to satisfactorily perform the onerous duties peculiar to the office. When pupils discover that a teacher entertains doubts of his own ability, they are sure to put his misgivings to the test, and will completely conquer him should his skill and resources fall short of the occasion. Fixity of will is the measure of ability in such cases. Resolution will give him the victory.

Fretfulness and frivolity to be avoided.

The teacher should never so far forget the high responsibility of his post as to wear an air of peevishness on the one hand, or of frivolity on the other; nor should he blend these characteristics together, as is done in many instances. The trials of life should never influence his conduct in school. In sickness or in health his manner should be uniform, calm, and genial. If not favored with a strong constitution, it may, at times, be difficult to overcome these frailties. We are inclined to believe, however, that they can be thoroughly subdued, even by a confirmed invalid, should he only consider how little his pupils have to do with the cause of his illness or the state of the weather. Unless a man learns to govern himself in such trivial matters, he cannot possibly govern others. How can the blind lead the blind?

To commence as he would continue.

In his dealings with his pupils, and with the public generally, the teacher should never forget his personal dignity so far as to "put on airs" (as it is called), nor should he ever assume a manner foreign to his natural character. "Be what you appear to be," is a good and wholesome motto. With children, as with full-grown people, attachment always follows respect—esteem and admiration always precede affection and love. To gain this esteem, affection, and love, he must be courteous and affable, yet firm and resolute—deeply interested in the welfare of his pupils. His future success depends, in a great measure, on "first impressions." On taking charge of a school, or class, he should be sure to commence as he would wish to continue, and *vice versâ.* In a day or two, each pupil in the school or class has formed his (or her) estimate of the new teacher. One has formed an opinion of him in one respect, another in another respect, and so on. If the individual opinions thus formed were written out in order, the aggregate would undoubtedly be a fair estimate of the teacher's character.

The teacher should be particularly careful not to exhibit distrust, or appear to entertain suspicion of his pupils, either collectively or individually. He should never let them see that he is watching them, or that he suspects they would do wrong. Such an act would not only decrease their respect for him personally, but would actually tend to make them what he desires them not to be.* If he has reason to believe that a pupil is vicious or idle, and inclined to be troublesome, he may possibly reform him by the exercise of a little stratagem—by apparently placing great confidence in him, for instance, or by appointing him to some responsible position in the school *pro tem.*, or by occasionally requesting his assistance in some responsible capacity. The judicious application of such incentives as these will be almost sure to transform "the backslider" into a good, industrious, trustworthy boy. To doubt an honest child is tantamount to doing all we can to make him a liar. Unless able to convict, we should never appear to doubt. *Not wise to exhibit suspicion.*

If a boy be wild, idle, and troublesome, it is not wise of the teacher to look altogether on the dark side of his char- *To look on both sides of a boy's character.*

---

* Page.

acter. He should be permitted to understand that the teacher's gaze is fixed on the bright side also—that his good qualities have been noted as well as his bad ones, and that, no matter how reprehensible his acts have been, still it is believed that many of his intentions were good. This course being in accordance with Nature, will probably be effective. At all events, it will exhibit to the pupil "a strong likeness of himself," so that as time rolls away he may gradually become conscious of his errors, and be strengthened to avoid his follies in the future. The teacher cannot be too careful in bestowing his commendations. Always strictly just and honest, he will not, of course, offer them unless they have been merited. Boys, like older folks, can distinguish between praise and flattery—they will not fail to look upon the one as honest payment of a just debt, and upon the other as a sinister present. Verbal bribes, like those of a more tangible nature, are certain signs of weakness, and he who offers them merits contempt.

Pupils not to be contrasted with each other.

The painful and malevolent passions of rivalry, arising from envy or jealousy, should be carefully repressed by the impartial distribution of affection and applause—by the due administration of exact justice, each receiving "what was justly due to him." When necessary, the plain truth should be spoken, as to their respective excellencies; but we should never contrast pupils with each other, nor should we censure one while we praise another. As Rousseau observes, "Let us compare the pupil as he *is*, with what he himself *has been*, or may be, but never compare his deficiencies with another pupil's excellencies." We naturally love those who are, to us, a source of pleasure. To prevent envy or jealousy, and make children fond of each other, we must place them in situations where no passion or appetite will cross their natural sympathy, and where they can dispense pleasure to each other. "It is true," as Edgeworth states, "that many of our most useful and agreeable actions arise from the desire to excel; yet, as a rule, we should avoid placing children in painful competition with each other."

Children should be encouraged, but not flattered. They should receive their just reward when they act so as to merit the approbation of parents, teachers, and friends. The teacher or parent who always scolds, and is never satisfied with a child's efforts, is sure to break his spirit, and to destroy in him the desire to please, since all his efforts, all his deeds (whether good or bad), meet with the same reception. Teachers, be gentle, but firm, with your pupils; watch over them constantly; reprove earnestly, but "be not bitter against them." Have compassiom on their infirmities; remember that you were children yourselves; recal your childhood days, and you will be better able to sympathize with your pupils in all their little trials, joys, and sorrows. Endeavour to discriminate between idleness and want of ability. Encourage as much and reprove as little as possible. Try to "overcome evil with good;" and remember that if a child has done its best, it can do no more. It then merits praise, and not censure, however insignificant the result of its efforts. *Children to be encouraged.*

The teacher should be careful not to appear to believe a pupil guilty of an offence until the charge is clearly proved by reliable evidence, and he should suspend judgment in all cases until such evidence is produced. He should avoid anything that would tend to produce the impression that he had pre-judged the case. "Innocent until proved guilty," should be the motto of the school as well as of the hall of justice; and the reputation of a child should be as sacred as that of a man or woman. Such kind and charitable feelings exhibited by the teacher towards the accused, will tend to show that he takes an interest in their welfare, and would fain consider them honorable and trustworthy; and his good opinion will have no small effect in making them so. As Marmontel observes, "This is the wisest plan, and also the *Offenders to be considered innocent until proved guilty.*

most just." Such a rule of conduct will foster sentiments of mutual confidence and esteem, and induce the pupils to feel that the teacher is their friend as well as their judge. "Respect their feelings, and they in turn will respect yours."

To maintain proper discipline. In the matter of discipline, the teacher should be strict without being severe. As Mr. Lancaster observes, "Each and all should always have something to do, and a motive for doing it." The various exercises should be so conducted that the pupils may feel that indolence and inattention are sure to be followed by detection, and that degradation and punishment will be the natural consequences. As order, quietness, and implicit obedience are characteristics of every well-conducted school, the teacher should not be insensible to any breach of the same, be it ever so insignificant.

A time for everything, and everything in its time. "A time for everything, and everything in its time," was the favourite motto of good old Lancaster—the motto which he placed over the door of his school in imitation of that of Plato;* and, without strict attention to its precepts, no teacher can be really successful. Should the teacher disregard its principles, irregularities will accumulate; indolence, mischief, and confusion will increase, until, perplexed and oppressed, he bows down beneath their united weight, and is finally led to believe that his profession is the most wearisome in the world—and that, far from being "a delightful task," it is a sore burden too heavy to be borne. However, if he adhere strictly to his "time-table," appointing a time for every duty and attending to every duty at its proper time—in other words, if he carry on business in a systematic manner—then order, regularity, and quietness will be the characteristics of his school; otherwise, it will become a babel—a pandemonium. Whatsoever the teacher finds to do let him do it with all his might, for, as an old couplet states—

> " One thing at a time and that done well,
> Is a very good rule as many can tell."

---

* "Let no one ignorant of mathematics enter here."

A person can only attend to one thing at a time with *all* his might, and at one and the same time can only do *one thing well*. If he attempt to do two things at one time, and does one of them well with all his might, the other must of necessity be done badly or imperfectly. Therefore, if a teacher be giving a lesson in geography, let him not mix it up with algebra, and if giving a lesson in geometry, let him not "interline it" with a lecture on grammar. While hearing the recitations of one class, let him not attempt to correct the exercises of another. So of individuals as of classes. When giving a lesson in any subject, he should not allow pupils to interrupt him with complaints against their fellows, or with requests of assistance in other lessons, etc. He should not tolerate extraneous interference by the members of other classes, but he may encourage the individual pupils of the class he is instructing to ask any questions connected with the subject. He should not, however, allow them to ask collateral questions until the close of the lesson. They should wait on him, not he on them. Were he to permit individuals to interrupt him during the delivery of his instructions by asking questions, etc., concerning extraneous subjects, the attention of his class would be arrested, *their* chain of thought and *his* broken, and a large amount of time squandered to no purpose. When the lesson has been delivered, he might profitably allow the pupils to question each other, beginning with the last and ending with the first in the class—taking care to revise the queries proposed when necessary.

Imprudence of dividing the attention.

If the teacher be not systematic in all his school arrangements, then frequent interruptions will occur during the delivery of the respective lessons. On the one side, James will ask for leave to go out; on the other, little Georgie will request permission to take a drink; Minnie will require some assistance in arithmetic; Maggie may want to know the position of some city, town, or river; whilst Philip,

Not to allow interruptions.

aggrieved by idle John, immediately cries out for justice
and protection. All this time the teacher must be attending
to these various requests and complaints to the neglect of
the lesson (the members of his class gazing listlessly at each
other) or *vice versâ;* or he must be attending to both. If
the latter, then he is attempting an impossibility, and is only
half doing his work ; if the former, then he is attending to
the requests and neglecting the lesson, or *vice versâ,* and the
class before him, and the children preferring petitions, are
slowly but surely acquiring habits of disorder, inattention,
and carelessness. It would be totally subversive of good
order to attend to the lesson exclusively, and permit the
complainants to prefer their petitions unheeded. On the
other hand, if he allows the interruptions, and attends to the
complaints, he must partially neglect the lesson, and thus
the chain of ideas will be broken, the pupils will lose all
interest in the subject, and the effect of this "dual work"
will be ruinous to the school. It is in the power of every
teacher to put an end to these unseemly things, and he should
do it. Of course, every one will admit that there will be
always some interruptions in a large school consisting of
pupils of various ages, many of whom were never trained in
habits of order and system at home, and are, therefore, heed-
less of these virtues abroad. However, while engaged in
delivering lessons or in hearing recitations, the teacher, as a
rule, should never attend to extraneous requests—never
allow complaints to be made, never inflict punishment, and
but seldom administer reproof. Then his teachings will be
effective, prolific of good to his pupils, and of comfort to
himself.

A time for
investiga-
ting irregu-
larities.

As he has a time for teaching, during which he should
permit no interruptions, so should he have a time for inves-
tigating irregularities of conduct, for administering reproof
or punishment—a time for receiving complaints, and for
attending to requests, and (as a rule) that time should be

during intermission or immediately before its commencement.

Most of the negligence, disorder, and insubordination, occasionally visible in some schools, may be traced to the monotonous character of the programme, and the lack of interest in the respective studies. He, therefore, will be the best disciplinarian who can excite and maintain the deepest interest in the various exercises. It is thus that he will wake up mind in the fullest and truest sense of the word. It would be well, perhaps, if the teacher were occasionally to introduce a little variety in the respective exercises. This he can accomplish by means of recitations, special readings, music—vocal or instrumental—etc. By such means he will seldom fail to interest the minds of even the most indolent ; and, in addition, will so engross the attention of the more unruly as to prevent them being troublesome. These exercises, like David's harp, will seldom fail to expel the spirit of discord, as they tend to elevate the mind, cultivate the taste, soothe the passions, and, in addition, are an excellent recreation.

Certain variations commendable.

-Now, thanks to the enlightened spirit of the age, music— vocal or instrumental, or both—is being introduced into all our public schools. Almost all the superior public schools are provided with a piano or melodeon. This is specially true in cities and towns, and the country schools are following suite. Many a time has the writer enjoyed the sweet performances in the public schools of New York, Ohio, and Illinois. In these schools, one of the pupils plays voluntaries whilst the classes are marching to or from their classrooms. Everything is done with precision and in silence. Not a sound is heard on such occasions but the music and the pupils' measured tread. When the weather is cold, wet, or boisterous, the respective divisions practice certain evolutions during intermissions in the hall or class-rooms. These evolutions are very graceful and becoming, and are

Music in schools.

10

sometimes accompanied by patriotic and soul-stirring songs. The principal, or the first assistant, superintends, and one of the pupils discourses the music.   Such exercises as these are calculated not only to refine the taste, elevate the affections, and create a love for the school and its officers, but likewise to educate citizens and patriots who shall rival the worthies of ancient Greece and Rome.   The pupils of "the music class" preside at the piano in turn, and, on ordinary occasions, many of them remain in to practice during recess —preferring the enjoyments of the school-room to the pleasures of the play-grounds.   Music, in fact, is one of the characteristic recreations of public school life in America. We would it were so in other countries also.   The cost of the instrument is a mere trifle in comparison with the benefits it confers on the rising generation.   It furnishes a continual feast to the pupils at school, and at home it is the source of much profitable amusement.   Give the young warblers a chance to speak their thoughts in music.

Military education in schools. If convenient, it would be well to put boys through a course of military drill.   No other exercise will be so effectual an aid in school government.   It trains the pupil to habits of prompt obedience—it predisposes him to observe the rules and regulations, and, to a certain extent, prepares his mind to receive durable impressions.   In a military and physiological point of view, it would be wise perhaps to have all school boys drilled, and trained to the use of arms.   Any country adopting this policy would, in less than fifteen years, be a nation of citizen soldiers—powerful as a friend, terrible as an enemy.

Quality, not quantity. In prescribing "home work," or in assigning lessons for the respective school exercises, teachers should be very careful not to require their pupils to master too large a task— more than they can well accomplish, allowing sufficient time for recreation.   If the lessons appointed be too lengthy, the pupils must necessarily learn them superficially—or possibly they may be induced to give up the task in despair, and not learn them at all.   Such habits, like all others, would "grow with their growth, and strengthen with their strength."   As a necessary consequence, they would lose their self-respect, be indifferent about their failures, reckless in manner, and, perhaps, acquire propensities which would materially injure their mental and moral character for time and eternity.   In prescribing lessons, the teacher should consider the minimum capacity of the children, rather than the maximum—he should appoint too small a lesson, rather than too large a one.   In this respect, as in others, his motto should be, "quality before quantity."

We have reason to believe that pupils would progress in their studies with greater celerity and more uniformity, if they were to learn their lessons under the immediate supervision of their teachers. Parents are seldom willing or competent to render much assistance to their children at home. Some, having the inclination to do so, have not the necessary time ; and others, having the time, are devoid of the ability or inclination.   As a necessary result, many pupils—even the most industrious, for want of a little aid—are obliged to prepare their lessons in a very imperfect manner, whilst the majority neglect them altogether.   The indolence and carelessness of even a few will divert the efforts of the more industrious, and check the progress of the whole class.   But when the work is done under the teacher's supervision it is generally well done—better done than elsewhere.   Pupils may, with propriety, be required to prepare their lessons in the easier branches at home ; but lessons in the more difficult subjects should be studied at school, under the immediate supervision of the teacher.   While engaged in this exercise, immobility and perfect silence should be maintained. *Preparation of lessons. Home work.*

The time fixed for the preparation of each lesson must necessarily be limited, and indolent pupils who fail to keep pace with the rest, should be " kept in" and required to study during the greater part of the intermissions and, if necessary, compelled to return and prepare their lessons after school is *Perfect recitation required.*

dismissed, so that they may make good their deficiencies, and keep pace with the more intelligent and industrious. Judging by our own experience and that of others whom we have consulted concerning this subject, we feel assured that we advance a good and wholesome rule when we say that, if the exercises be performed in a careless or slovenly manner during school hours, the teacher should have them properly done *after hours*, retaining for that purpose (after the usual time of dismissal) those pupils who may have exhibited laxity of discipline or application. This privation would be a disgrace as well as a punishment, and the offenders would probably soon endeavour to avoid both by attending more strictly to business ; so that instead of gazing on their books in a passive listless manner, their minds, aroused to activity by a sense of duty, would be absorbed in their studies during the appointed hours. If a pupil, convicted of indolence or wilful negligence failed to remain in, or to return to study his lessons after hours, as instructed, he should be subjected to corporal punishment. If his parents or guardians object to this arrangement and discipline, the young offender should be expelled forthwith, so that his example may be a warning to his companions and save them from similar errors. The teacher will seldom have occasion to adopt the latter expedient. He may never have occasion to exercise such authority; but its possession will have a material effect on his labours, and will tend to keep youthful feet on the right path—the path of duty and of peace.

The Alternate System. The carrying out of the foregoing principles, regulations, and suggestions, is not so difficult as may appear at first sight. For instance, the teacher can give instruction to one of the classes, sections, or divisions of his school, or hear them recite, while the remainder would be engaged in the preparation of their fixed or prescribed lessons or tasks. During the succeeding hour he could examine or instruct the latter, and while doing so, could have the former engaged at the work of preparation, and so on alternately, the time occupied in the delivery of any lesson not to exceed three-quarters of an hour in length—thirty minutes would be sufficient in the junior classes. This plan has been adopted in most of our public schools, and is specially applicable when circumstances do not permit trustees to secure the services of a teacher for every class. The system has also been adopted in the public schools of the United States, Canada, Prussia, Ireland, and in the superior schools of England—countries whose inhabitants have been long noted for their intelligence, prowess, and patriotism. "The Alternate System," as it has been called, is a special feature in the public schools of Massachusetts—a State whose school system has long been a model for America, and the admiration of distant nations.

Frequent reviews are necessary with every student, but more particularly with the young. They strengthen and improve all the faculties, whilst impressing useful facts on the tablet of the mind, but if carried to excess they will weaken the power of attention. When skilfully conducted, they are a source of never-failing interest. One of the most successful teachers now living, once informed us that he ascribed all his success to "grinding;" another, speaking in the same spirit, attributed his "fame in the art" to frequent reviews and searching private examinations. The teacher should know by the manner, voice, and countenance of the pupil, when he clearly understands, and is master of the ideas advanced. The mind should then be directed to the consideration of some other topic—prompt, active, and unremitting attention being required in all cases. The teacher should never indulge in the habit of calling special attention to certain questions or parts of lessons to the exclusion of others. Such a practice would weaken and perhaps ultimately destroy the powers of attention. On the whole, we are inclined to believe that, in the nature of things, no sys-

Reviewing and grinding

tem can be successful without "grinding." It will always
be a mighty lever in the hands of a judicious instructor. If
possible, the teacher should review his work, at least once a
month—we allude to the studies of the more advanced
pupils. The work of the younger children should be re-
viewed once a week. At the close of each lesson the teacher
should call on the members of the respective classes to give
him a summary of the facts adduced, (in their own words,)
taking care to arrange them in logical order or natural
sequence. The pupils should be encouraged to furnish any
personal incidents or other matters likely to explain or
illustrate any of the subjects under consideration. He
might profitably devote five minutes or more to this purpose at the close of each lesson, and at the same time encourage the pupils to mention any difficulty which may have
occurred to them in connection therewith, or any statement,
etc., which they may have failed to understand or comprehend. No pupil should be allowed to put questions, or interrupt the class during the time a lesson is being given,
more especially if the subject of his enquiries has nothing to
do with the matter under consideration.

Loitering, etc., on the way to or from school. The teacher should prohibit pupils from loitering around
the gates, or on their way to or from school, as such a prac-
tice tends to promote indolence and slovenly habits. Such
habits exhibited *outside* the school have a tendency to impress strangers with the idea that discipline is lax *inside*.
Pupils should be taught to be kind and courteous to their
companions, polite and respectful to their teachers and elders,
" to hurt no person by word or deed, to be true and just in
all their dealings," ever zealous to promote the honour of
the school, and always desirous of deserving a good name.

Suspension of privileges Suspensions, or total loss of privileges accompanied by confinement, is an effectual aid in school government, and in
compelling the observance of all rules and regulations. The
infringement of laws, human or divine, entails punishment ;

and the abuse of privileges should be followed by their temporary or permanent suspension. If a pupil be guilty of improprieties of conduct, or neglectful of his duties, or if he disregard the rights of his fellows, then punishment, in some form, should follow as a necessary consequence. The voice of conscience, the code of right and wrong, should be the common law of the school ; and parties interested should be made to feel that the teachers will, and the pupils must, obey its precepts—that no infringement of its principles will be permitted—that all without exception must conform to its enunciations.

Before proceeding to consider the infliction of the minor or major punishments, we will venture to treat of the "Merit System" and its registration of "credits"—a system deservedly popular on both sides of the Atlantic. Having carefully studied its effects as applied to the Collegiate Schools of England and Public Schools of the United States, we have no hesitation in affirming that in the hands of a skilful teacher, the registration of merit and demerit marks is a most effective medium of good government. It is a most powerful ally in stirring up the minds of the pupils—a valuable aid in inciting them to honourable rivalry, to renewed application, to persevering study, so that if possible they may surpass themselves and each other. This system is carried out more perfectly in the Upper Canada College (Toronto) than in any other school or college with which we are personally acquainted. We will therefore venture to give a synopsis of the method as practised in that Institution under the vigorous supervision of its kind and excellent Principal, G. R. R. Cockburn, Esq., M.A. *The Registration system.*

In the Upper Canada College (and similar institutions) the delivery, or recitation, of a lesson occupies about forty-five minutes. The janitor rings the College bell on the expiration of the allotted time, and the students then change classes or go out to enjoy "recess." Each master or pro- *How applied in U. C. College.*

fessor teaches his particular subject to all the classes in turn, and in his own particular room. The classes, it will be observed, change rooms, but the teacher never does so. Each master, or teacher, is supplied with a " Daily Register" and a "Demerit Book." Each of these books contains the names of all the students in attendance, classified in their respective classes according to the order in which they wait on the teacher. Before commencing his lesson, or lecture, the master reads out the names from the "Daily Register," and the standing (individually) held at the close of last lesson on the same subject. Each boy takes his place in the order and position indicated thereby. After this process has been completed, the teacher commences his lesson, and the pupils, during its delivery, change places according to the *value* of their answers. A pupil invariably goes above all the pupils he has corrected. If, perchance, he happens to be third from the head, and corrects the pupil tenth from the head, the question having meantime been passed round to all below number ten, and to the first and second boys, he takes the position number nine from the head, and counts one Round. When the lesson is over, the boy who has most Rounds, or supposing the number of Rounds equal, the boy who is nearest the head is ranked one, and the others follow in rotation according to their standing. The boys who are idly disposed and desire to keep together, are thus shaken up, and idle coteries destroyed. By this method no boy can come out head by a mere chance correction, made perhaps just before the end of the lesson. When "the lesson is over," (*i. e.*, about three minutes before the bell tolls,) he desires them to "number." In response, the first boy says "one," the second "two," and so on to the last. Then the teacher calls the name of each individual in order, as at the beginning, and as he does so, the party named mentions the number he holds in the class, and the same is entered opposite his name in the Register.

At the end of each month the numbers opposite each individual's name are added up, and the total divided by the number of lessons he attended during that time. The quotient indicates his average standing in the class for that particular month in that subject of study. When the average places of all have been thus ascertained they are "numbered off;" the lowest quotient will be the first in the order of merit for that class during that month ; the next lowest will be second ; the next third ; and so on to the highest, which, of course, indicates the last in the order of merit.

On entering the college each pupil is supplied with a neat Private Report Book, into which his absolute and his average standing in each class (and also his absolute and his average for all the classes united) is copied every month by the respective masters ; by whom also, remarks are recorded opposite each subject, stating whether the pupil is progressing satisfactorily or otherwise, The total number of pupils in each class is also stated, so that the efficiency and progress of each boy can be seen at a glance. The demerit marks accorded, the fines, penalties and punishments inflicted, and sometimes the offences committed, are also recorded ; so that teachers and friends may judge of a boy's character, whether good, bad, or indifferent, by this barometer of conduct. These reports are made out and entered in the Pupil's Private Report Book on the last school day in each month—after which the said Report Book is forwarded to the parents or guardians for inspection. Should they reside at a distance, the principal sends them a copy by mail of their son's " Report" as exhibited in the Report Book, and retains the latter until the close of the session. In this way the parents and guardians receive a " monthly reminder" of the capacities of their children and of the progress made ; and the pupils, from love of parents or other motives, take a pride in study, so that they may attain a higher position and, if possible, obtain a better report each month. On the whole, we are inclined to believe that the foregoing is a most excellent plan for exciting an honest and praiseworthy emulation.

The Demerit Book. The Demerit Book is used for recording any breach of discipline, any acts of insubordination, negligence, etc., with the kind and degree of punishment inflicted. A separate book is sometimes kept for recording the latter items. In all such institutions corporal punishments are inflicted by the principal alone, or with his approval, and only for the graver and higher offences, such as obstinacy and insubordination. Pupils guilty of any of the minor offences, are punished (at the discretion of the teacher in charge) by allotting additional lessons, or by " the imposition of demerit marks, or the deprivation of some privilege." The demerit marks are entered in the Demerit Book opposite the offender's name ; also, the date and nature of his offence. On the last school day of each month these marks are summed up and added to his " sum of averages,"—which is, of course, a very severe punishment, as it removes, or rather degrades, him so many places in the relative order of merit in his class. As "1" is the highest number a pupil can get in his class, it follows that he who has " the smallest total will have the greatest merit." Generally speaking, boys would prefer any amount of corporal punishment to this moral one. The application of a moral punishment is not unfrequently found to be conducive of more good, individually and collectively, than either "public or private flogging." A teacher should be judicious and sparing in awarding merit (or demerit) marks. To be lavish of them would decrease their value and lessen their effect.

American system of registration. The following is a good method of keeping a school record. Some may prefer it to the foregoing, especially if the classes are very large and the teachers too few in number, as in most of our common or public schools. The former system is the more exact, the latter the less laborious on the teacher.* Let the number "5" be adopted as the maximum standard of perfection for a recitation, or for a day's deportment. Should the pupil recite lessons in a subject every day, he will (if able to answer all questions perfectly) obtain 25 marks for that subject every week, or 100 every month—there being five days in the school week, and about twenty in the school month. [It simplifies the work to regard each week as a unit of time complete in itself—four such weeks to make a school month.] Should a class recite in a subject only twice a week, then "40" will be the maximum for the month in that subject. The principle of the system is unaffected by the number of recitations. His own convenience, the necessities of the school, and the requirements of the law, must guide the teacher as regards the frequency of recitations in any particular subject or number of subjects.

At the close of each month the marks obtained in the several subjects should be added up, and the result placed in the margin under the heading "monthly summary." *Monthly Roll of Honour.* From this summary, or rather from the aggregate arising from the addition of the several summaries, a monthly "roll of honour" should be prepared—the order of sequence of the pupils' names corresponding with their order of merit, as indicated by the maximum of marks. This "roll of honour" should be placed in a neat frame, to be provided by the school board, and hung up in the school, until replaced by the "roll" for the succeeding month. As in the preceding system, the average standing may be found by dividing the maximum of marks by the number of lessons the pupil has attended. This is done in U. C. College, and in each succeeding roll of honour the ranks previously obtained are also

* For specimens of both systems see Appendix. The samples of the mode of registration of merit marks, etc., in U. C. College, furnished us through the kindness of the principal, have been copied directly from the books of that institution. The samples of the second method have been taken from the "Record Books" of Clifton School, Niagara Falls. They, therefore, have the advantage of being the exponents of actual practice.

recorded along-side the name of the pupil, so that the Form
Master may judge by a glance at the list whether a pupil is
rising or falling in his class.

Value of
marks and
time of
entry.

The record of scholarship should be entered at the close
of each lesson—a perfect recitation (as aforesaid) being
marked "5," and a total failure "0" or "●"—the inter-
vening numbers being awarded according to the degree of
intermediate merit. Before the close of each day the roll of
deportment and attendance should be called. If a pupil has
conducted himself to the teacher's satisfaction—not requiring
or receiving admonition, reproof, or other punishment—he
will be entitled to a record of "5," and will answer accordingly. The number "10" is taken as the maximum of merit
for a recitation in some of the public schools in Philadelphia,
whilst "5" has been adopted as the maximum in most of
the schools in the cities of New York and Boston. Any
number may be used, but we believe that, in practice, "5"
will be found most convenient.

A word to
trustees.

Of late years we have seen the "registration system" practised in schools of every grade, and invariably found that it
worked well in all.   It is popular with the pupils and well
received by intelligent parents, wheresoever adopted. Unfortunately, very few teachers give registration a fair trial, very
few receive it with favour, feeling that it entails a large
amount of additional labour for which, under present arrangements, they would receive no additional remuneration. The
system does, undoubtedly, entail much additional labour ;
and the managing officers of schools would find it to the
advantage of their several communities were they less nig-
gardly in money matters. The teacher cannot be expected
to make himself the "scape-goat" of the community, or to
perform extra work without extra pay. "Good teachers,"
as a learned writer remarks, "cannot be paid too highly,"
and, "if trustees want good hands," they must give good hire.
We have no doubt, judging by our own knowledge of the
foregoing system, and the observations made by us of its

successful working in Europe and America, that it will gradually be introduced and finally prevail in all our schools. Oregon, quite a new State, has inserted an article in its School law in Oregon. constitution providing for the registration of progress, etc., of pupils of the public schools; and another, prohibiting any person from assuming the office of teacher who has not a diploma from the State Normal School, or a certificate from the Board of Public Instruction. In these respects she has set a worthy example, not only to her sister States, but to the proud and boastful countries of Europe.

CHAPTER V.
SCHOOL GOVERNMENT.

Children will naturally practice such habits as are associ- Effects of associated pleasure or pain. ated with pleasure, whilst they will soon learn to avoid such as are followed by immediate or even prospective pain. Punishment will, therefore, be more intelligible and effective with *young* children, if it be immediately and uniformly associated with actions from which we wish them to refrain. The same principle holds good in the use of rewards. By associating pleasure or pain with certain actions, habits may be formed long before reason can be sufficiently developed to be used as a means of government. We should make reason our friend and ally as soon as possible. Otherwise, it may become an enemy. As pointed out elsewhere, it is natural for children to dislike everyone, and everything, that gives or causes them pain, and equally natural that they should like all that gives them pleasure. To secure and retain their affection, the teacher or parent must respect his own authority, be consistent in its exercise, and particularly careful not to enforce it in a fretful, peevish, or ungenerous manner. The little sufferer will then attribute his pain to his offence, and regard it as the natural consequence of his own conduct, instead of associating it with the person of his just, but generous ruler.

Natural con-
sequences.

He will, unconsciously, perhaps, reason on the philosophy of natural consequences, and gradually learn, by experience, that trust and confidence are the reward of sincerity and truth, that all the useful virtues give birth to esteem, that the heroic virtues command sympathy and admiration, and that the amiable virtues engender affection and foster love. Good and bad actions should be referred to their proper source, and receive their due meed of praise, censure, or pain, without unnecessary delay; and a repetition of an offence should, on detection, be inevitably followed by a repetition of the punishment.

Obedience,
and how to
secure it.

The virtue of obedience should be taught as a habit, inasmuch as we expect it from children long before they are capable of yielding it on rational grounds. The best way to secure it is, at first, to command children to do agreeable things, then those which are less agreeable, and so on to the repugnant. They will thus by degrees become accustomed to the habit, and then the observance of disagreeable orders will not be so difficult. Frequent prohibitions, and contradictory commands, promote disobedience, peevishness, and other infirmities of disposition. The voice of command should be gentle, but decided. However disagreeable an order may be, the pupil must regard prompt obedience as an imperative necessity. Authority is placed in jeopardy by giving a command without enforcing it; and, if we condescend to entreat compliance, we abdicate our functions, and give the child the impression that he may refuse if so disposed. Before giving commands we should be sure that the child is able to obey them, and, in case of refusal, that we are able to compel him. If we are not exact in requiring prompt obedience, we will never succeed in obtaining it.

We should endeavour to lead our pupils to perceive that we wish to promote their welfare and happiness, and that obedience to our commands will facilitate, if it does not ensure, this object. If children entertain a love of glory—and many of them do—the courage and fortitude, which would otherwise have a tendency to degenerate to obstinacy, may be admired and extolled; for they will impel their possessors to travel in the path of honour. The love of glory enlarges the understanding, transforms obstinacy into magnanimity, and strengthens every noble feeling of the heart. It is, therefore, a worthy ally in educational work.

The teacher may be regarded as the common parent for the time being, of all the children under his charge, and is justified in treating them in every respect as if they were really his own. His responsibility is, however, much greater than that of any individual parent—his "collective family" being much larger than that of any "home circle." There is scarcely a domestic circle in the land in which "the head of the house" (notwithstanding his moral influence and other parental advantages) has not more than once deemed it his duty to inflict corporal punishment on some member of his family. This he did with the view of reforming the "little culprit," and for the sake of example; hoping thereby to deter his other children from committing similar offences. The teacher, for identical reasons, uses similar means to produce like results, being the parents' substitute, or *locum tenens*, in all educational matters. *The Father of the school.*

The abolition or continuance of corporal punishment in our schools, is a subject which has been discussed with much interest throughout the length and breadth of the land; and, strange to say, it is a question on which the greatest teachers and most learned men of the age have taken opposite views. Some of the States—New Jersey, for instance—passed laws prohibiting corporal punishment in the public schools; but ere many months elapsed, the respective legis- *Legislation concerning corporal punishment.*

latures had to repeal these enactments, "the moral suasion system" not having been successful in winning "little offenders" to a right sense of duty. Events proved that a middle course was best—that corporal punishment should not be abolished, but that it should be resorted to as seldom as possible ; only when all other means had been tried and found to fail. Efficient school government is not a tyranny. It is an arrangement for the public good, placing the teacher temporarily in the position of parent to each and all under his tuition—to children not his own. This arrangement, made by the common consent of parents and guardians, has been founded upon the experience of ages past, not for the teacher's special convenience, but for the pupils' public and private welfare.

Section 1. THE MINOR PUNISHMENTS.

Objects of punishment

The "minor punishments" are frequently and thoughtlessly used and abused by both parents and teachers. We will therefore take the liberty of considering them before proceeding to treat of the infliction of corporal correction. This is regarded by the vulgar as the "major punishment," but we believe that children of a refined nature will frequently regard it as "a misfortune" far more easily borne than any of the minor or moral punishments. Reformation of the culprit, and the detention of others from committing like offences, are the principal objects in view, when we inflict punishment of any kind. When these objects are united, the motive for punishment is doubly just and proper. Legitimate authority, having praiseworthy objects in view, has an unquestionable right to inflict legitimate punishments to accomplish legitimate ends. It is so with civil and military governments, in every country on earth. It is so in the private family, and should be so in the public school. No punishment, not proper nor legitimate, should be inflicted on any pupil : no unseemly or disagreeable epithets should be applied to him. As Mr. Page well observes, "he should never be scolded or abused, never be struck with the hand, and never subjected to any punishment partaking of the nature of prolonged torture. The teacher must avoid the appearance of inflicting punishment as if it were a *pleasing* duty—as if he were glad of having the opportunity of paying the pupils off for some real or imaginary crime. He should administer it with regret and sorrow, and in obedience to the claims of justice. Punishment should be administered in love, and because the little sufferer is beloved; otherwise the teacher would be a tyrant, and the pupil a martyr.

If we express censure or indignation, it should be against the child's fault not against himself; and even then it should never pass the bounds of exact justice. Should it do so, the little culprit will command the sympathies of his school fellows. It is not advisable to punish or censure a whole class or division at once, as numbers keep each other in countenance, and, to a certain extent, modify the shame of guilt. *Censure faults.*

Solitary confinement, in a properly lighted and well ventilated room, is one of the most commendable of the minor punishments. It affords time for reflection, and, if exclusive and effective, will seldom fail to produce repentance, contrition, and reformation. It will, therefore, be found an important aid in preventing the repetition of offences, as it will eradicate or stem the evil at its source. But to be successful, it must be effective—it must be really solitary, and the offenders must have no means of communication during its continuance. In school the confinement must necessarily be limited, but at home it may be prolonged if necessary. In the former case, the refractory pupils will feel that should they "hold out" a certain length of time, they must be liberated unconditionally. It would be better that they should never be confined than that this should occur. How- *Solitary confinement.*

11

ever, they might be required to attend school on Saturdays,
or other holidays, to undergo this punishment.   In the
nature of things, solitary confinement is better adapted for
domestic discipline than for school government.   We cannot,
therefore, recommend its general application.

Admonition and advice.   In the event of a pupil being condemned to "solitary confinement," the teacher, when releasing him at the close of
the allotted time, should administer a " proper dose " of kind
reproof, showing the guilty one how his conduct appears in
its various phases—leading him to "see himself as others
see him".—after which he may give him some good and
friendly advice as regards the future.   The skilful teacher
will seldom find this course to fail, even with the most obdu-
rate, and will probably have the satisfaction of feeling, ere
many weeks elapse, that he has converted another "prodigal."   Advice is better received in private than in public.
Were reproof administered to a pupil publicly, a spirit of
obstinacy might be developed in him, the manifestation of
which would be anything but agreeable or edifying.   Human
nature is weak at best, and inclined to be rebellious on such
occasions—more especially if the reason and judgment be
not well developed.   For this cause, if for no other, reproof
(like advice) should always be administered in private, unless the offence be a *very grave* one.   The kind consideration exhibited in respecting the offender's feelings so far as
not to expose him in the presence of his companions, will
tend to open his heart to receive better impressions, and
may possibly stamp on his conscience the seal of contrition,
besides increasing his affection for the teacher personally.

Ridicule and Reproach.   Ridicule and reproach are objectionable as aids in school
management.   The former tends to loosen the ties between
the teacher and the taught ; and the latter, though not quite
so objectionable, has much the same effect.   Both should be
avoided.   They generally fall on the awkward, innocent,
and over-sensitive pupils, whilst the idle and vicious, having

no reputation to forfeit, are quite indifferent or insensible to their application or effect. The unskilful use of either reproach or ridicule could not fail to destroy the harmony and mutual affection which exists between the pupils and teacher of every well-regulated school. It would annoy and degrade one section of the pupils, whilst it unduly elevated the other. Besides, it would foster a tendency in the latter to regard themselves as much better individuals than the former. In fact; it is wrong to sneer at pupils, and not prudent to rail at them, or to work much on their feelings. On the whole, it must be apparent to every reflecting mind (particularly to every experienced teacher) that reproach and ridicule are extremely dangerous as school punishments, if not wholly pernicious or reprehensible.

Humiliation, as a means of school discipline—though a legitimate punishment—should be used, if resorted to, with much caution and extreme delicacy. If not skilfully used, it might possibly produce the same effects as ridicule, and be followed by disobedience and rebellion. Before resorting to it, therefore, the teacher should be careful to satisfy himself that it is requisite. Sometimes the public confession of an error or offence, may be absolutely necessary; and when made it should be accompanied with a request for forgiveness. To condone the offence, this confession should spring from a contrite heart. The confessor should be *really* penitent—*really* sincere; for, as Blair well observes, "sincerity is the basis of every virtue . . . . Ingenuousness and candour possess the most powerful charms, and carry an apology for almost every failing." The teacher should always encourage his pupils to frankly acknowledge their offences, commending them to pursue the wisest, best, and most gentlemanly policy under the circumstances, namely— *make a free confession with a suitable apology.* If they confess their offences, regret their occurrence, and resolve not to be guilty of such conduct in future, the teacher may with pro-

<small>Humiliation considered.</small>

priety overlook the past, and agree to receive them into favour again.   Should the "little culprits" fail to do (or decline to do) these things, and that the offence is a grave one, the teacher being morally bound to investigate the case, will be legally (and naturally) justified in using every legitimate means, even corporal punishment, to bring about the desired reformation.

"Quickness of apprehension" in children.

"Grown persons often make an incorrect estimate of the understanding of children, and judge them by what they know, rather than by their capacity of comprehension." Their knowledge is "very limited," but their power of comprehension is very great.   They are close observers in small things, and can draw correct inferences from few and insignificant actions.   People often wonder at the grotesque mixture of wisdom and folly in the sayings and doings of some "solitary little one," whose old-fashioned ways indicate its inexperience and want of genial companionship.   Its sayings are foolish, from comparative ignorance; and wise, from quickness of apprehension.   It behoves the educator to train and develop the latter faculty, so as neither to depress, repress, or over-exert it.   Like all other faculties it should be duly exercised, not prematurely forced.   No human being can overstep with impunity the intellectual boundaries fixed by Nature.

Courtesy to juveniles.

Juvenile inquisitiveness is a natural thirst for knowledge, and should, therefore, be encouraged rather than discountenanced.   The pupil should not be ridiculed, or laughed at, if he fail to convey his ideas in suitable or intelligible language.   Rather let him be requested to put his question in other words, so that the teacher, if possible, may discover his meaning.   This being done, let the teacher courteously furnish the required information, taking care to use words suitable to the child's capacity.

Children not to be rebuked in anger.

No teacher should forget himself so far as to lose his temper, or to become what children call a "scold."   It is very objectionable to chide pupils frequently or passionately—such "indulgence" would certainly lessen the teacher's authority, and diminish the pupils' respect for his person. If they have violated, or infringed on, any of the rules, a few words representing the reprehensible nature of their offence, spoken in a kind and sober tone, with coolness, courtesy, and becoming dignity, will be far more effective in producing sorrow and amendment than many hasty rebukes or sundry angry allusions. In fact, the teacher who would command respect and professional success, must diligently study the temper, disposition, and character of his pupils individually, and fill them, "not so much with learning as with a desire to learn,"—not so much with the fear of punishment as with the desire not to offend.

He must lead them to discover at an early age that virtue and wisdom are the great objects of all learning—" that the end of education (as Milton affirms) is to repair the ruins of Eden by regaining to know God aright ;" and that the more they advance in learning, the nearer they approach to Him who is the fountain of all knowledge. *The end of education.*

People naturally love liberty, and dislike anything that tends to curtail their privileges. So is it with children. By nature they have an antipathy towards the performance of compulsory duties, and have an aversion for anything enjoined as a task, particularly if it tends to limit their pleasures, or control their freedom. The skilful teacher will therefore induce them to perform their various duties without giving them reason to feel, or even suspect, that they are in the harness of restraint, and must be obedient to the whip of compulsion. He may even succeed in creating in some of them, if not in all, a desire to be taught for the sake of the honour, delight, and recreation the information may afford ; but, if possible, he will never allow them to suspect that the acquisition of any subject, or part of a subject, is imposed as a compulsory task. The moment he does so, its *How to make study pleasant.*

study will be shorn of its attractions, and may be regarded as "a punishment rather than a pleasure."

Natural tendencies of children. Children love dominion, and take much delight in exacting obedience to their will. During infancy this tendency displays itself in frequent fits of crying, and in "unreasonable peevishness;" in boyhood, the presence of the "disease" is indicated chiefly by sullenness of temper, or the desire of personal acquisition—a longing to have "things as their own." This love of power and inordinate possession, being the foundation of many evils, and the roots of contention and injustice, must be promptly rebuked, and, if possible, extracted from the system. If children strive together for the mastery, as often happens, and the case be duly reported to the teacher, he should, as a rule, give judgment against the originators of the strife, calling attention to the spirit of the Saviour's words—"Whosoever would be chief among you, let him be your servant."

Personal recriminations not to be countenanced. Though it be necessary for the teacher to curb the insolent and unruly, and to check ill-nature, yet, as a rule, it would not be prudent of him to countenance the accusations or informations of pupils against each other. Such charges are generally the result of anger, envy, or malice—feelings which need repression, not development. However, if on investigation, he finds the accused "guilty," he would do well to reprove him in private, and if possible induce him (1st) to solicit pardon from, and (2nd) make reparation to, the injured party—both to be done as if the offender were acting of his own free will. Such a course will make the apology more easy to the one and more acceptable to the other, whilst it mutually engenders and promotes feelings of good nature, civility, courtesy, and respect. In well-regulated homes, children never get what they cry for, or basely ask. Of course their necessities are supplied, but the desires of passion or fancy are firmly denied: so should it be in every well-ordered school. Pupils should be taught, so far as pos-

sible, to practice the virtues of resignation, submission, mod- The practice of sundry virtues.
esty, and self-denial, so that they may cheerfully "bear and
forbear," cordially sympathizing with each other in every
little trial and difficulty incident to "school-life," being ever
ready to assist each other—ever willing to divide and share
their little stock of delicacies or curiosities.

Faults arising from inadvertency, mental weakness, for- Certain shortcomings to be treated with indulgence.
getfulness, unsteadiness, and absence of mind—when not
wilful—may be treated with some little indulgence, more
especially if the pupil be dull of comprehension or perception. Probably the best way to correct such errors, or irregularities, is to recognize them as constitutional, but conquer-
able misfortunes, whose subjugation will require continued
efforts on the part of the pupil, and continued tenderness and
good-will on the part of the teacher. The influence of mutual affection will be almost sure to sharpen the intellect of
the pupil, opening and expanding his mind, so that he may
do his duty faithfully and well. Without this incentive to
action (as Locke truly observes) "there would probably be
much uneasiness, and but little learning."

Section 2. CORPORAL PUNISHMENT.

The greatest happiness and ultimate good of the whole, Object of punishment.
should be the chief objects of school government. The punishment of the few is not only to be tolerated but commended, when it is necessary for the public or general good,
more especially when there is reasonable hope that its infliction will reform the offender, and deter others. The least
possible amount of pain which can produce the desired effect,
is the just measure of punishment; and the best system of
government is that which reduces to a minimum the temp-
tation to do wrong.

Children favoured with reasonable and affectionate parents Shame as a punishment.
are under judicious discipline at home, and, as a necessary

consequence, they will seldom need punishment at school. Intelligent and well-disposed pupils require little restraint. Shame is a more powerful feeling than that arising from bodily pain. Hence the advisability of leading children to perceive that it is shameful to *need* government by force.

Corporal punishment justifiable.

Many educational writers seem to think (with certain legislators) that the use of "the rod of correction" is inconsistent with the spirit and progress of this enlightened age. They affect to regard corporal punishment as a relic of barbarism, and as a crime against juvenile humanity. On enquiry it will generally be found that these writers have never been practical teachers, and have never raised a family of their own. The theories of such kind-hearted gentlemen are seldom founded on experience, and (we regret to say) will not stand the stern test of practice. In teaching, as in other things, we must take human nature as it is—as we find it, and not as we hope it may be some centuries hence. Guided by the experience of mankind, we must deduce our inferences from general principles and actual experiment. It would be folly to draw our conclusions *from* (or to found a theory *on*) isolated cases of permanent success, as the result of mere moral suasion. The oldest book in the world declares with divine authority, that " He who spareth his rod hateth his son ; but he that loveth him chasteneth him betimes."* "Chasten thy son," says Solomon, "while there is hope, and let not thy soul spare for his crying, . . . for if thou deliver him thou must do it again."† "Foolishness is bound in the heart of a child, but the rod of correction shall drive it far from him."‡ "Correct thy son and he shall give thee rest, yea, he shall give delight unto thy soul."§ While extracting these precepts, our mind reverts to the writings of a sage of an anterior age. We remember that it is recorded in the first book of Samuel, that God

---

*Prov. xiii. 24. †Prov. xix. 18-19. ‡Prov. xxii. 15. §Prov. xxix. 17.

Himself punished a certain parent, and pronounced a fearful doom against his posterity, because he neglected his duty in this respect. We allude to Eli, Judge of Israel. When informed of the evil deeds of Hophni and Phineas, the soft·hearted old man (believing, doubtless, in the omnipotence of moral suasion), merely pointed out the enormity of their offence, hoping probably that they would repent and reform ; but he did not inflict any tangible degradation or punishment, or take any steps to produce contrition or reformation and for these reasons the Lord declared that both his sons should die in one day—that his priesthood should be given to another, and that all his posterity should die in the flower of their age.* What a dreadful punishment of the old man's apathy, and of his weakness in neglecting to "train up his children in the way they should go?† Well might Solomon say : "Withhold not correction from thy child, for if thou beatest him with the rod of correction he shall not die. Thou shalt beat him with the rod and deliver his soul from hell."‡ And to the young he says in another place : "Apply thy heart unto instruction and thine ears unto the words of knowledge."§ "Hear counsel and receive instruction, that thou mayest be wise in thy latter end."|| These precepts give a divine sanction to the judicious application of corporal punishment—to the discreet use of the rod, and not only invest the parent with the necessary authority, but absolutely require him to exercise it efficiently ; and, moreover, the practice of all nations, ancient and modern, barbarous and civilized, seems to indicate that such a right has always been recognized by mankind generally.

In the early ages of the world, parents were the principal (and in most cases the sole) teachers of their own children. Every father had to instruct his sons in the arts of peace

The origin of public schools.

---

*1 Sam. ii. 22-36. †Prov. xxii. 6. ‡Prov. xxiii. 13-14. §Prov. xxiii. 12.
|| Prov. xix. 20.

and war, so that he was tutor, chaplain, judge, and military commander—all in one. In like manner, the mother had to teach her daughters the arts of domestic life, attending also to the education of her sons during their younger years. But, as civilization advanced, the arts of life became more numerous and complex, so that domestic or public obligations compelled parents to delegate their educational duties and privileges to another, who thus became the *locum tenens* of the parent. Then, after the lapse of years, another change took place, as men became conscious of the advantages to be derived from "a division of labour." A number of families residing in the same locality made arrangements to transfer the education of their children to one such officer—thinking, doubtless, that this plan would be more economical than for each to keep a private tutor. This officer, through "immemorial custom," and by virtue of his election, became the common parent (so to speak) of all the pupils entrusted to his charge—being authorized to treat them in every respect as if they were really his own. Probably it was thus public schools first originated; and, in this way, instead of every parent in a town or district being of necessity compelled as of old to assume the office of private teacher to his own family—thereby neglecting other duties—a common tutor was (and is) appointed to represent them all, who, by reason of his special training and experience, is far more skilful as an educator than each individual parent (or private tutor) could possibly be.

The teacher's commission.

In the present age, the teacher is not only recognized as the legal representative of the parents in all scholastic matters, but is likewise considered as endowed with full parental powers while in the school-room. Public opinion supports his influence, and the laws confirm his authority. Indeed, it seems to be tacitly understood, if not generally conceded, that "the teacher, in the school-room, stands in the parents' shoes." Let him, therefore, make the most of the position

accorded him by the law, by public opinion, and by immemorial usage, always acting towards "the little ones" as if
they were really his own—judiciously and discreetly exercising his delegated authority according to his superior
judgment, and "the light that is in him;" not scrupling to
inflict even corporal punishment when he considers it necessary, and conscientiously believes that, under similar circumstances, an intelligent and prudent parent would do likewise.
"Tenderness is a very requisite quality in an instructor,
yet there is often the truest tenderness in well-timed correction." *

The teacher should be careful never to threaten his pupils, *Teachers never to threaten pupils.*
more especially if he is not prepared to carry his threats into
execution. If a boy be innocent, no one has a right to
threaten him ; if guilty, justice or good example call for his
punishment. The ruler who continually threatens his subjects, will gradually alienate their affections, and ultimately
be "favoured" with their hatred and contempt. They will
hate his person, scoff at his words, revile his actions, and at
last rise in rebellion and deprive him of power if not of
his head. He who strikes without previous threats, is the
man whom people honour and obey. An old proverb tells
us that "the dog which barks the loudest is not the quickest
dog to bite." Children acquire a knowledge of this fact as
if by instinct, and soon learn that the loudest and greatest
talker is usually the weakest and smallest actor—that the
firmness and decision of a man of many words are confined
to his tongue. They feel that he does not really mean what
he says, and, if they do not actually learn to despise their
ruler, they, at least, acquire the habit of listening with
indifference to his words. Parents and teachers who understand human nature, will never threaten children. If a
grave offence be committed, and the teacher is of opinion

---

* Goldsmith.

that the imposition of a certain task—say "double home work," so many hundred lines, loss of privileges for a term, or confinement, followed by admonition or advice, etc.— would be ineffectual in producing reformation, then let him resort to corporal punishment without "scolding" or previous threats. The teacher must never "give in to disobedience or wilful neglect."

Corporal punishment to be inflicted publicly. Corporal punishment should be inflicted in the presence of the whole school, and in as solemn a manner as possible. When inflicted publicly, it tends not only to reform the offender, but deters others from committing similar offences. When inflicted privately, its example is lost to the school, and the disgrace to the sufferer is not lessened. Inflicted publicly in a proper manner, with a right spirit, and for sufficient cause, its effects on the school will be lasting and salutary. The degree of severity cannot be exaggerated to parents and guardians, nor ridiculed and "made light of" to school-fellows and other associates. The teacher cannot be misrepresented; nothing can be mis-stated, or erroneously reported, as dozens of anxious eyes will witness its application, dozens of attentive ears will listen to the investigation, and dozens of expanding minds will moralize on the relations between cause and effect. If this punishment were administered in private, (in a room where there would be no witness,) its example would be lost, and the teacher might be misrepresented, and the degree of severity erroneously reported. Punishment should be inflicted as early in the day as may be convenient, and, as a rule, it should never be administered during the last hour of the school session.

To establish authority by force, if necessary. The teacher can scarcely expect prompt obedience from *all* his pupils (on taking charge of a school). He must first win their love or affectionate regard; and this he cannot do in a day, a week, or perhaps in a month. Without a will of his own, and an affectionate, straight-forward, gentlemanly manner, concurrent with an unalterable tenacity of purpose, he will never win their esteem; and, without enjoying their esteem, he cannot secure their love. What, then, is he to do? Should he allow some of them, desirous of being troublesome, to run riot for weeks or months, and thus set a pernicious example to the remainder, whilst he—endeavouring to convert them by softer means—declines to establish his authority by force? Were he to do so, he would never win their affection, and never succeed in ruling by love, by reason, or persuasion. No half measures ever succeed in such cases—"he fears to strike," would be the motto of all. Things would go on from bad to worse; "the sickly sheep would infect the flock," and, as a last and only resource, a new physician would be invited to attend to the case, and the old one paid off. If the pupils abuse their freedom, and disregard or disrespect the immortal principles of law and order, the teacher must act promptly, and do as governments do in extreme cases—"suspend the constitution, and rule by martial law." A ruler, abolishing fines, prisons, penal servitude, and capital punishment, would soon have no country to rule, no servants to obey him, no friends to love him—all would be confusion, riot, and bloodshed; so of a teacher who, on failing to establish his authority by reason and love, would decline to do so by force. At the very first, the teacher must establish habits of order and implicit obedience at any cost. When this has been done, he will have to resort but seldom to the rod of correction. Habits of order and obedience being promulgated and firmly established, his appeals to higher motives than fear or force will seldom fail. He can thenceforth rule by the power of reciprocal affection, and rely for success on the finer feelings of human nature. These will carry conviction to the conscience through the avenues of the heart, and the pupils can then be easily led to exercise their mental faculties under the teacher's supervision, even as they would exercise their physical powers without his instructions; for activity of

mind is as natural to them as activity of body.   Both need
direction and exercise.   Good government is essential to
progress, and it can be maintained only through "eternal
vigilance."   "Aimez les enfants," says Archbishop Fenelon,
"n'oubliez rien pour en etre aimé. La crainte est nécessaire
quand l'amour manque ; mais il la faut toujours employer
à regret, comme les remedes violents et les plus dangereux."

Punishment
to be made
effectual. Corporal punishment is the last resource, and, when used,
its application should be made effectual.   The punishment
should be continued until the offender is thoroughly subdued; otherwise its application will only "make bad worse."
The rod should be used only when absolutely necessary, and
when other means have failed or would be likely to fail.
Slight offences should not be followed by a slight application
of the rod ; nor should the teacher be so deficient in wisdom
and good taste as to keep this instrument in his hand when
he visits the several departments and classes, or when going
from one part of his school-room to another.   It should be
kept in the desk or drawer until required for use, and deposited in the same place after it has done its work.   Its
constant appearance, or its frequent and slight application,
will familiarize the pupils with its terrors—and familiarity,
it is said, generates contempt.   "All punishments," as Seneca
observes, "are either for amendment or example, or for
both. . . . .   The custom of offending will take away
the shame of it . . . .   and for these reasons, punishments should be effectual, few, and far between."   Moreover,
it is as dishonourable for a teacher to have too many punishments, or rather occasions to punish, "as it is for a prince
to have too many executions, or a physician too many
funerals."   It would be far better never to attempt to administer corporal punishment, than that it should fail in
design, or soon need repetition.   As a rule, it should be
inflicted on the hands with a cane of moderate thickness.
The child should never be struck on the head, or on the

front part of the body. Good discipline is the foundation of good teaching—the fundamental basis of education—yet it should be always tempered with mercy, and administered in love.

The teacher should never be in a hurry to inflict corporal punishment. He would do well to remember that one thoughtless word, one unjust blow, may nullify the laborious inculcations of many days. Quiet deliberation and long-forbearing justice, are fundamental elements of success in school government. When inflicting punishment he should, therefore, be perfectly calm, self-possessed, and *free from anger;* but at the same time, he should exhibit a just sense of the reprehensible nature of the offence. If not free from anger he should defer the punishment. Except in the case of very young pupils, it will always be wise to allow some time to elapse—a day or two, or more, according to circumstances—from the investigation of an offence and delivery of judgment, until the infliction of punishment. During the interval, the offender will have the opportunity of reflecting on the nature of his crime and the justice of his sentence, and may perhaps become truly penitent. Thoroughly understanding the teacher's character, and knowing by experience that silence and delay do not mean exemption, he will feel certain that nothing will arrest the course of justice except due contrition and immediate reformation—the exhibition of a heartfelt repentance and timely amendment. The teacher should carefully avoid the appearance of "favour" or prejudice during the investigation of a case; but above all, he should never execute judgment or inflict punishment while under the influence of anger. It is related in ancient story that on a certain occasion the great teacher Plato being incensed with the conduct of one of his slaves, thoughtlessly raised his hand to inflict punishment. Suddenly recollecting himself, he checked his uplifted arm, but still retained it in its elevated and menacing position. The poor slave

A supplementary duty.

ran away after some hesitation, although his master remained "fixed to the spot," as if he were a statue. One of his intimate friends, having observed the occurrence, asked the philosopher what he meant by such singular conduct？ "I am now (said he) chastising an angry man." He had postponed his servant's punishment, and was punishing himself for having given way to anger. Seneca states that on another occasion this individual committed some offence for which Plato thought it advisable to administer corporal punishment. But being under the influence of anger, he addressed his friend Speusippus, who happened to be present, saying—"Do you chastise that fellow, please. I am angry, and might go farther than becomes me." This is the spirit we would commend. The modern teacher, like his Grecian predecessor, *should never inflict punishment while under the influence of anger.* He, also, is liable to "go farther than becomes him." It is true, he cannot legally delegate his executive power in this respect to another ; but he can stop his uplifted hand, and allow the offender time to repent, and his own anger time to evaporate.

The teacher to be free from anger when inflicting punishment.

The teacher should not rest satisfied with the mere infliction of corporal punishment. A much higher and nobler duty awaits him. Coercion prepares the way for persuasion. Negociations and amicable arrangements are often impracticable until after a satisfactory trial of arms. The infliction of punishment does not terminate the teacher's opportunities or responsibilities. Every act of coercive discipline should be carefully followed up by sound suggestions and friendly influences, until the subjugation of the will is supplemented by the conquest of the heart. The more critical the case, and the more violent the treatment, the more pressing is the need for the watchful and unwearied application of the necessary subsequent restoratives.*

---

*Jewell.

The teacher teaches wherever he is. His daily walk and conversation are living lessons—practical inculcators of every praiseworthy quality, or the opposite. Calm, steady, and gentle, he should be consistent in all his actions—a standard of justice and honour, a model in manners, and a bright example of patient self-control. Whilst insisting on the due observance of all rules and regulations of the school by his pupils, he should be particularly careful not to infringe them himself; nor should he ever allow himself any indulgence which duty or principle would compel him to deny to others. Whatever he would wish his pupils to do, *that* he must also do himself; for, as Seneca well observes, "the best instructors are those who teach in their lives, and prove their words by their actions."

Not to indulge self and deny others.

The divine Seneca, in his "Cautions Against Anger," advances many useful hints concerning the education of children. We take the liberty of transcribing a few of them, which may possibly be interesting to parents, and useful to the young teacher. The noble Roman affirms that "a careful education is a great matter in enabling us to conquer our evil propensities, for our minds are easily formed in youth; but bad habits once acquired are very difficult to cure. Children should be trained to avoid provocations and the beginnings of anger. Nothing breeds anger more than a soft effeminate education. The choice of a healthy nurse and a good-natured tutor, goes a great way in eradicating or eliminating its germs from the system; for the sweetness of the blood and manners pass into the child. . . . The teacher's favourite or mother's darling, seldom come to good. Flattery and fortune nourish touchiness, and as he grows up he becomes a choleric coxcomb . . . It is a very nice point to check the germs of anger in a child, so as not to take off his edge and quench his spirits. In this matter, care must be taken that he be neither too much emboldened by license, nor too much depressed by severity. Commenda-

Seneca's remarks on the education of children.

12

tions give him confidence and courage; but, if dispensed to excess, they seldom fail to promote a spirit of insolence. . . . When to use the bridle and when the spur, is the main difficulty." Parents or teachers should never put the child to the necessity of begging anything basely; and if he demeans himself in this manner, let him go without what he desires—he is unworthy to receive it. They should give him nothing that he cries for, until the dogged fit is over. However, if convenient, they may let him have it when he has regained his equanimity, and assumed a cheerful and becoming demeanour. "He will thus learn that nothing is to be gained by peevishness," and, as a necessary consequence, will, day by day, become less waspish and quarrelsome. Let him be led to understand, in his various exercises, that it is not generous nor just to injure his competitors and opponents, or even to wish them harm, but that it is praiseworthy to overcome them without wishing to depress them.

SECTION 3. MUTUAL DUTIES AND OFFICIAL RELATIONS.

Powers and duties of principals.

In Canada and most of the States, the principal of a public school is invested, by law, with full power and authority in the management and control of the school. In such cases he is bound to conduct the school according to law, and it becomes his duty to observe and enforce the rules and regulations prescribed by the State, or Provincial Council of Public Instruction, and any other rules or regulations consistent therewith, which himself and the school board may, from time to time, think expedient or necessary for the efficient government of the respective departments or classes. It is also his duty (with the concurrence of the school board) to prescribe the work of the assistant teachers. The law, or public opinion, holds him responsible for their work; hence the necessity for continual vigilance. It is the principal's duty, also, to prescribe a general plan of teaching for the whole school; but without sacrificing harmony of arrangement or development, he may permit its provisions to be slightly modified in application, so as to meet the peculiar necessities of each division or department. There *may* be variety in method, but there *should* be unity in design. We here venture to advance a few suggestions which may be of material service in effecting these objects.

1. Each assistant in charge of a division, department, class, or section, should rule in accordance with the prescribed general plan or method, and in its administration be guided by the principles of government adopted for, and applicable to, the whole school. There will then be uniformity of discipline and no clashing of interests—no occasion, and no opportunity, for invidious comparisons, or internal jealousies; each individual division will supplement and sustain the whole. *Uniformity of discipline.*

2. As a rule, each teacher of division (*i. e.* an assistant in charge of a class-room) should receive authority and, in fact, be required to investigate and decide on all matters of discipline within his (or her) particular realm. But the graver offences, and all matters affecting other divisions, or the order and government of the school in general, and such as may be committed on the grounds, or in entering or leaving school, or on the way to or from school, should be referred to the principal. *Powers and duties of assistants.*

3. All cases of suspension, expulsion, or of corporal punishment, should be entered in a book, to be kept for that purpose, by the principal. Before inflicting corporal punishment, each teacher should enter a statement of the case in this book, names of witnesses, amount of punishment, etc., and then affix their signature. The principal should revise these reports occasionally, and give such advice (privately) to the teacher concerned as he may think judicious. This book should be open for inspection by parents; and it might not be amiss to lay it before the school board at their regular meetings. *A Record of punishments.*

Proper channel of inter-communication.

4. The principal is the only proper channel of communication between the assistant teachers and trustees, or public at large. All letters relative to the pupils, or other school matters in this connection, should pass through his hands; and should any of the people, ignorant, or otherwise, of this rule, address an official communication to an assistant teacher, said teacher as a matter of courtesy, if not of right, should immediately lay it before the principal, who should reply (if necessary) in such terms as he may think judicious; or the assistant may reply under his instructions.

Signatures to notes.

5. "All notes presented by pupils should bear the signature of the parent or guardian, known as such to the teacher."

Local supremacy of teachers.

6. "A teacher," says Tracy, "should not be interfered with in the Government of his or her class while in actual command—not even by the principal. The teacher, of whatever grade, should, in the estimation of the pupil, be principal of his or her own class. Any suggestions or advice from the principal should, in all cases, be apart from the observation of the school or class; otherwise the authority of the teacher is, in the minds of the pupil, weakened; for, if the principal manifest a lack of confidence in the teacher, so will the pupil. It is a great mistake for the assistant to appeal unnecessarily to the principal in maintaining order in the class; for the pupil is thereby impressed with the idea that his teacher is incompetent, or he would manage without assistance. Pupils should not be sent to the principal for punishment or reproof, except for absolute disobedience. All else being settled by the teacher unaided, increases his authority and secures for him the respect of the pupil. When a teacher is obliged to send an unruly pupil out of the class-room, he should, at the time, explain the nature of his offence to the principal, said explanation to be made to the principal alone."

To report cause of absence to principal.

7. Teachers should not allow anything but impossibilities to prevent their attendance at school; for, when a teacher is

absent, not only his class but the whole school is more or less embarrassed. When a teacher is absent through any cause, he should never fail to apprise the principal of the circumstances.

8. The principal should visit each class, division, or de- *General supervision.* partment at least once a day. It would be advisable that he should note the state of discipline, the character of the work being done, etc., on these occasions, and make an entry of same in the Report Book of the division, or in the General Report Book of the school. He should review the work of each division, at least once a month ; or require the respective teachers to do so under his direction. He should then make an entry of the result in the General Report Book, after (privately) calling attention to defects, or publicly pointing out excellencies.

The adoption and observance of such rules and regulations as the foregoing, cannot fail to create a unity of influence, effort, and design amongst teachers of the same school.

PART III.—METHODS OF TEACHING.

CHAPTER I

HINTS ON THE GENERAL ORGANIZATION OF SCHOOLS.

Moreau's
plan the
best for
Moreau.

It is said that when Napoleon was about to send Moreau (A.D. 1801) to fight the Austrians, he drew up a plan of campaign, such as he himself would have used, and presented it to the General with his commission as Generalissimo. Moreau read it over, and then, after a few moments' deliberation, declined to accept the command, affirming that should he fight as directed, and in accordance with the instructions contained in the document before him, he would certainly be defeated. The First Consul was not pleased with the gallant officer's blunt but honest declaration, as it reflected on, or apparently depreciated, his own military talents. However, after a little consideration, he very wisely resolved to let the General have his own way, stating that "he believed Moreau's plan was the best for Moreau." That gallant officer fought according to "his own plan," and the total defeat of the Austrians under Klenau, at Hohenlinden, was the result. As it was with Moreau, so is it with almost every individual teacher. His own plans and expedients (or methods) are the best for him. We do not mean to imply that the teacher should decline to enquire into the nature and positive success of other methods, and blindly follow his own. Quite the reverse. We mean that the teacher, like General Moreau, must have diligently studied and thoroughly mastered the theory and practice of his art, before he can take rank, or assume any very responsible position in his profession; and that, having thus posted himself—duly graduated, so to speak, in all the principles and applications of his calling— he should strike out an independent and original course.

In writing the preceding sheets, we have not taken it upon ourselves to particularly recommend any individual system or method of education, nor have we wittingly spoken dogmatically to our fellow-citizens and co-labourers on any contested subject or theory; for, as aforesaid, we believe that, in the majority of cases, each teacher's "own plan is the best for him." *Still, in practice as in theory, there are general principles and a common basis from which no teacher can materially diverge, without suffering the penalties of failure and defeat. Each teacher should be careful to found his plan or system on these fixed and eternal principles,* and not, as is too often the case, on his own or other men's hobbies. As Wickersham observes, "Teaching is an art based on scientific principles that must always guide its practice . . . it lays under contribution all science and all art, in working out the grandest end that human conception ever realized— the perfection of the human race." Let the teacher, therefore, be just and honest towards himself and his charge —let him act like Moreau, or like David of old, who preferred his own simple weapons to those which he had not tested nor proved. But should he have cause to doubt or suspect the comparative efficacy of his own weapons, let him lose no time in discarding them, so that he may acquire the use of others more efficient. Prussia was the first nation in Europe to arm her soldiers with the needle gun. The victories of Konnigratz, Sadowa, Gravellotte, and Sedan, were the result of this intelligence and promptitude. Had she been content with her old weapons, Alsace, Lorraine, Schleswig Holstein, and the minor German States, would not have been annexed; Sadowa and Sedan would have had a different ending, and her King would never have reigned over a "united Fatherland." These facts tell us we should never

To have an original plan.

despise new principles, or ignore new discoveries; and that, while revering the old, we should acquire an intelligent, practical knowledge of the new. Having treated of some of the general principles on which all good, sound education should be based, we will now proceed to consider matters which involve the practical application of the great truths advanced in the foregoing pages.

The school-room and its decorations. The class-rooms of the public schools in the more respectable towns and villages, as well as in the cities of the respective States (of America), are generally decorated with life-size paintings of Washington, Jefferson, Franklin, and other worthies of the Republic. This decoration speaks volumes for the taste and generosity of the people. Apart from the decoration of the walls and consequent beauty of the interior, it cannot fail to have a powerful influence on the minds of the rising generation. Besides cultivating the taste of the pupils and developing their ideas of the beautiful, it creates a certain emulation which tends to incite them to the performance of patriotic and heroic deeds. As time rolls away, we trust the class-rooms of our public schools will become more and more like the private drawing-room. Then will children look upon them as the most pleasant as well as the most profitable places in which they can spend their time. The decoration of our educational institutions deserves the consideration of every citizen. The legislature of every civilized community should make a liberal provision for this purpose. It behoves our legislators to make the school attractive so far as money can do it; and by doing so, they will discharge one of the most important duties which they owe to posterity. No capital will bring in such a large interest as that which is invested in education. The United States have generally acted in accordance with this principle, and Canada—following the example of her southern sisters—has already taken the initiative in decorative matters. The Canadian system of education is

said to equal that of Massachusetts, but in artistic arrangement, decorative attractions, and architectural design, the
schools of the States far excel those of Canada.

We are of opinion that large public schools should contain *Plan of class-rooms.*
a special room for each class, and also a room of sufficient
capacity to allow all the pupils to assemble together during
opening and closing exercises, and on special occasions, such
as exhibition or celebration days, etc. In this room pupils,
with their teachers, should assemble every morning for
prayers, etc., after which they should be dismissed by the
principal, class by class, to their respective class-rooms.* At
one end there should be an elevated platform, from which
the principal or his assistant may overlook the whole school,
and direct the various movements of the classes. It would
be advisable for the principal and his assistants to have
desks or seats on this dais, as it would be their most appropriate place at the commencement and close of business.
But if the school is not a very large one, and all *must* find
accommodation in one room—that room should be rectan-
gular in shape. At the further end of the room a gallery (or
galleries) should be erected, with fixed seats or chairs for pupils, during the delivery of collective or object lessons. This
gallery should be separated from the rest of the room by
means of a movable glass partition. There should be a partition, because without it the classes will interrupt each other

---

* Some years ago while engaged as a master at the Upper Canada College,
Toronto, we had the pleasure of studying practically the excellencies of this
system—the arrangements alluded to being strictly observed in that Institution.
So far as we know, the principle has not been hitherto adopted in any other Canadian schools. It is coming into general favour in the States, and is fully exemplified in the new State Normal School, at Buffalo, under the kind and able supervision
of its excellent principal, Mr. Buckham. Officers charged with the erection of
Normal or other large schools, would do well to visit both of these Institutions,
and study their arrangements, before adopting plans or awarding contracts. Standing, as it does, at the head of the great public schools of the continent, U. C. College should have buildings more worthy of its fame. The interior arrangements
are excellent, but the style of architecture is not such as we would recommend.
The Toronto Provincial Normal School Buildings are, on the whole, worthy of
much commendation—particularly those sections allotted to the Education Offices,
Library and Museum. The Model Schools (or schools of practice) are neither as
commodious or convenient as we would wish to see them, and, in reality, detract
from the beauty and symmetry of one of the prettiest and best ordered institutions
in the Province.

during recitation, etc., and it should be of glass, so that the principal may see through it, and, if necessary, overlook the work of the whole school or department at one and the same time. The part of the floor occupied by desks, if the room be very large, should gradually rise towards the rear, and the smaller pupils should occupy the first seats. The desks should be arranged so that the pupils when seated may face the teacher's platform. Behind the recitation gallery, and at other convenient places, maps, diagrams, etc., might be suspended. The walls of all class-rooms should be lined with slate (three feet three inches wide) for "black-board" purposes, the lower margin being about three feet from the floor. The windows should be elevated about four feet from the ground, so that outside transactions may not attract the attention of the pupils. The wall behind the teacher's platform, and also certain portions of the side walls, should be adorned with historical paintings and with life-size likenesses of the great and good men of other times. The ground space of a school-room laid out according to the foregoing plan would consist of four divisions :—(1) The teacher's platform, (2) the recitation or object lesson gallery, (3) the space occupied by desks in the body of the school, and (4) the open space between the front desks and the platform. In small schools the gallery may be dispensed with. All classes, when at recitations, should be separated from each other by movable glass partitions; but if the attendance be very large, the accommodation sufficient, and the staff of teachers in proportion, each class, division, or department should have its own particular room; or the pupils should change class-rooms as often as they change subjects. According to the former plan, the teacher in charge of this class or department would teach them every subject; and according to the latter plan, certain teachers would teach them certain subjects, and they would daily pass under the jurisdiction of each individual teacher in the school. Both arrangements have their advantages and objections; but of the two, the latter is the more commendable. In either case the respective classes (having separate class-rooms, and, for the time being, different teachers) would meet together in the assembly room of the school only twice a day—at the commencement and conclusion of business. The tolling of a bell would announce the intermissions or respective changes, and each class would of course know by its "time table" what subject would come next, and what teacher (and in what class room) they should attend during the ensuing hour. Each class-room should possess the most approved means of ventilation, and, unless in very rare cases, the building should not exceed two stories in height.

Desks should not be larger than what may be necessary to accommodate two pupils. The distance between each desk, from front to rear, need not be more than twelve or fifteen inches; but the distance between the "ends of each range" of desks and seats should not be less than two feet four inches. That is to say, the aisles should be between two and three feet in width. The centre aisle should not be less than four or five feet. If a school "be seated" according to this plan, each pupil can get to, or from, his particular seat without disturbing his companions: the space lost in width, and occupied with aisles, will be more than gained in length, as more desks can be made to fit from front to rear, than under the old system. In addition, a more general air of comfort and respectability will pervade the establishment; the teachers can preserve better order, and there will be less "crowding" on entering or leaving the school-room. But instead of being made for two, it would be better if the desks were constructed for the accommodation of only one pupil. In many of the more respectable public schools in American cities,* the desks and

Isolation and arrangement of desks.

* Normal School, Buffalo, for instance

seats are isolated; each pupil has a desk and seat for himself, and this desk and seat have no connection with other desks or seats. We affirm without hesitation that this is one of the great improvements of the age—one which only needs time to be generally adopted. The upper part of these desks resembles a gentlemen's writing case when open— being elevated in front, and dipping as it approaches the body. It is fastened to a cast iron pillar, (or to two iron castings,) which, in turn, is fixed to the floor. Immediately in rear of this pillar is a seat resembling a small arm chair, which is also fastened to a pillar fixed to the floor at a convenient distance from the former. These desks are placed together in pairs to the right and left of the regular aisles, and only two feet apart. Being thus isolated from each other, no pupil can hold communication with his companions without detection, as there is no covering in front to hide from the teachers "the telegraphic movements" of "little hands and feet." There is another feature in these primary arrangements which (so far as we know) is peculiar to America—a feature which deserves not a little attention. It has met with much favour in New England, especially in "the old Bay State." We allude to the practice of placing the principal's platform in a large and commodious recess in the side of the school-room, the pupils being faced as usual towards either end. By this arrangement the teacher has a full side view of each pupil—a better view, perhaps, for all practical purposes than he could enjoy were he to gaze on them from front to rear.

The play ground and cloak-rooms.

A good play ground, well stocked with gymnastic apparatus, should be attached to every school. Part of it should be covered in, so as to protect the pupils from the extremes of temperature. Flowers, fancy shrubs, and trees might be cultivated in another portion of it, if the grounds are large enough. There should also be a suitable place for cricket and other such games. The grounds should be enclosed with a high wall, and a good pump should be situated in some convenient place therein. In the respective cloak-rooms there should be a wash-stand, looking-glass, some brushes and other apparatus for arranging and adjusting the toilet. These things are necessary in every respectable school, and *all schools should be respectable.* The articles required cost but little, and they tend materially to promote habits of taste, cleanliness, and good order amongst the pupils.

Scholastic exercises should be conducted with considerable military precision. When the bell "calls school," the pupils should arrange themselves in files on the play ground or some other convenient place. When it ceases to ring, they should march into the school and to their respective class-rooms, keeping time to the music of an organ or piano. Should there be no instrumental music available, they may be allowed to sing some patriotic soul-stirring song. The piano should be situated on the platform, to the right or left of the principal's desk. One of the assistant teachers, or some of the older pupils, should discourse the music; or each pupil competent to do so might take the post in turn. The music, whether vocal or instrumental, should be continued until all the pupils have entered, and are standing in line beside their respective seats. Then the principal should command "the halt" by touching his bell, and, by a second sound thereof, order them to be seated. *Exercises to be conducted with military precision.*

If it be the custom of all the teachers and pupils to assemble in the large common hall or assembly room at the commencement and close of business, the principal, after conducting the religious exercises or other "collective business," should dismiss the classes to their homes, or to their respective class-rooms, not altogether, but separately, and at short intervals. He should first (by touching his bell) dismiss the lowest class with its teacher, then the second class with its teacher, and so on, until all have left, or until none remain, except the principal's own particular class, *"Calling" and "dismissing school."*

should he have one. During their departure some patriotic tune should be played on the piano : so that as a rule they should march into, and out of, school (or their respective class-rooms) to the sound of music. Though the dismissal of the pupils should not be *en bloc*, it should be continuous —class after class in succession.

The school may be conveniently organized into three divisions or departments, each division into two classes; and, if the school be a large one, each of the classes should be sub-divided into two sections, each section to number from twenty to thirty pupils. In Ontario the pupils of the public schools are supposed to be divided into six classes, the qualifications of each class or grade being fixed by the Council of Public Instruction. Under this system a teacher may be placed in charge of each class, as in central schools, or two or more classes may form a division under the superintendence of one teacher, as in the generality of public schools —the head master being responsible in all cases for the classification, management and control of each class or division, as well as for the general progress of the whole. In conjunction with the School Board, he has the power to prescribe the duties of all his assistant teachers, and the school laws require him to see that these duties are efficiently performed. Generally speaking, the head masters of the public schools have little cause to find fault; for there is no "class of workers" in the world more faithful, diligent, and zealous than Canadian female teachers—the class whence the supply of assistant teachers is usually drawn.

As a rule, pupils should pursue all their studies in the same division, or class. But, although it is desirable that their progress from class to class should be uniform, still, a pupil may be allowed, if qualified, to study reading in one section of that class, and arithmetic in another, or *vice versâ;* and so of the other subjects. These may be regarded as the most appropriate test subjects for the younger children, (*i. e.* those best adapted for enabling a teacher to determine the section, class, or division to which each child should belong,) but dictation, composition, (with accurate punctuation, spelling, etc.,) mathematics, and the elements of natural science, may be more suitable for senior pupils; as difference in skill, in their case, is more easily ascertained in the latter subjects than in the former. They are also more appropriate to the supposed mental calibre of the pupils of advanced age.

It has been ascertained that in almost all schools classified Grading. as above, the third or lowest division will contain about twice as many pupils as the first; and the second about as many, and half as many more. In large schools the foregoing classification into divisions, classes and sections, is the best that can be adopted. Taking *fifteen* as the average number in each section, a school arranged as indicated would stand as follows :

First Division or Department, two classes, each
    class two sections .... 60 pupils
Second Division or Department, three classes, each
    class two sections .... 90 "
Third Division or Department, four classes, each
    class, two sections .... 120 "
             Total average attendance .... 270 "

If *twenty* be taken as the average number in each " section," it will give a total of 360 for the whole school ; but schools are seldom so large, even in our most prosperous cities, as to exhibit such a high average. As a rule, a "section" should not contain less than ten, nor more than thirty pupils; and there should be an assistant teacher for each class of two sections, or "a teacher for every thirty in the average." In many English schools what we call sections are called classes and *vice versâ :* but the name is a matter of little import, provided we have the principle. In small schools the intermediate grade should be omitted, and the pupils classified as

follows—at least we think the following classification will
be more appropriate in rural schools than that given above.
The following is to be considered as merely an approxi-
mation :

First Division, one class of, say...............	20 pupils.
Second Division, two classes, fifteen pupils each.	30 "
Third Division, two classes, twenty pupils each.	40 "
Total average attendance....	90

In very small or very large schools, the classification should
be somewhat different still to the foregoing : we merely
submit these examples as guides to classification. They may
serve as a basis for that purpose. It would be unwise, if
not impossible, to lay down any fixed or rigid rules on this
subject, as so much depends on circumstances—circumstances
not general. However, enough has been said on the subject for all practical purposes.

Uniformity of progress. If the teacher be desirous of promoting *uniform progress*,
the classes must be of uniform size ; the pupils of the same
class, if not of the same section, must be of the same intellectual attainments ; and whatever assistance he thinks proper to furnish should be given, not to one individual but, to
the whole class collectively. If a pupil ask for aid, the
teacher should note the difficulty, and explain the same to
the whole class at a fit and convenient time, when, if possible, he will lead " the youngsters" to solve it for themselves.
Unless he attend to these things, and that the pupils present
at collective lessons be endowed with the same, or nearly the
same, degree of mental capacity, his teaching cannot possibly
be very efficient or successful. He will be like the sower
who went forth to sow, whose seed fell amongst thorns and
on rocks, as well as on good soil. We may remember, it is
said, that the seed which fell on the latter, grew up and came
to maturity, whilst that which fell on rocks and amongst
thorns, remained unproductive. The child's mind is the
ground on which the seed is cast. It behoves the teacher

to see that the soil is duly prepared for the seeds of instruction—properly cleared of rocks, stumps and weeds—so that in days to come, he may reap where he has sown.

The teacher should be careful to suit the subjects of study, and the mode of treating them, to the mental capacities of the children under his charge. Starting with common things and long familiar ideas, he should lead them on gradually to higher objects—to more enlarged acquirements, more extensive views, and, so far as possible, to the maximum of excellence in everything. The subjects or branches of learning, likely to be useful in after life, should be made the instruments of moral culture and mental development. The lessons of the lower sections and classes should be specially adapted to the exercise of the perceptive faculties. At this stage, observation and curiosity are the "working organs," and, so far as possible, the pupils should be taught through the medium of the eye. As the children grow older, or advance in their respective classes, as aforesaid, memory, imagination, reason and judgment, should be developed in *natural order*. This development is the foundation of good education. The healthy cultivation of the mental, moral and physical powers is far more desirable than the mere acquisition of knowledge.

Subjects of study to be adapted to mental capacity.

The various methods of instruction may be reduced to two—the synthetical and the analytical. By the former we combine, construct, or put together; by the latter, we reduce compounds to elements. The one ascends from particular facts to general principles, the other descends from general principles to particular facts.

Systems of teaching.

When the essential particulars of any subject are so numerous as to be likely to fatigue the attention, pupils may commence its study by learning the general principles first, and then proceed to the consideration of the respective facts. However, as a rule, they should proceed from the simple to the complex, from the concrete to the abstract, from the homo-

Order of development.

13

geneous to the heterogeneous.   If possible, the mind should
be introduced to principles through the medium of examples, and gradually led from the particular to the general.
Every study should have an experimental introduction.
The facts a child acquires in this manner should be made
the basis of communication of more advanced or more complex ideas.   When he fully understands these ideas, we may
aꞁke a further step in advance.   As he thus gradually digests
each lesson, we may supply the knowledge he craves, and
thus make the mind self-developing.   As M. Le Compte
well observes, " the genesis of knowledge in the individual
must follow the same course as the genesis of knowledge
in the race."   "In mode and arrangement," says Herbert
Spencer, "the education of children must harmonize with
the education of the race, considered historically."   "There
are stages of development in the immature growth of individuals," says Hugh Miller, "which seem to correspond with
stages of development in the immature growth of nations."
There is in every child, as we may ascertain by looking
back on our own individual history, an aptitude to acquire
information in the order in which the race to which he
belongs mastered its various kinds of knowledge.   The
education of the individual may be facilitated by leading
him through the steps traversed by the general mind —
those steps being taken in their order of sequence.   Hence,
education should be a repetition, in miniature, of the successive stages of development in the civilization of the race.
The more fully we consider these facts, the more firmly are
we convinced of their truth.   The history of educational
progress amongst the race (or mankind generally) is a potent
ally in enabling us to understand " child nature," whilst it
suggests many useful hints as regards the true principles of
teaching.   One mind is a type and representative, more or
less, of all minds; hence, if we understand our own conceptions, and duly comprehend the power and effect of the

laws which regulate the action of thought, we will be able to divine the thoughts and ascertain the motives of other people. We may generally read a parent's character through that of his child; and, *vice versâ*, the evil passions and infirmities of disposition to be checked or eradicated in children, are traits of character which have been more or less transmitted from their progenitors. Hereditary transmission hands down mental and moral characteristics as well as physical excellencies or defects.

The order in which subjects of study should be presented to the understanding, deserves much thought. By judicious *Natural and logical order of study.* arrangements and careful elimination, the accumulated knowledge of ages may be condensed into a small compass, and imparted to children in such a form as will create a thirst for more light, whilst saving them useless labour. An experienced teacher can impart as much information in a few hours, as the unassisted tyro would fail to acquire in as many months—perhaps years. The subjects embraced in the programme of studies should follow each other in natural and logical order. The primary, or elementary subjects should invariably be presented first, and the elements of each, thoroughly understood by the pupil before the teacher proceeds to the inculcation of higher truths. In other words, the subjects best calculated to promote the right cultivation of the mental powers, should be presented to the mind in the order of sequence which nature follows in the development of these faculties. For these reasons, "natural and logical order" should be a motto with every student and teacher; otherwise, success, if possible, will at all events be doubtful. Pupils desirous of acquiring any branch of knowledge should learn to regard it in an applicate as well as in a theoretical sense, and *vice versâ*. For instance, in the acquistion of geometry, arithmetic, grammar, geography, or any other branch of learning, *they should study the subject*, and regard books relating thereto as mere tools or means for that purpose. As matters stand, they frequently fall into the error of studying the author more than they study the subject, implicitly adopting *his* views without the least reflection or personal investigation. Mind should not be a passive recipient, like the sponge. It should be the great and constant aim of the teacher to make it an active agent, so that it may exercise its divinity, and assert its near relation to the Creator.

CHAPTER II.

COLLECTIVE TEACHING.

Sundry ob-
servations.

In collective teaching the teacher's success will depend, in a great measure, on his personal carriage and general appearance. His manner of address should, therefore, be easy, fluent, and graceful. He should be animated, without being "flouried." Being careful to avoid such characteristics as "meaningless pauses," stammering, and unnecessary repetition, he should state exactly what he means, and in as few words as possible. It is far better to be a man of too few than too many words. Simplicity should be one of the characteristics of every teacher—simplicity of language, simplicity of illustration. In fact, simplicity may be regarded as "the maximum of excellence." During the delivery of a lesson, prior to its commencement and after its close, the teacher should test his pupils' comprehension of the subject by a series of skilful questions. As explained more fully elsewhere, the time occupied in the delivery of a lesson should not be prolonged so as to weary the class, and create a dislike for the subject. A lesson extending over the space of half an hour will be quite long enough for junior classes, and forty-five minutes will be sufficient for the senior divisions. The teacher can easily guess how long a lesson may be, and also ascertain the effect of his teaching, by noting the interest he is able to inspire and maintain. He should never continue a lesson until the pupils lose their relish for the subject. He must stir up and partially satisfy their mental appetites, but he must not allow them to feed to the verge of satiety. Better to stop short of this point and bring the lesson to a close, while the pupils are yet anxious to learn more about it. They will then return to, or resume, its investigation at some future time with renewed pleasure, and study it in private with an ever-increasing interest.

With very young children, the elliptical method of teaching is, perhaps, the most effective—at all events, it will be most successful in maintaining attention. It has its dangers, however, and, to be successful, must be guided by a skilful "hand." As a rule, the practice of this method will be successful if accompanied by many questions, and but few ellipses. Both skilfully intermixed, will be effective. The pupils should not be required to fill in an ellipsis which, in the nature of things, they could not be expected to supply. The ellipses should not be ambiguous nor uncertain, and should consist of but few words. If the class be composed of very young children, one word will be sufficient. *The elliptical method.*

The analytical and synthetical methods may be used with great advantage in collective teaching. In conducting his instructions according to the collective method, the teacher should be particularly careful that the pupils in each class be of the same degree of mental capacity; that he educate as well as talk; that they be instructed as well as pleased; that he be supplied with specimens, models, or diagrams, to illustrate his lesson; that whatever maps he may require be at hand, and that any subjects needing illustrations, additional to those provided, be sketched on the black-board. If the members composing a class be not of the same (or *Same class, same capacity.*

nearly the same) degree of capacity, the subject, and the teacher's method of treating it, will be too simple for some, and incomprehensible to others. Therefore, neither party will be edified—probably both will be injured, fatigued, or "disgusted." Imperfect classification is one of the greatest impediments to success, and one of the most serious obstacles with which the conscientious teacher has to contend. The difficulty arises from many causes, such as irregularity of attendance, want of sufficient help, the natural though foolish anxiety of parents to have their children promoted, the desire of teachers to comply with parents' wishes, etc. The teacher who would be successful must exhibit a will of his own, and classify his pupils according to their natural and acquired abilities, irrespective of exterior influences. But to return :

Arrangement of lesson in its natural order and sequence.

The teacher must thoroughly understand his subject, and arrange the matter in natural and logical order, if he be really desirous of practising collective lessons successfully. He should prepare a sketch of the subject, and after the delivery of the lesson, file the same for future reference. This sketch should exhibit the heads, divisions, and subdivisions of the lesson, arranged in their natural order of sequence, so that the treatment of the matter, and manner of delivery may be apparent at a glance. It would be wise to note (as a P.S.) the specimens, models, charts, or diagrams, necessary for illustrating the subject. Object lessons are generally collective lessons; and every collective lesson, should be more or less an object lesson.

Recapitulation.

When the teacher has deduced and explained all the particulars of the first section of his lesson, he should lead his pupils to recapitulate what they have learned, whilst he writes the headings or sketch of same on the black-board, from their dictation—taking care to ascertain whether they have gained ideas as well as words. He should then take up the next section and treat it in like manner, and so on to the end of the lesson, when there should be a general recapitulation of the whole, the teacher pointing to the headings on the board. At the close, the black-board should exhibit a perfect sketch of the principal points of the lesson, duly numbered in their order of sequence—then each idea will have been developed, deduced, and expressed in its logical order. Each of these lessons should form part of a regular series—of a complete whole—being naturally connected one with another, links in the development of the great chain of intellect, well-prepared stones in the great arch of science.

From what has been stated in this and preceding chapters, it will be seen that successful teaching depends chiefly on the following characteristics, namely: (1) *Simplicity*, by which we mean that the mind should be fixed upon only one thought at a time: (2) *Gradation*, or logical and natural order: (3) *Repetition*, which is necessary to due impression: (4) *Illustration*, which groups and associates examples of same facts: (5) *Precision* in the use of words, whereby the elective faculty selects the best and most appropriate: (6) Enunciation or *Definition*, whereby principles are clothed in words: (7) *Application*, which applies the results of the lesson to the benefit of the pupil, by solving or confirming some principle in religion, science, or morals.

Characteristics of good teaching.

Every collective lesson should have an introduction, and an application. The object of the introduction is to connect the lesson with the preceding lessons on the same subject. It should be short, clear, useful, and interesting; so that it may open the mind to receive additional light, and fix the attention on what follows. The illustrations used should be apposite and natural, interesting, clear and graphic, the essential points of resemblance being distinctly and prominently placed before the mental gaze. Illustration to be effective must be ample, without being redundant.

Introduction to lesson—its object

Lesson to
have a prac-
tical appli-
cation.

The practical application of a lesson should grow naturally out of the lesson. It should not be forced, nor introduced as a mere statement, but as a reflection associated with, and arising from, the subject. It should not comprise more than one or two inferences. Were they increased in number, the impression of each would be lessened, and the mind confused. The teacher should have a definite purpose in every lesson he gives, and should not rest satisfied until he has accomplished the object in view. Should he have a just conception of his work, he will be able to describe beforehand what he aims at, how he expects to attain it, and what effect each lesson may be expected to produce. The collective lesson, if skilfully delivered, is a potent agent in developing noble ideas, habits, and actions. It is the most effective instrument he can use to influence the affections, or draw out and develop the various faculties of the mind. Under the management of a skilful teacher it is one of the most powerful aids in doing good. We know of no means more efficient in "pointing a moral or adorning a tale."

SECTION 2. THE ART OF CATECHISING.

Socratic
method.

The art of asking questions admits of two divisions. The first division may be used as a means of instruction, and is then called the catechetical or Socratic method. It is a well-known fact, that by means of a few judicious well-connected questions, pupils may be easily led to discover principles, and to solve difficulties, which would otherwise be insurmountable. Full many a time does the bosom of the pupil glow with honest pride when he remembers, that personal efforts have enabled him to overcome such literary obstacles. But to effect these objects, the questions should naturally grow out of each other, beginning at some familiar point and proceeding step by step to the unknown—until the answer to the last question of the series reveals the mystery, and unfolds the knowledge sought.

The second division of the art comprehends queries pro- Tentative and examination questions. posed as test questions at recitations, reviews, and public or private examinations, and also such as may be proposed to ascertain the extent of pupils' knowledge of a subject before giving a lesson. In proposing questions, as in performing other educational work, the teacher's chief object should be to exercise and strengthen the respective mental faculties of the pupils. The test of their actual knowledge (except at certain examinations) is a matter secondary to these considerations. A question, admitting of such an answer as "*yes*" or "*no*," should never be proposed. Queries should be of a searching nature, and be proposed in such a manner as to find out how much or how little the pupil knows of the subject. This course will tend to secure careful and thorough preparation. It will improve the pupil's power of expression, cultivate his memory, increase his knowledge, make his information more definite, and thereby enable him to acquit himself with credit and satisfaction. The pupil's answers, like the teacher's queries, should be clear, full, and exact— free from ambiguity and uncertainty. As a rule, the pupil should not be interrupted or corrected until "quite through with his reply." The tact or skill requisite in asking questions aright may be regarded as one of the mysteries of the teacher's art—and not the least of them. This tact is, in fact, one of his most important qualifications, and (if not naturally possessed of it) he must necessarily acquire it, should he be desirous of more than ordinary success. It is a real test of the teacher's aptitude and ability. However, it must be remembered that the true measure of his skill is not what he can do and say himself, but what he can get his pupils to say and do.

Individual questioning is impossible in a large class; and, To be general in application. if possible, it implies a loss of power, as each pupil will receive only a fraction of the whole instruction. Questions should be addressed to the class, not to individual pupils. To be effective, they must act upon the whole, not upon any part or unit. After all have held up their hand, or given some other sign of their ability or inability to reply, the teacher may call on one individual to give the answer; but he should never designate the individual before giving the question. In this manner, all the pupils will profit by the questions addressed to one, and the whole lesson will be continuous to the whole class.

Effective questioning must combine the individual and simultaneous methods. Under such a combination the pupils will acquire a tendency to answer mentally, and, if the questions be fairly distributed, the class will imbibe the maximum amount of knowledge. Thoughtfulness and distinctness are the best characteristics of good answering. Hence, replies are to be judged by a double standard—by the amount of truth they contain, and the amount of thought they indicate. In rejecting an answer, the teacher should give credit for the amount of truth or evidence of thought expressed or implied therein—the class, or the pupil himself, being led to amend or enlarge, as necessary. This course will encourage the diffident, and check the thoughtless ardour of the over-confident, whilst it develops instead of repressing intelligence. Should the teacher detect any inattention on the part of a pupil he should instantly ask him to answer the question proposed, or to repeat it. If unable to do so, he should forfeit his standing in the class.

Error is the result of ignorance, prejudice, or habit. Personal correction on the part of the pupil is the only true safe-guard against its repetition. The correction of errors is no small part of the work of both teacher and pupil; but unless a sense of error be felt by those who make it, there can be no real or thorough correction. It is not always expedient to insist on rapidity of thought. Hasty answers are often the result of impulse, and then imply the absence of reflection. For these reasons pupils should be encouraged to "think twice before they speak once."

CHAPTER III.

S P E L L I N G.

Having treated of the school building, of the order or plan of instruction and classification, and of the general principles which should guide every teacher in the intelligent practice of his art, we will now proceed to consider the more important of those branches of knowledge supposed to be imparted at every public school. Feeling that theory should give way to practice, and science develop itself in art, we will venture to submit, at least, one of the more approved methods of teaching each particular subject. However, we would not bind the teacher to adopt this method, seeing that "Moreau's plan was the best for Moreau." There are circumstances in which other methods will work equally well. The teacher, however, must remember that all systems of education should be founded on well-established scientific principles, and that life is too short to waste much time in visionary experiments. Doubtless the following pages may be useful to the young and inexperienced teacher, and not wholly uninteresting to the Nestors of the profession. *Methods of teaching should be based on scientific principles.*

Keeping the foregoing objects in view, we will now proceed to consider the more important subjects of popular instruction. First on the list, and first in the order of sequence, is spelling—the foundation-stone of all literary education. This subject may be taught to very young children by means of a box or spelling apparatus, containing a chart *Spelling, and how to teach it.*

of pictures and words (names), which, by the agency of
cranks, can be moved like a panorama behind an opening—
the said opening, through the action of flexible slides, to be
closed, enlarged, or decreased, at the will of the teacher.

The pictures are of great value, as they prepare the mind to
receive the name of the object presented.   Then the crank
is turned again, and, as it slowly revolves, letter after letter
of the name is exposed in regular sequence; so that the
little ones actually spell the word by naming each letter as
it appears.   By these means, they first receive a strong impression of the object; they then obtain its name, (through
the teacher, if necessary,) and finally learn to spell the same.
This done, they should write the word on their slates (if
able to write), after which the teacher may write the word
on the black-board, and direct them to compare it with the
word on their slates, making any necessary corrections.
They may then proceed to consider the next object, and to
spell and write its name in like manner—the new object
being revealed, and the former one concealed, by another
turn of the crank; and so on to the end of the lesson.   It
will be seen that this system combines real amusement with
genuine intellectual instruction.   The fact of a portion of
the lesson being concealed, tends to excite the curiosity and
to hold the attention of the pupils, so that they are sure to
be on the *qui vive* as to "what will come next."   This spelling apparatus is specially adapted for the use of primary

schools, and may be said to supersede the use of primers.
Besides making instruction pleasant and profitable, it saves
much time and labour, and materially increases the instructor's teaching power. It will be seen that reading (and
even *viva voce* composition) can be taught young pupils by
means of this apparatus ; but the reading machine is a much
better aid in this respect.

The Reading Machine, of which the above is a cut, was
devised (with some necessary alterations) from a model seen
by us some years ago in the Royal Museum at Naples. It
is simple in construction and very easily managed. It may
be described as a frame, or box, mounted on a movable
support and fixed so as to revolve on a horizontal axle, E, F.
It may be of any height or length, but its width from front

to rear need not exceed two and a half inches.   The face or front of the machine may be divided into as many vertical sections containing words, as the teacher may desire;—each section being covered with slides which can be moved upwards or downwards at pleasure, one slide being absent in each column.   Inside these slides is a card, of suitable dimensions, containing sentences arranged so that at any stage of an expression the words will suit and make sense, no matter which of the slides may be moved in the adjoining column.   The teacher may remove the card and substitute another by opening the base-board, c, d.   The iron feet are sufficiently heavy and far apart to secure stability.   It would be advantageous to mount them on rollers.   The card headings, corresponding to the spaces from a to b, contain pictures representing the subject of the lesson (the lion for instance) in various attitudes or relations.

Reading to precede spelling.

According to Nature's mode of teaching, reading should precede spelling in the order of sequence.   The young child acquires the use of words long before he is required to analyze them into sounds, or express them by letters.   After he has learned to read and write the letters of the alphabet (small script or italic) he may, by means of the "reading machine," be taught to read *short* sentences.   After reading a sentence, the words may be resolved into syllables and letters, and then written by the teacher on the black-board, the children dictating the letters.   The children may then copy same, letter for letter, on their slates; after which they should be required to read it collectively and simultaneously—finally spelling each word as they have written it. The machine used for teaching spelling in some of the Massachusetts primary schools (see fig., page 196,) is about three feet long by one and a half in breadth and two in height, and when in use is fixed on a table set apart for the purpose.   The respective objects, and their names, letter by letter, are exhibited to the class by the movement of the crank turned by the teacher's hand—bevelled wheels acting on the cylinders inside cause them to revolve, and thus roll the canvas round the drum at one end of the machine (*a*), whilst it is unrolled at the other (*b*). In some primary schools the "spelling stick" (see cut) is favoured with a prominent place.

This instrument consists of a piece of wood, or iron, properly fashioned and grooved for holding the card-board letters. By the aid of this simple device the teachers of primary classes will find it easy to command the attention of their pupils, teach the form of letters, and show how to combine them into words. It has been well said that "by its use words and their spelling may be taught to a large class with less outlay of time and patience than is required for teaching a single pupil with the book alone." It will be seen that if words, instead of letters, be placed on the card-board, the Spelling Stick will be transformed into a "Sentence Stick"—an instrument which may be very advantageously used in teaching children how to construct sentences, just as they had previously been shown how to construct words. In fact this is done in the ordinary manner, as above, with but little effort on the part of the teacher. By means of "The Stick" the teacher may (without the use of the rod) lead his primary classes to acquire, almost unconsciously, a good working knowledge of the first principles of composition.

How the higher classes should be taught.

Pupils of the higher classes should be taught spelling by means of dictation, composition and analysis of words. Spelling is needed chiefly in writing, and is taught best in connection with that exercise. Its acquisition, in this manner, will cost comparatively little time or labour, and the necessary practice in writing words will ensure the pupil a degree of facility in expressing his thoughts, which will be no small help when he comes to study the art of composition. Each pupil should provide himself with a dictionary, and also with a spelling book "without meanings." During the preparation of his lesson he should write on his slate the words prescribed, and attach their meanings as given in the dictionary. The time fixed for spelling exercises having arrived, and the class being called, the pupils will erase any words they may have on the slates, and take their places according to their order of merit in the last spelling class. The teacher will then give out the words of the prescribed lesson *in irregular order*, and the pupils will write the same to his dictation. This being done he will instruct them to write the meanings, allowing a fixed time to do so. He will then tell them to hold down (or exchange) slates, after which he will glance over each and mark the errors, beginning at the head of the class. When all the slates have been examined thus, the pupils who have no errors will take precedence, according to their order of merit, of those who have. In like manner those who have only one error will take precedence of those who have two, whilst those who have more than two may be "plucked," *i. e.* sent to their seats with instructions to remain in during intermissions, or to remain after school hours to study the lesson. The former,

Order of merit.

that is, those who had but one or two errors, correct the same, while the latter are returning to their seats. The teacher examines the corrections and instructs the class to "number." He then reads aloud the name of each individual in the spelling class, from the " Daily Register of Progress."

While doing so, each pupil, as mentioned, states the "number" indicating his standing in the class as acquired during the present lesson. This number is immediately entered by the teacher opposite the pupil's name, under the proper date, and so on from first to last. Pupils sent to their seats will have no standing, and must take places in the class next time after all their companions, and in the relative order indicated by their register numbers on the roll of the school.

The pupils of intermediate or junior classes may not be compelled to give "meanings for words" as indicated above, but should be required to write them correctly, dividing each into its proper syllables. The correct copying of prose or poetry is an agreeable exercise, and also an excellent method of teaching this subject. Pupils making mistakes in spelling should invariably correct them in writing—on paper or on the black-board—this will tend to fix them on the tablet of the mind. Some teachers require pupils to prepare their spelling exercises at home, but the circumstances of each being different, and the facilities of acquisition variable, we believe it would be better to have the work done in school under official supervision. The higher classes should study the philosophy of spelling while labouring to acquire perfection in the art. This is often neglected by modern students, but was never forgotten by our fathers. They were also more skilful in the art than we are. They seem to have had more time for practice than their sons and grandsons of the present age. In former times, besides the ordinary daily lessons in spelling, there were what might be called general field days. On these occasions the pupils (by "choosing sides") divided into two parties, and were ranged in lines opposite each other. The two best pupils in the school made the "selections" alternately, under the supervision of the teacher. Sometimes, instead of "the whole school being ranged against each other," irrespective of sex, the girls became the opponents of the boys, or a class was

How errors should be corrected.

"Field days" in spelling.

14

ranged against a class.   The words were then given out by
the teacher, or by one of the pupils elected for the purpose,
and the lively contest commenced; or the pupils on either
side gave words to their opponents — words taken from
lessons that had been learned.   Each pupil who missed a
word, fell out of line and took his seat, and at last only a
few remained standing on the "bloodless field."   These
"heroes" then commenced the contest anew (if time permitted), and waged "war" until one had the high honour of
standing alone, "monarch of all he surveyed."   This pupil
was then hailed as "champion speller" of the school, until
the varying fortunes of another battle gave his laurels to
some industrious rival.   If time were limited, the side which
had the greater number standing after "the first round of
spelling" had been finished, might, of course, be regarded as
having won the match.   We would not be so minute in
describing this method were it not that it has fallen into
disuse, and may be forgotten, unknown, or misunderstood
by young teachers.   It was formerly very popular, and is
so still, wherever used.   It forms an agreeable variation
when the mind is fatigued with heavier studies, and, if
introduced, the teacher may rely on its favourable accept-
ance and general success.

CHAPTER IV.

READING.

Reading,
and how to
teach it.

In reading, as in spelling and other exercises, the teacher,
of course, appoints the lesson beforehand.   It is the custom
in many schools for pupils to go through their reading exercise in their desks, each standing up when it comes to his

turn to read; but, if convenient, it would be advisable for the pupils to go through this lesson at the class stations, taking and changing places according to merit. Having duly prepared the lesson, and taken their respective positions, the teacher gives the signal to "begin," and then the first pupil in the class commences to read, previously naming the page, subject, etc. As a rule, before giving the order to commence, the teacher should propose a few searching questions, so that he may ascertain what the pupils really know about the lesson. By this means he gains several necessary advantages; he leads the pupils to perceive how much they have still to learn in connection with the subject; he excites their curiosity to know more; he gains and concentrates their attention, and places himself in a position to adapt his teaching to their mental capacity and general acquirements. If consistent with his convenience, he should also ask a few leading questions concerning the lesson, on the same subject, immediately preceding the one under consideration. This practice will enable him to retain and continue the thread of succession. In reading exercises, strict attention should be paid to the clear, distinct utterance of each word, to correct pronunciation, proper inflection, and just emphasis— the teacher himself occasionally reading a sentence as a model. Pupils detecting errors in the reading of their companions should raise their right hand in token of dissent; and one of them, specially selected by the teacher, should make the necessary correction. If it be the custom of the school that pupils are to be permitted to "change places" in their classes, taking precedence according to merit, then, if several of the pupils have their hands up, the teacher, as a rule, would require the correction to be made, or the correct answer to be given, by the nearest boy to him who had erred, and who may have his "hand up." Should this party answer satisfactorily, he should be allowed to "go up," that is, to take precedence of the erring boy, and all the inter-

Precedence according to merit.

Some questions to precede the lessons.

mediate pupils, if any. At the close of each paragraph (if the class be a junior one) questions might be advantageously proposed relative to the meaning of the respective sentences and component words. If necessary, explanations should be given, diagrams and other illustrations exhibited, and, finally, the pupils should be required to express the sense of the paragraph in their own words. At the close of the

Pupils to give a summary of the lesson at its close.

lesson (whether the classes be junior or senior) a general summing up is desirable. Each pupil should be required to name in order (wholly or in part) the successive steps in the argument or discourse. The pupils may be occasionally per-

To question each other.

mitted, as a favour, to propose questions to each other concerning the lesson—each taking "place" according to his skill and ability. The last or lowest pupil in the class would, of course, ask the first query, and the head of the class would ask the last, according to this arrangement. This exercise will form an agreeable variation, and will never fail to excite general interest, and to create an honest rivalry amongst the pupils. It will cause them to seek assistance at home, so that they may be able to come to school with a select stock of questions on the reading lesson. This is a subject in which almost every parent will be able to render assistance. Of course, all questions proposed by pupils will be subject to such alterations, additions, or omissions, as the teacher may think necessary; and all pupils must "ask questions having answers in the lesson." The observance of this rule is necessary to the success of the plan. Every Friday afternoon, the pupils may be allowed to question each other on general topics—on the contents of the several lessons learned during the week, for instance— but no idle or unruly pupil should be allowed to take part in this recreation. It will be observed, that these remarks

Things to be observed.

concerning exercises in reading, are equally applicable to

Lessons to be of moderate length.

lessons in history, geography, and several other subjects. Reading lessons should be of moderate length—the limits being always fixed beforehand by the teacher. Every pupil in a class should be required to pay strict attention to the reading of his companions, and occasionally required to criticise same. Should the teacher have reason to believe that any pupil is careless or inattentive, he should stop proceedings immediately, and ask him a question. Let him be asked to read, for instance, and, should he not know the place, let him be degraded and sent to the foot of the class.

The best way to correct a bad style is to call the pupils' attention to the characteristic excellencies of good reading— instructing them to carefully note the peculiar causes of bad reading. If a boy read badly, or in a slovenly and careless manner, the teacher should ask if any of his companions can read better. When he has ascertained how many of them feel desirous of "offering improvements," he should call on each pupil (having his hand up) to point out some defect, and finally require one of them to read the sentence again. He may then encourage them to point out the difference between the reading of the former and that of the latter, and so on until all have read. The following is also a good method of improving style, viz., let the children be requested to relate some anecdote, or a short history of their own life and experience. After it has been stated *viva voce*, let them be required to write it on paper, taking care to observe the same order of narration. This being done, let each pupil, in turn, be requested to read his own composition. It will be found that pupils can read their own productions, of this nature, much more efficiently than they can read other compositions. They may thus be led to discover, that, as a rule, good readers must deliver a piece as they would recite it, were the composition their own—that they must read as they would speak, or as they would relate a personal anecdote.

How to correct and improve style.

The concert method. The pupils should be occasionally required to read in concert—that is, all together—taking the time from the teacher, or some of their more efficient companions. This exercise will cure them of many defects, such as false emphasis, etc. At the close of each sentence or paragraph the teacher should call for criticisms, or point out such defects as he had noticed and wished them to avoid. In reading exercises, attention should be directed to the ideas expressed, rather than to the form of expression. The lesson should be repeated until the ideas contained therein become familiar. Should the pupil fail to observe or understand these ideas, they must be pointed out and explained; after which, his attention may be directed to the form of expression—to the spelling, derivation, and syllabification of the more important words, etc., the black-board being freely used.

Pupils to learn the position of places mentioned in lessons. It would be advisable to get the pupils to point out on maps or globes the position of all places mentioned in historical or geographical lessons, as well as in reading exercises. If maps or globes are not convenient they can point towards the places, giving their positions with respect to some known locality. At the close of the lesson the pupils may be directed to ask for any additional information—direct or collateral—which they may desire concerning it; but they should not be allowed to ask "idle questions," or queries, which have nothing to do with the subject. During the progress or delivery of the lesson they may be allowed to take or "change places," according to their efficiency or ability in answering. At the close of the lesson the teacher orders them to number, and then copies these numbers into the register of daily progress, as described elsewhere. Before dismissing the class, the teacher should always fix the limits of the next lesson on the same subject. The register of progress, if properly kept, will present an accurate daily record of each pupil's scholarship and deportment. However, it cannot be accurately kept unless the record is made at the close of each lesson; and without accuracy it will command no confidence, and its moral effect will be lost. When the staff of instructors is small in comparison with the number of pupils, it is questionable whether the teachers can spare time to keep such a register of daily progress as that alluded to. In this case "merit cards" may be used as a substitute. By their aid, teachers may secure most of the good results of accurate records with less expense of time.

A substitute for the register of daily progress.

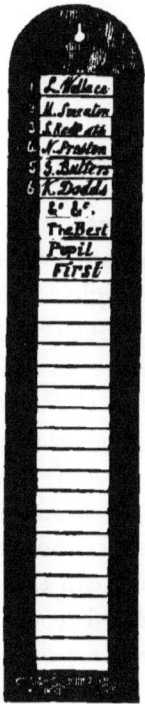

SCHOOL INDEX.

We may here remark that teachers who keep Class Records or Registers of Progress should never fail to summarize same on or about the first day of every month, so as to ascertain the relative merit of their pupils and give each his proper position on the Monthly Roll of Honour. In New England and New York it is the custom of the teachers of the more respectable public schools to prepare a Monthly Register of Merit in the form of a "School Index" (see cut); and, so far as we could learn, its introduction and constant use has been attended with the happiest results. The School Index is hung on the walls (generally in some conspicuous place), where it can be easily seen and examined by the pupils, parents and visitors. It consists of a black walnut or other frame, in which are arranged, inside a glass front, small pieces of wood, or slate, the names of pupils being written on same once a month, in their relative order of merit. One side of the frame is hinged, so that it can be opened whenever the teacher desires to make any change in the order or position of the names. This machine may be used to indicate (1) the standing of each pupil as to Scholarship alone ; or (2) Deportment alone ; or (3) Scholarship and Deportment, with attendance, the marks obtained in all subjects being added together for this purpose. When used, there should be an "Index" for each Class or Division of the School.

CHAPTER V.

WRITING.

To be taught at an early age. The practice of writing is often foolishly delayed until the child reaches a certain age or certain class, etc. We believe it should be one of the first subjects taught. So soon as children have learned the names of the letters of the alphabet, they should be permitted to indulge in the pleasure of writing—"making" each letter on their slates as they learn (or even before they learn) its name, the teacher first printing same on the black-board. *The first letters* First lesson. *taught should be the smaller script or italic ;* and, if brought before them in a proper manner, they will know, and be able to write, the alphabet in a few days. They can then learn to write small words. Attention should be directed, at an early date, to the proper manner of holding a pen or pencil. The teacher will guide, modify and correct the pupils' attempts in writing, but it would not be wise to insist on too rigid a uniformity in the style. No two persons are alike, mentally or physically, and handwriting, like a man's face, will always be characteristic and personal— similar, yet different. Let the pupil's capacity in this respect, as in others, be developed, disciplined, and regulated, but never artificially forced.

When the time prescribed in the Time Table for the How to teach it. practice of writing arrives, the teacher should call the school to attention by touching his bell. He then gives his preliminary command as follows, " First division (second or third as the case may be) prepare to write." Then the slates, books, etc., of the division, or divisions, addressed are quietly returned to their proper places. Pens, ink, and copy books having been conveniently arranged, the pupils sit perfectly still until they receive the signal to " Begin," from the teacher. When the time allotted to writing has been completed, the principal or his assistant should close proceedings as follows :—" Writers! finish lines"—a pause. "Clean pens"—a pause. " Deposit pens." He then touches his bell, and all the writers rise, holding their copy books in their hands. Another stroke of the bell (or the command, " Places") orders them to their class stations—each pupil taking his place according to his standing or order of merit in writing on the preceding day. Then the principal and his assistants, (if there be two or more classes) pass round the class (beginning with the "head") and examine the writing ; and while doing so, assign to each individual the place he deserves in the order of merit. The order to " Number" is then given, and the standing of each pupil is entered in the " Register of Progress." This being done, the command " To seats" is given, and all march off to their desks " in Indian file." Each pupil should lose a place in his class (i. e., be degraded one place), for every blot or error in his copy. If the " Merit Card System" is in use, the teacher may give a merit to every one deserving of it, taking care to give none to those who have blots or errors. In such cases pupils are generally fined a " merit" if their exercise in writing exhibits more than one blot or one error.

Before concluding this subject, it may be well to say that Working arrangements. children can be classified for the practice of writing, in classes, sections, or divisions. The children of the lower classes should sit in front, and those of the higher in the hindermost desks. When arranged and sub-divided in this way according to their proficiency in the art, the senior classes engage in copying from a head-line in their copy books, or from one on the black-board, or from copy slips placed before them for that purpose (as aforesaid); whilst the principal or his assistant (taking a convenient position before the same or another black-board) gives instruction to the junior pupils in the general principles of the science.

Primary classes. Teachers of writing in the primary department must, of necessity, devote considerable time to instruction of this kind; and, if properly managed, children of very tender years will take a great delight in the exercise. The pupils being furnished with slates and pencils, and having learned how to sit and how to hold the pen, the teacher will draw the straight stroke on the board, and direct attention to its slope, uniform thickness, and other characteristics, after which the little ones will copy it, each endeavouring to profit by the instructions received. When they have grown expert at this exercise, the upper and lower "ties" or "crooks" (as they are called) may be introduced. Then the characteristics of the curve may be pointed out, the children copying it after receiving the necessary preliminary explanations. When sufficiently posted in these exercises, lessons should be given on the formation of letters—each pupil being required to copy the same accurately from the black-board. This preliminary course "may be gone through on the slates." But the use of pen and paper should be introduced at its close. If the pupils copy from the same kind of head-lines (whether from the copy book or black-board) uniformity and similarity of writing will be the result. "Young beginners" may, for a short time, have the lines "pencilled."

Supervision and correction. While the pupils are practising their writing exercise, the principal, or one of his assistants, should pass up and down the aisles, pointing out errors, or leading the children to discover them by comparison with the original head-line or copy slip. It would be advisable that he should take a pupil's "copy" to the black-board and copy the errors in spelling, the malformation of letters, etc., and then require the pupils to point them out, deducing from themselves personally (by reference to the original) the principles to be observed in connection with the subject. In writing, as in all other subjects, the teacher should prefer quality to quantity, being more desirous that all should write well, than that a few should write *par excellence*.

CHAPTER VI.

ARITHMETIC AND ALGEBRA.

Arithmetic should be made an exercise of the mind, and not a mere application of rules. The science of numbers and art of computation afford, perhaps, the best facilities for the healthy exercise of the mental faculties. An intelligent knowledge of the powers, principles, and properties of numbers, combined with precision and despatch in their manipulation, effectually cultivate all the faculties of the mind, and in after years will enable the pupil to transact the business of daily life with credit to himself and employers. It is, perhaps, one of the best subjects for teaching pupils methods of thought, and how to reason; as well as what to do, and how to do it. *Arithmetic as a mental exercise.*

Children generally acquire their first knowledge of number by learning to count their own fingers. In primary schools the first ideas of number are usually imparted in this way, or by means of the ball-frame, the pupils being occasionally required to reckon marbles, pins, maps, the panes of glass in *First ideas of numbers.*

a window, etc. Children should be taught the elementary rules on a sort of common-sense principle. Beginning with simple things, they should be "inveigled" (or led) on by degrees to the comprehension of more complicated ideas. Children always seem to experience some difficulty in understanding abstract numbers, and for this reason they should (at first) be taught to connect them with visible objects. In the elementary exercises, they should be gradually led to discover that the name and kind of the articles reckoned, do not affect the result—that numbers, in themselves, are abstract; that 2 and 3 make 5, whether they be marbles, cows, horses, or abstract units; that the different orders of units increase from right to left, and decrease from left to right in a ten-fold ratio; and that the removal of a figure one place to the right or left, increases or decreases its value ten-fold.

Written arithmetic.

Having acquired the names of the numerals, formed correct ideas of their simple and local values, and learned how to solve easy questions in multiplication and division, they may commence the study of written arithmetic—the rules being deduced from the examples in all cases. The exercises in arithmetic (and in algebra also, so far as practicable), should always be thickly interspersed with questions occurring in, or applicable to, the transactions of daily life. The teacher may occasionally introduce a little variety into the subject, by writing the queries on the black-board. The various classes (standing at the draft stations, or sitting at their

Rapidity and accuracy.

desks), copy and solve these questions as rapidly and correctly as possible. "The first done" (if his work be correct) takes the first place, the "second done" takes the second place, and so on to the end. This exercise is conducted in some places in the following manner: We will suppose the pupils to be standing at their class stations, "armed with slates and pencils." The teacher writes the query on the black-board; the pupils copy and solve it. The first done calls out the word "one," and deposits his slate on the floor —first writing his name thereon. He then stands erect as before. The second done calls out the word "two," and follows the example of his predecessor. Each party writes a large figure on his slate to represent the number he called out. When all have done, or a reasonable time has elapsed, the teacher writes the answer on the black-board, and all the pupils raise their slates and hold them immovably in such a position as will enable the teacher to conveniently examine them as he passes round to "inspect the work." This being done the pupils, whose work is correct, take places according to the order of merit indicated by the "numbers" aforesaid. Another plan is as follows : As each pupil solves the question, let him deposit his slate on the table, taking care to place it on top of that of his predecessor. When all have done, the slates will thus be piled one on top of the other. Let the teacher then *reverse* the pile, and the slate of the boy who had done first, will be on the top. The teacher can then examine each slate, and, if the work be correct, the pupils will take places according to the order in which the slates come to hand. If many of the pupils fail to solve the query, the teacher should solve it himself on the black-board, explaining the different steps of the work. He should occasionally call on one of the pupils to exhibit and explain their solutions on the black-board. This is a wholesome and laudable practice. Such variations are highly commendable, and never fail to make school work attractive.

The following is, we believe, a more excellent way for teaching algebra, arithmetic, etc., than either of the foregoing: We will take it for granted that the walls of the school are all set with "liquid slating," or other material for black-board purposes. Let the black-boards be divided into spaces by upright lines 30 inches apart. Let each of these spaces be numbered, and a supply of crayons and brushes placed on the shelf beneath. On a signal from the teacher let the

A more approved method of teaching mathematics

pupils arrange themselves in class-form all round the room
—a pupil in front of each space, armed with a crayon. Let the
teacher divide the pupils into sections—the odd numbers
being section 1, and the even numbers section 2; or *vice
versâ*. By this arrangement no two pupils of the same
section will be together—the individuals of each section
will be alternate, and there can, therefore, be little or no
"copying." The teacher will then dictate a question to
section 1, and they will instantly commence its solution. He
will then give a different question to section 2, and they in
like manner will set to work with such energy and vigour
as to command our sympathies and admiration. As each
pupil finishes the solution, he deposits his crayon and faces
the centre, awaiting further orders. To procure despatch, as
well as accuracy, the pupil in each section who first solves
the question, is allowed a higher "mark" than his companions; and to prevent confusion he is required to say
"First," as he faces the centre. When all (or nearly all)
have done, the teacher, standing in the centre, or at his desk,
calls on the "first pupil" to read his answer. If it be correct
he (the pupil) marks a $\times$ opposite the name or register number on his portion of the black-board, and he underlines same
(thus $\underline{\times}$) to show that he was first in the order of merit in
that particular exercise. Two underlined $\times$'s count "three,"
i. e., the first pupil receives an additional "half mark" as
the reward of his superior despatch. All others, whose work
is correct, will mark $\times$ alone. Those who are wrong will
mark — instead of $\times$. Each pupil registers his own work
in the presence and under the inspection of his rivals. At
the close of the lesson the pupil writes three figures on the
black-board; the first indicates the number of "problems"
read to the section; the second, preceded by a minus sign,
indicates the number missed; and the third, preceded by the
sign of equality, shows the number he has solved correctly,
as indicated by $\times$'s. The teacher then records each pupil's

merits in the class register, glancing, if necessary, at the marking on the black-board. Should any pupils of a section fail to work the question, then some of the successful ones are required to go through the work and explain the respective stages of difficulty, the remaining successful pupils being required to assist from time to time. When arithmetic is properly taught it becomes a sort of mental recreation, and will always be popular in school—not only for the means of improvement it affords, but for the agreeable excitement and peculiar pleasure which always accompany trials of skill when the opponents are of the same, or nearly the same, mental calibre, and inspired by the desire to excel.

Teachers should see that every pupil is well grounded in the various arithmetical tables and elementary rules, so as to be able to apply them rapidly to the practical (or business) affairs of every-day life, and the general manipulations of numbers. As correctness and despatch are the principal objects aimed at, the pupils should be instructed in all contracted methods of calculation, and encouraged to "read, mark, learn, and inwardly digest" the laws and principles on which such systems are based; so that, if necessary, they may be able to discover other methods for themselves. As a rule, mental arithmetic should be taught to every class in the school, always being preliminary to the study of the written work. In fact, every "rule" of arithmetic should be preceded by a mental course bearing specially on that particular branch of the subject. The principles on which *the rule* is founded should be duly explained and thoroughly understood—practically and theoretically—before the pupils commence the investigation and solution of the exercises contained in the text-book under that heading. The skilful teacher will have little difficulty in leading pupils of average ability to discover these principles for themselves. When they understand the laws, and have discovered the principles on which the subject of study is based, they can be easily

[marginal notes:] Pupils to be well grounded in tables.

Mental arithmetic.

Principles before rules.

led, by a few judicious, well-connected questions, to give expression and form to "the rule." Each pupil should then be required to solve some exercises in accordance with the rule thus formed—explaining the principles involved in each step of the work; after which they may refer to their books and read the rule there given, comparing it with the one discovered by themselves. They will then see with their eyes and "understand with their hearts;" for they will have discovered with their minds, heard with their ears, and worked with their hands. Things thus learned will never be forgotten.

How to ensure the acquisition of knowledge.

In teaching mental calculations it would always be wise to commence with sensible objects—objects familiar to the pupils. Should a difficulty arise in treating of *abstract* numbers, the pupils will frequently solve it if referred to familiar things; that is, if the respective numbers be applied to things within their comprehension. The numbers (or quantities) treated of in the lower classes should be of small value (or dimensions)—so small as to be easily comprehended by young minds of average ability. Teachers conducting arithmetical (or mathematical) exercises should never forget to elicit, by frequent questions, whether the pupils understand the reason ("the why and the wherefore") of each step in the process in the respective solutions. Such diligent and persevering labours will be sure to produce much fruit.

CHAPTER VII.
GEOGRAPHY.

Geography—hints on its study.

Every school should be provided with a compass, a globe, and two sets of good maps—one set filled in and the other blank. It would be advisable, perhaps, to commence the study of geography by directing the attention of the pupils to the natural features of their own immediate neighbourhood. The peculiar characteristics of hills, mountains, valleys, islands, peninsulas, lakes, gulfs, seas, bays, straits, etc., may thus be deduced. The distribution of animals and vegetables may then be pointed out, and the phenomena of springs, fountains, deserts, volcanoes, etc., fully explained. Lessons on winds, currents, tides, climates, latitude, longitude, eclipses, and other such matters would, of course, follow in regular order. The "cardinal points" should be the subject of one of the early lessons in geography. Having learned how to "box the compass," the pupils may be required to *Boxing the compass.* point to any places named (or indicated on the maps), giving their "bearings" or position with respect to some well known city, country, or district. "Beginning at home," they should first give the position of all places in the immediate locality, the school (or their personal residence) being taken as "the fixed point." They may then be required to point in the direction of remote towns, cities, or countries. A map of their own city, vicinity, or county (if convenient), should then be introduced, and the pupils thoroughly grounded in the contents. When teaching geography, the scale of the map, (or chart) of the part of the world under consideration, should be one of the first things to which attention ought to be directed. Indeed it would not be amiss to give them a preliminary lesson on the measurement of space as exhibited on maps, charts, or globes. Latitude and longitude can be *Latitude and longitude, and how to teach them.* effectually explained by drawing two chalk lines on the floor (or on the black-board) at right angles to and cutting each other. One of these would represent the equator and the other the first meridian. The pupils could then be easily led to perceive that all objects on either side of the line representing the former, would be north or south, whilst those situated on it (or immediately under it) would be neither one nor the other—in other words, that all places

15

under the equator have no latitude, and that those on either side of it have north or south latitude according to their position. In like manner they would easily discover that all places under the first meridian have no longitude, and that all places to the right or left of it are in east or west longitude respectively. The globe may then be introduced, and the pupils led to perceive how the respective meridians (marked thereon) "come under the sun" in regular succession during the space of twenty-four hours—the earth in the meantime making one complete revolution on its axis, every point on its surface, except the poles, describing a circle or 360°. Having thus learned that the earth revolves on its axis at the rate of 360° in twenty-four hours, they will easily perceive that it rotates 15° in one hour, or 1° in four minutes. Hence, people say that "fifteen degrees of longitude make a difference of one hour in time." The calculation of time from difference of longitude (or of longitude from difference of time) will originate many questions of an instructive and interesting nature. The pupils will easily perceive that time varies as the longitude changes, but the fact that all places east of them have earlier time than they have, and that all places west have later time, will at first cause some confusion. The action of the sun and moon with reference to alternate light and darkness, etc., being explained and understood, the attention of the pupils may be directed to the orbitual motion of the earth, when the causes of the seasons and other collateral matters may be fully discussed.

Rotation of the earth, and differences of time.

The first map introduced, in teaching political geography, should be that of the city, township, or county in which the school is situated ; the second should be that of the state or country ; the third, that of the continent which includes their particular nation. Map-drawing should go hand in hand with these subjects, each pupil being requested to sketch maps on the black-board, or to fill up those drawn

Hints on the use of maps and charts.

(in outline) by the teacher, correctly locating the cities, delineating the rivers, mountains, etc. As a preliminary exercise to this, the teacher should point to certain localities on the blank map, desiring the pupils to name the places, and mention their natural characteristics, historical associations, etc. The difference of countries (or parts of countries) in physical appearance, mineral wealth, and geological formation, should be pointed out. Attention should be specially directed to their agricultural productions, manufacturing enterprise, and commercial facilities; nor should the national character of the modern and ancient inhabitants be overlooked or forgotten. The maps of the great empires of antiquity should be studied in connection with ancient history. It should always be borne in mind that a vast amount of geographical and historical information is acquired incidentally. For this reason every city, river, mountain, etc., mentioned in the respective lessons, should be pointed out on the maps, and then a short summary should be given of their historical associations.

The principal things to be attended to in teaching geography are as follows—to commence with some known locality, and direct attention to its physical features, or rather by a series of skilful questions to lead the pupils to state its natural peculiarities, political importance, etc.; to draw (or cause the pupils to draw) an outline map of the district under consideration; to require the pupils to point with their finger towards any place mentioned, or to indicate its position on the map, globe, or chart, relating, at the same time, the characteristics of the locality and the historical events associated with the name. At the close of the lesson the pupils may be allowed to question each other on the contents of same. *Order of teaching geography.*

The following may give some idea as to the order in which the geographical facts of a country, continent, or island should be introduced to a class:—(1) Boundaries, (2) Extent *Geographical summary* and divisions, (3) General character of surface, (4) Internal waters, (5) Nature of soil and climate, (6) Productions, (7) Cities and towns, (8) Facilities of internal communication, (9) Inhabitants—Race, (10) Education, religion and government, (11) Science and art, (12) Miscellaneous facts.

Weekly Reviews.

During a short time every Friday the pupils may be permitted (as aforesaid) to examine each other on the subjects of study during the week. When each pupil has asked his query, the teacher, if so disposed, may propose a series of general questions on the present and preceding lessons, and also mention such collateral matters as occurred to him during the "mutual examination."

CHAPTER VIII.

ACQUISITION OF LANGUAGE.

How Nature teaches "the languages."

Nature, when teaching a language, always commences with nouns. She impels the young child to begin with simple sounds—words of one syllable, such as ma, pa, ba, da, etc. She then prompts him to repeat them at short intervals—hence the combinations of ma-ma, pa-pa, da-da, etc. His words, at first, are all names (nouns); adjectives, and certain pronouns, follow in regular succession. By imitation, he gradually acquires the use of verbs—and all this time he has no knowledge of the grammatical relations of words. The ideas expressed are stored up in his mind; a language has been learned, but the memory has not been burdened with words. In fact, Nature has never called upon him to exert his memory for that purpose She required him to remember the ideas, but allowed him to let the words take care of themselves. Yet, by preserving the ideas, she has made the words his own. They return with the respective ideas, but he is unconscious of having ever occupied himself in acquiring them. While exercising his faculties in the acquisition of knowledge, he has, without any special exertion, learned to speak and understand a language—the elements of which he uses correctly, without knowing when or how he acquired them. The ideas comprising this knowledge were impressed on the mind by the action of the judgment or will; but the words must have been committed to memory unconsciously and unintentionally.

When Nature uses words as a medium for conveying ideas, they are always kept in the back ground. The ideas exist first in the speaker's mind, and often suggest the words which give them expression. Should the ideas be vigorously conceived, words will follow naturally, correctly, and in the form and order required. Should the mind attempt to grasp both the ideas and words at one and same time, the attention will be divided and distracted, and the understanding little benefited. Should the mind attend to words alone, the comprehension will be weakened, and the intellect degraded. Ideas should, therefore, precede words.

Mental conceptions to precede words.

It is injudicious to cultivate the memory at the expense of the reason and judgment, as the mere acquisition of lessons by rote will not promote intellectual improvement. In such cases, the recurrence or expression of ideas depends on a set form of words, and can, therefore, never make a permanent lodgment in the memory. If words be preferred to ideas, the texture of the mind will be injured, and its impressions weakened. Such a preference would not only enervate the understanding, but ultimately produce, more or less, incapacity of thought. It would, moreover, cause children to dislike study, and thus injure or destroy their chances of success in after life. A chapter, first read for the sake of its ideas alone, and for the sake of the pleasure it

Nature's method of teaching.

affords, will produce impressions far more clear and permanent than if it were first "learned by rote," and then "sifted for ideas."

In committing lessons to memory, the *first object* of the pupil should be to understand the ideas; *second*, to arrange them in natural or consecutive order as in the book; *third*, to clothe them in appropriate words; *fourth*, to commit them to memory for future use. In this, as in all other educational matters, the powers of the mind must be concentrated upon one thing, and only one, at a time; and the attention must not be diverted until that thing be thoroughly known. Nature first imparts ideas, and then supplies appropriate words or terms. Her order of instruction should never be reversed. Such a course would, more or less, be sure to paralyze physical effort, and promote mental debility. Let us, therefore, study her means, follow her methods, and conform to the order of sequence and development exhibited in her teachings; we may then entertain a reasonable hope that success will crown our efforts.

CHAPTER IX.

ENGLISH GRAMMAR AND COMPOSITION.

In the nature of things, English composition, both spoken and written, should precede or accompany the study of English grammar. Grammar should be introduced in connection with sentences composed by the pupils, and written from their dictation by the teacher on the black-board, or it may be introduced through the aid of the Reading Machine (see page 227). By these means its study becomes an intellectual exercise, and the children are taught the principles of the science through the medium of the eye.

The method of treating the subject will, of course, depend very much on the age and mental capacities of the children. If they be very young, the subject may be introduced by asking them to mention the names of some things or places they see or have seen. Such answers as house, tree, field, boat, book, river, etc., may be given in reply. The selection of the names should be left to themselves, as it is a matter of importance that they should have a clear idea of the meaning of each term. The words, thus given, are written vertically on the black-board, in their order of sequence— the plurals being placed in an opposite column. The teacher then points to the word house, tree, or field, etc., and asks what kind it may be? In all likelihood they will answer "nice," "pretty," "green," etc., and then these qualities— these words—are written before the names of the things to which they allude—the pupils spelling as the teacher writes. They are then asked "what these" new words "tell us of the names?" and will probably answer—"Their kind, their quality." They may then be informed that another word for names is "nouns"—and that both words are similar in meaning. The word "nouns" is then written over the list of names, and the pupils are informed (because they could not be expected to discover it themselves) that words which express "kind or quality" are called "adjectives." They are then asked what the nice house, the pretty tree, the large field, etc., might do? and may reply, "The nice house falls," "the pretty tree blossoms," etc. They are then asked to mention something they themselves could do? and will probably give some such reply as—"We talk, learn, eat, drink, jump, and sleep," etc. If asked what these words tell us, they may reply—"They tell us of the *doing* of some-thing." The teacher may then inform them that "words which tell us of the doing of something," are called verbs. The question is then asked—"What have you been learn-ing?" and they will probably reply, "We have been learning

How to teach grammar to junior pupils.

about nouns, adjectives, and verbs." They are then required to define these words *viva voce*, or on their slates or blackboard, giving examples of each. The other parts of speech should be taught in much the same manner.

The pupils should then be "practised" in the construction of sentences containing all the parts of speech. The pointing out of the several parts of speech as they occur in an ordinary reading lesson, is also a good method of impressing them with correct ideas of classification. Occasionally, they may be required to write out the different parts of speech in a certain number of sentences, taking care to place each word under its proper heading. A few preliminary exercises on the Reading and Parsing Machine will afford material assistance in this respect.

The properties or inflections of the different parts of speech may then be taught on the same common-sense principle, each being attended with so much "practical drill" as may be sufficient to permanently fix the subject on the pupils' mind. The parts of speech, and their variations or inflections, being thus "imprinted on the tablets of the memory," the principles of concord and government may be introduced, the teacher taking care to lead the children to discover the laws and rules of syntax for themselves. He can do this by a series of judicious questions relative to the composition, or verbal construction, of certain sentences, written specially on the black-board—said sentences to contain the principles (or violation of principles) involved in the rule to be deduced.

Grammar is usually considered "a very dry subject," and one of which the pupils of many schools entertain a certain undefined dread, or suspicious awe, arising principally from imperfect methods of teaching. The pupil, left to himself and the usual text book, finds that he is expected to acquire, and even love, that which he does not comprehend or esteem; and he is whipped or disgraced if he fails to perform the allotted task.   Poor fellow! his lot is not an enviable one.   I fear that we teachers have a great deal to answer for.   We often lose sight of the fact that we were not always wise or learned men ourselves.   Perhaps we are still wanting in this respect.   We seldom take the trouble to bring ourselves down to the pupil's mental level, so that we may look out on his difficulties from a child's standpoint.   Yet, it is only by such condescension that we can discover and remove these obstacles.   In fact, we have yet to learn how to deal with children as we would wish teachers to deal with us, were we children once more.   To be successful teachers, we must become as little children.   Grammar, being considered "a dry subject" by children, it behooves the teacher to aim at making it as interesting as any other subject.   If he can do this, and also duly impress the pupils with a just sense of its utility, they will smile at the idea of its being "dry," and become as thoroughly posted in it as in any other subject—if not more so.

It is a matter worthy of note that pupils "well up" in grammar, are invariably well posted in the other school subjects.   This probably arises from the fact that owing to imperfections in the method of teaching, and to non-development of the reason and judgment, pupils are generally on the confines of manhood before they thoroughly understand "what grammar is all about"—before they can comprehend its principles, or intelligently apply its rules.   By the adoption of the common-sense method, previously alluded to, pupils will be enabled to educate themselves (so to speak), and the teacher will skilfully lead them, by the judicious exercise of their own minds, to discover the various laws and principles peculiar to each element of the language—merely supplying them with the proper terms as occasion requires. *An observation.*

As aforementioned, when the pupils are thoroughly posted on "the Parts of Speech," the teacher must retrace his steps and—considering them one by one—lead the children *The Grammatical variations.*

to discover the variations of each. By inducing them to observe the genius and common usages of our language, and by leading them to illustrate the same by reference to familiar examples, they cannot fail to discover the rules of syntax for themselves — the teacher giving *form* to the expression of their ideas when necessary.* In this way they will be led to think for themselves, while acquiring the ideas and experience of others; their thoughts will become more original, and their conceptions, like the rose-buds of early spring, will gradually unfold until they expand into full-grown flowers. The pupils will thus be educated in the true sense of the word.

Composition and grammar should be taught in conjunc- *Composition —secondary and original.* tion—they naturally go "hand in hand with each other." In practising composition, the pupils will be enabled profitably to employ the principles learned in grammar. It may consist of two kinds—original and secondary. In the order of sequence (or study), secondary composition should always precede original. In first-class schools, one hour a week should, at least, be devoted to the study of the science and art of composition; two hours would not be too much. In some cases parents and friends will be likely to render considerable assistance, and it may, therefore, be advisable to occasionally appoint it as a "Home Exercise." If it be a "Secondary Composition," the ideas may be appropriated from the works of some standard author, or from some lesson given by the teacher; but they must be neatly dressed in the pupils' own language. When criticising the MSS. of pupils, the teacher should pay strict attention to the veracity of the information, the style, orthography, penmanship, punctuation, use of capitals, etc.

The best teacher of grammar and composition. Before concluding this subject we may observe that English grammar, regarded as a text-book, is a collection of the laws and principles which should govern the expression of English thought. It should therefore be borne in mind that

---

* Rev. Dr. Davies.

the rules of grammar are merely the expression in words of the recognized usages of language. He who can most successfully lead his pupils to discover these principles and usages for themselves, before they attempt to learn the rules by rote, will be the most successful teacher of grammar and composition.

One hour per week, at least, should be set apart for the practice of "letter writing." This is one of the most useful and important branches of composition. Other branches may be regarded as an accomplishment, but this is a necessity in every sphere of life. It behoves every respectable citizen to be an expert correspondent. It is a matter of fact that there are many intelligent and respectable people in this enlightened country (and fair scholars too) who are totally unable to write a passable letter. This defect should be remedied at once so far as the rising generation are concerned; and there is no more effectual way for doing so than by introducing "correspondence" into all our schools—taking care to prescribe it as one of the regular periodical exercises. Its importance should be duly recognized on the programme of studies. In every stage and condition of life it is one of the most useful and agreeable exercises. Nevertheless, at the present moment its study and practice are neglected or ignored in more than three-fourths of our public schools. This gigantic defect is partially remedied by "our commercial colleges." These private institutions profess to teach business correspondence; but the subject should be thoroughly taught in all schools and seminaries, without restriction. The public school is the crowning glory of this favoured land—one of the institutions of which we feel especially proud. By its means alone can we reach the children of the masses. The desire, therefore, of the people, and the common object of both teachers and legislators, should be to equip the rising generation with the armour of intelligence, and to educate them

Importance and utility of correspondence.

in the use of all weapons, or tools, essential to their success
in the battle of life.

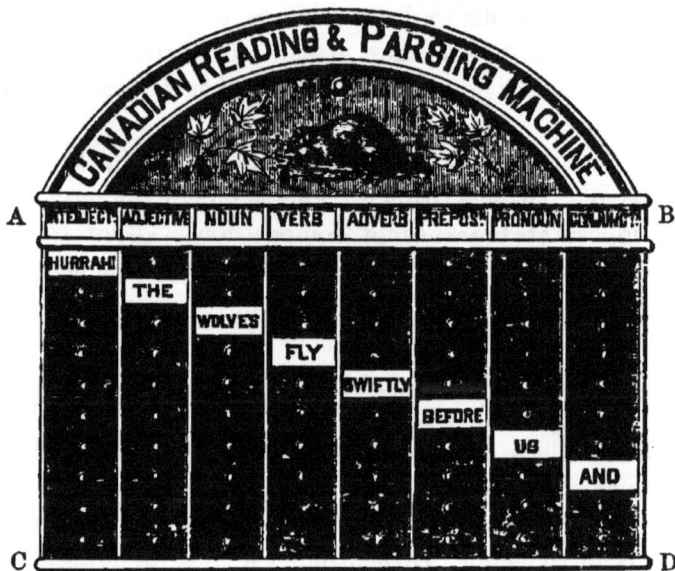

The above is a modification of the Reading Machine already described. Its face or front is divided into eight vertical columns or sections, to correspond with the Eight Parts
of Speech. Slips containing the names of the Parts of
Speech, in print, are placed at the head of the respective
columns—from A to B—in such order as the teacher may
desire; or these "headings" may appear on the card selections if preferred. The card may be inserted or removed
by opening the base-board, c, D. Its dimensions should correspond to the arrangement of the machine; and it should
embrace sentences comprising all the Parts of Speech,
arranged so that each word will make sense with what has
gone before, no matter which slide is opened in the vertical
section immediately succeeding. After half an hour's intelligent practice at this Machine the youngest children in
primary classes will feel little or no difficulty in classifying
the words of any sentence so as to place them under their
proper headings or respective Parts of Speech.

CHAPTER X.

HISTORY.

There are two methods of teaching history, each perhaps *History—methods of teaching.* equally useful in its way—both very different in form. According to the first method, the pupils receive a lesson *viva voce* from the teacher on the events, manners, customs, etc., of some particular time or era, and are then required to read at home the account of the same as given in history. On the occasion of next lesson they are questioned closely on the subject. This is, perhaps, the method best adapted for junior pupils. According to the second method the pupils read history at school as a reading lesson or as a recitation. Prior to the commencement of this exercise the teacher should examine them to ascertain how much they know of the subject, and to excite an interest therein. During the progress of the lesson he should occasionally question them as regards the positions, etc., of the localities *Incidental questions.* mentioned, and also as regards matters alluded to, which he may have reason to believe they do not thoroughly understand. Their attention should be specially directed to the effects likely to be produced by the invasion and subjugation of one people by another—to the changes which follow amalgamation of races—to how people were housed, clothed and fed in different ages—to the manners, customs and facilities of intercourse which existed at different periods— how railroads, canals, steamboats, etc., promote the general happiness, preventing local famine, equalizing prices, and extending commercial intercourse—to the advance of science the invention of paper, of printing, etc., etc., to the fact that the poorest citizens are now in the enjoyment of privileges and advantages, comforts and conveniences denied to kings in olden times. Children should thus be "introduced to the events of other ages," and not confined to the acquisition of dry chronological facts. Let the teacher exert his professional skill so as to interest the pupils in their work. They will then find every lesson instructive, and cannot fail to improve the future by reflecting on the past. When the prescribed lesson has been read, the whole subject (or the substance of it) should be recapitulated in the answers to a series of searching, well-connected, well-arranged questions judiciously proposed. During the progress of the lesson, or at its close, the teacher may (as hinted elsewhere) furnish any additional information connected with the events mentioned, and relate any incidents of interest associated with localities named therein. Then, with a view of impressing the principal facts of the lesson on their minds, he may require each pupil to write a skeleton of same ; or he may desire each in turn to mention some one idea in its order of sequence some " one step in the argument," so that when put together they may exhibit a chaste and logical outline of the subject under consideration. He may then allow the pupils to question each other—the last in the class commencing, as described in the Chapter on Reading. Finally he may require them to prepare (at their convenience) an abstract of the lesson, the same to be presented for inspection at some specified time.

General recapitulation.

Pupils to write sketches of the lesson.

How to study history aright.

It is not necessary that a large number of studies should be mastered in youth, but it is essential that pupils should acquire the art of studying aright, and that whatsoever is taught should be taught livingly, philosophically, profoundly. In teaching history, for instance, it is not necessary that the pupil should be taken though the minutiæ of the subject from the creation until the present day, or that he should be compelled *nolens volens* to pore over the fragmentary records of lost races, much less "the gigantic" volumes which relate the story of modern nations. Rather let the pupils be taught to study—"read, mark, learn, and inwardly digest"—the history of an individual nation. As he proceeds, let the teacher show him how to apply the principles of historical evidence to the statements contained therein; let him then be led to trace the causes and effects of events, and directed to investigate the motives of actions, so that he may observe the workings of human nature in what has been done and suffered;* let him endeavour to detect the ruling spirit of each successive age, sympathizing with what is noble and abhorring what is unworthy; let him master the great truths and impulses which formed the basis of human action in the past, and learn to judge impartially of men and things, whilst recognizing a moral Providence, a retributive justice, amidst all mutations and corruptions. He will thus acquire the art of tracing all events to their origin, whilst forming a judicious conclusion as to their ultimate effects. The exercise thus afforded will enable him to study aright, and as he grows in years he will extend his researches (should time permit) until he has studied the whole course of human history. One book studied in this way will afford him more educational discipline than would all the histories in the world read in the usual cursory style.

CHAPTER XI.

GEOMETRY.

Geometry presents us with one of the most extensive and attractive fields for the exercise of the faculties of memory, reason, and judgment. Some mathematicians exhibit a disposition to ignore Euclid, and go so far as to assert that trigonometry and mensuration may be mastered without the aid of pure geometry. They might as well assert that a stone bridge could be built on a basis of sand. Supposing

Excellency of geometry as a mental exercise.

---
* Canning.

that a knowledge of Euclid were unnecessary for the acquisition and right application of other branches of mathematics, it would still be worthy of study, as no other subject affords such mental discipline. Other subjects may equal it in positive utility, but none can surpass it as an invigorator of the mind. Euclid is not so popular in America as in the British Isles. The fact that our people prefer utility to abstract excellence, is the only reason we can offer for such a singular anomaly; yet it is possible that defective teaching ability may have something to do with the matter. It is a matter of notoriety that the subject is highly appreciated in our universities, while partially ignored in our public schools. It is a well-known fact that pure geometry is better adapted for cultivating and invigorating the reason and judgment than for developing the inferior faculties. Those who degrade it to a mere memory exercise, mistake its real objects, and divert it from its legitimate province. In attempting to cram, they fail to educate; and, as a necessary result, the youthful students learn to dislike the subject. This can scarcely be wondered at when we consider the mode of study adopted in some schools. We will venture to illustrate our meaning by an example which came under our own notice in a land famous for its mathematical scholars.

A common method of teaching Euclid.

Some years ago we held the position of First Assistant Master in one of the High Schools of England. Occasionally the duties of general superintendence devolved upon us, and in that capacity we had to visit the respective classrooms once or twice a day. On one of these occasions it happened that we were present during the delivery of a lesson in Euclid—the class being the highest in the institution. The method of teaching having attracted our attention, we remained until the close of the lesson. This method was as follows: The young men, seated at their desks during the first half hour, read the proposition (or lesson prescribed) over and over, the books being open before them. During the succeeding fifteen minutes they were engaged in writing *verbatim* (from memory) the words of the text—the book being closed. Each pupil used the diagram lettered as in the book. During the next fifteen minutes each pupil had to read what he had written, and the teacher—glancing at the book—told him to "sit down" if his composition failed to coincide with that of the text. If he happened to remember the words of the book, and suc‐ceeded in giving a *verbatim* report, the teacher smiled and informed him that he was a "good boy." The good boy then resumed his seat with an air of conscious pride, and was asked no further questions.

We represented the weakness and inutility of this system to the teacher—a graduate of a famous university—and like‐wise explained our views to the principal who happened to be the teacher's father; but both gentlemen informed us that such was the method in use at Cambridge, and that as most of the pupils were preparing for matriculation in that university, they thought it advisable to adhere to the "Cambridge System." We were under the impression at the time that these gentlemen had been misinformed, but on making enquiries as to the practice at other colleges, we found that the system was a favorite one in several of the great educational institutes though it had not been formally encouraged by Cambridge. On further enquiry, we learned through Professor Stokes and others, that Professors in the great English universities had no fixed plan of imparting information on this subject, but generally followed the method of teaching practised in the sister institutions of Scotland and Ireland. *A change of system.*

Geometry should always be taught as a real intellectual exercise. The enunciation of each proposition should first be analyzed, and each statement clearly understood. Then the different assertions should be written in logical order on *"The more excellent method."*

16

the black-board.   The teacher, pointing to these, should require the pupils to enumerate the queries, or things to be done, and also the data or things given.   Having described the diagram—each part in the order in which it is mentioned in the enunciation—he may ask the pupils if they can suggest any way for solving the theorem (or problem) or any of its individual assertions.   Perhaps one boy can do one part, and another boy the next, and so on until the proposition is solved.   Should they wander from the right path the teacher will, of course, lead them back, occasionally making such suggestions as he may think necessary to throw light on the subject.   When they have gone through the solution in this way, the teacher may solve the proposition himself in the presence of the whole class; after which they may be allowed to take their seats and study the solution as given in the text book.   On referring to the text they will be delighted to find that they have successfully solved the proposition—they will be proud of their discoveries, pleased with themselves, and grateful to the teacher.   But a new exercise is before them.   After some time they are called to their places or class stations, and one by one required to perform the solution without assistance, using the diagram without letters.   Each pupil, while solving the proposition at the board, is closely watched by his companions, who listen to his words with the ears of critics.   If he happens to go wrong, up go the hands of his comrades—the teacher points to one, down go the hands, and the pupil indicated instantly corrects the error, and takes his place in the class accordingly.   After they have been well drilled in this exercise, they are required to solve the proposition in *general terms*—no diagrams being used.   Each pupil takes precedence according to his merit.   The latter is, perhaps, the most interesting as well as the most useful exercise in the study of Euclid.   It improves the memory, strengthens the judgment, sharpens the reasoning faculties, increases the

To use diagrams without letters.

Solution in general terms.

power of expressing ideas, stores the mind with new terms, and tends to make the pupils eloquent by enabling them to speak effectively and concisely, with accuracy and precision, whilst creating and fostering a love of truth in general, and of mathematical knowledge in particular. Such is the "more excellent way" for teaching geometry.

In teaching Euclid, especially the second, fifth and sixth books, the teacher should lead his pupils to discover its intimate relation to Arithmetic and Algebra. After analyzing the enunciation of each proposition, as before described, the teacher, by directing the pupils to take numbers to represent the respective lines, or parts of lines, and to operate on them as indicated in the same (enunciation), will greatly facilitate their comprehension of the subject, and thereby indelibly imprint on their minds the facts elicited. After doing so, he may proceed with the diagram as before described, and conclude with the solution in "general terms." During the pupil's progress through the various books, the teacher should point out the connection of the respective propositions with the kindred sciences, whensoever that can be done with advantage. In teaching mensuration or trigonometry, frequent reference should be made to the principles in geometry on which each rule, proposition, or exercise is based. If the pupil be thoroughly posted in the latter subject, he will experience no difficulty in acquiring an efficient knowledge of the former.

The connection with kindred sciences to be noted.

CHAPTER XII.

A SCIENTIFIC HABIT.

Thirst for knowledge is a desire for novelty and change— a wish for more than we have—a disposition not to be content with what we know—a longing for information. In

The cultivation of a scientific habit.

early youth, having no experience and but little knowledge, we need instruction in the best and most approved methods of acquisition. Whether old or young, as students, we must learn to despise nothing; we must investigate and strive to understand the nature and use of everything that comes under our observation. In other words, we must carefully cultivate a scientific habit, and labour to acquire a thorough knowledge of the more useful and important branches of science. Nature generally endows children with every requisite necessary for the formation of this habit. They naturally notice everything they see or hear, and seldom fail to draw right conclusions from the data thus afforded. Nature impels them to study her wondrous workings by implanting in their breasts the curiosity and inductive propensities necessary to unravel her mysteries; but at first they may need a tutor or guide, just as at an earlier stage of existence they required the services of a nurse. The scientific habit once acquired, time and opportunity alone can define its limits. The play of the pupil may be made to afford him the most useful and instructive lessons. Circumstances alone can determine whether he is to become a Newton, a Herschell, or a mere average scholar; but in either case he must have a beginning—teaching of some sort must initiate and drill him in the earlier stages of progress.

Natural history.

In the cultivation of a scientific habit, care must be taken to present such subjects of study as are likely to be attractive to youthful minds, the less difficult and more popular subjects preceding the more difficult and less attractive, in their order of sequence, each branch being introduced and treated in a manner such as will ensure its comprehension by youthful and inexperienced minds. *Natural History* is, perhaps, one of the most popular subjects with the generality of children. Besides presenting them with rich and inexhaustible mines of information, it will be a powerful aid in inculcating scientific habits, and for these reasons should be taught in every school. Children, if favoured with a little assistance, are capable of understanding every department of natural history. They have eyes, and a lively curiosity which impels them to investigate and make enquiries, so as to satisfy their natural desire of acquisition. Nature compels them to use the faculties with which she has endowed them. It is the teacher's province to train and develop said faculties, and to ensure this result he is justified in pressing science and art into his service.

CHAPTER XIII.

BOTANY.

During the spring, summer, and early autumn months children indulge in the habit of bringing flowers and branches of trees to school. They adorn their desks with these "spoils of the season." Nor will they forget their teacher. His desk will receive its share of the regalia. We remember the little devices occasionally practised by some dear pupils to induce certain teachers to leave the class-room at intermissions, and mingle in the sports on the play-grounds, so that some of them in the meantime might decorate the teacher's desk with flowers and evergreens. How slyly the little flower "without a name" used to be laid apart by itself, so that its character and history might be discussed on the occasion of the next lesson in botany. How delicate and yet how devoted are the attentions of children—artless yet full of art, cunning yet delightfully innocent—they seldom fail to please. *Children's love of flowers*

Children enjoy their teacher's pleasure and surprise, and when they learn that he is fond of flowers, etc., they are *To be turned to account in teaching botany.*

sure to keep him well supplied. He may easily turn these little attentions and civilities to good account in imparting a knowledge of botany. Holding up a flower (for instance) he may direct their attention to its form, colour, number of its parts, and the functions of each part in the floral

Arrange-
ment.

economy. Directing attention to the uniformity in number and size of the sepals, petals, stamens, pistils and shape of leaves characteristic of one class, he may compare or contrast them with corresponding parts of another class, and thus

Adaptation
to circum-
stances.

lead the pupils to form correct ideas of classification. By directing attention to the form and shape of the root— whether fibrous, bulbous or tap-rooted—and inquiring where the flower was found, in what situation and under what conditions, he may easily lead them to discover that different kinds of plants grow in different situations and in different kinds of soil ; each in the soil best suited to its habits; some in the shade, some in the sunlight, some in water, some on

Characteris-
tics of parts.

dry land, whilst others grow on their fellow plants. The attention of the children may then be directed to the charac- teristics of the roots, trunks (or stems), twigs, branches, leaves and leaflets of different trees, the parts of one being compared with the corresponding parts in another. They may be thus led to distinguish between flowering and flowerless plants, being occasionally required to state points of likeness and points of difference. Their attention may then be directed to the characteristics of exogens and endogens, the outside growers and inside growers (a sample of each being produced for inspection.) Each pupil should note the point of difference in the appearance of the plants while growing; the difference in the wood, in the leaf, branch, stem and bud or embryo, as the case may be.

Season
rings.

Having learned that the layers of wood of an exogen are called season rings, and that one ring is formed every season, they will easily discover that the number of "rings" indicate the age of the tree. Looking closer, they may perceive that the concentric circles or season rings are not all of equal thickness, and when informed that these inequalities may be ascribed to some variety in the seasons of former years—such as a cold or dry summer—they will not be slow in perceiving that they can thus ascertain the probable character of the weather during every season since the tree commenced its growth. Having thus become acquainted with the kind, *Classification.* form, manner, and term of growth of the various plants and organs of vegetation and reproduction, and the particular uses and peculiarities of arrangement of the respective parts, the attention of the young botanists should be directed to the principles and practice of botanical classification.

CHAPTER XIV.

ANIMAL PHYSIOLOGY.

Animal Physiology may be taught to children at a very *Teach them through the eye.* early age. It is a very interesting subject, and one in which they specially delight. Most of its details may be taught through the medium of the eye, and for these reasons it can be easily adapted to their comprehension or capacity. Their attention should first be directed to the domestic animals, after which they should be led to study the structure, outward appearance, habits, and other peculiar characteristics of each class, order, genus, and species. Attention should then be directed to the changes which the food undergoes during the process of mastication, digestion, etc., before its conversion into blood. A series of lessons should be given on this subject, so that the pupils may thoroughly master its difficulties, and fully and clearly understand its nature and effects on the physical peculiarities of each class of animals.

To these should be added a series of skilfully arranged lessons on the circulation of the blood, the organization and action of the heart, lungs, senses, arteries, veins, etc.

Lessons about birds.

In teaching that branch of animal physiology which relates to birds, the attention should first be directed to the form, habits, and other characteristics of those varieties with which the pupils are most familiar. The birds themselves (or "their pictures") should be produced before the class. Those which migrate should be distinguished from those that do not indulge in this propensity. The times of their departure and arrival may be noted, the reason for these observances, etc. The pupils may then be required to state the characteristics of water birds (the Natatores,) and to point out the various ways in which they differ from (the Insessores) those that roost or perch, etc.—characteristics of those that sing, those noted for brilliancy of plumage, etc.—characteristics of the cursores, scansores, grallatores, and raptores, and how each differs from the other according to mode of life, etc.

Lessons about fishes.

A few lessons may then be given on the construction, characteristics, habits, etc., of fishes and reptiles; after which the pupils should be required to learn by rote the classification of the animal kingdom, as given by some writer of eminence. Having acquired a passable knowledge of the sub-kingdom vertebrata, the pupils may now (if time and circumstances permit) direct their attention to the sub-kingdoms invertebrata, duly studying the various structure and peculiarities of the Mollusca, Articulata, and Radiata.

Human Physiology.

Human physiology should form an important branch of study in every school, and be placed in a prominent position in the programme. No pupil should be left in ignorance of the laws of health and physical development; nor should they be uninstructed as to what they should eat and what they should drink, and how human food, in all its varieties, should be prepared for use.

CHAPTER XV.

ELEMENTARY GEOLOGY.

Geology, though still one of the infant sciences, should not be altogether ignored in the public school. The attention of the pupils might profitably be directed to this subject some time before they commence their studies in agricultural chemistry. Geological science is useful, necessary, and interesting. When properly taught it cannot fail to be the source of much pleasure. The teacher need not necessarily enter into the technicalities of the science. By reference to charts or to some locality in the vicinity of the school, the pupils may be led to distinguish between stratified and unstratified rocks. Their attention may then be directed to the divisions and sub-divisions of the former—to the order of sequence of the different strata irrespective of locality—to the manner in which the different strata were deposited through the agency of water, the materials being originally of igneous and metamorphic origin—to the fossils characteristic of each stratum—to the degradation, denudation, and erosion of rocks under the influence of water, heat, cold, frost, and thaw—to the action of glaciers and the accumulation of alluvial débris. *First lessons in geology.*

The formation of soils will thus become an interesting study. The pupils will easily understand, by due attention to the foregoing, how the mineral ingredients are derived from underlying rocks or from the detritus of neighbouring mountains—how the high hills are being ground down and the valleys elevated—how the depth of the soil increases from year to year—how great rivers form deltas in one locality, whilst "they wear away the stones" in another, as at Niagara Falls. *Formation of soils.*

Peculiarities of location.

Having taken a course of lessons in these subjects, and committed the order of stratification to memory, the attention of the children may be recalled to the consideration of the unstratified rocks, such as granite, syenite, etc., the agency of their formation and protrusion being explained as clearly and fully as possible. Having learned that the unstratified rocks generally appear on the summits of mountains as well as at the base of the aqueous formations, the class may be easily led to perceive that the cause of their elevation must be referred to internal violence; and that during their upheaval the concentric crusts, coats, or layers of the secondary strata were broken and laid bare for inspection, and that the internal treasures of the earth were thus brought within the reach of man.

Utility of geological knowledge.

While directing the pupils' attention to the laws of geological super-imposition, the teacher may justly refer to some of the many instances in which vast sums of money were needlessly and uselessly spent by miners, ignorant of the principles enunciated by the discoverers of "the order of sequence." He may then question the pupils as to their knowledge of the preceding subjects, and the general application of geological science, being careful to ascertain where they would look for coal?—the names of the strata underlying and overlying the coal measures?—where they would bore for oil, water, or salt, etc., etc.—the names of the creatures which characterized the Silurian, Devonian, and other eras?—their dimensions, structure, and habits?—the names of creatures which have become extinct during the human era?—the probable causes of their extinction, etc.—alterations in climate?—cause and consequence?

CHAPTER XVI.

AGRICULTURAL CHEMISTRY.

There is no knowledge of a secular nature more interesting than that which is furnished by chemical science; and of all the branches of chemistry there is none so useful or so important as that which relates to agriculture. We are a great agricultural people, and likely to continue so for ever. Our farmers should, therefore, conduct their field operations on scientific principles, being careful to leave their profession better than they found it. "Head rules muscle, and (as a learned writer well observes) all farmers who educate only their muscle must occupy the inferior relation of muscle."* Hence we infer that the elements of agricultural chemistry, or the theory of farming, should be taught in every public school—more especially in rural ones. Human forces are mere developments of nature. Man's nourishment and strength are her gifts; and through her the student of humanity learns the true relationships of things, and through them finally succeeds in understanding the wonderful workings of the human mind.

Importance of agricultural chemistry.

The great object of the farmer is to make his lands yield the most productive crops at the least possible expense. To effect this laudable desire, he must be guided in his agricultural operations, by science and experience. Science teaches him that all soils, plants, and animals are composed of two kinds of substances, whose proportional ingredients vary in different species—that one kind of substances is organic and volatile; that the other is inorganic and incapable of growth except by accumulation; and that these again can be analyzed into their separate elements, the number, nature, and amount of which will indicate the composition of the original compound. These things are

Different kinds of substances.

---

* Rev. E. Ryerson, D.D.

not difficult of comprehension, and should be taught in the laboratory and on the farm, by practical experiment. The pupils must first learn "the chemical alphabet"—the names, symbols, and atomic numbers of the respective elements. After which, the teacher, by a series of judicious, well-selected experiments, may lead them to discover the law of multiple proportions. After going through a series of lessons on the metals, metalloids, acids, bases, etc., attention should be directed to the composition, conservation, irrigation, and drainage of soils, the nature and structure of plants, etc., the rotation of crops, and general economy of the farm.

Rotation of crops.

Science teaches us that different species of plants require different kinds of nourishment—or the same kind in different proportions—that every crop deprives the soil of a portion of its elements; that no soil, however fertile, can yield an indefinite succession of crops without being manured; that rotation preserves the soil from impoverishment, clears it of pernicious weeds, turns each element to account in favour of reproduction, and enables the farmer to "replenish and recuperate the soil," while relieving him from the necessity of directly applying manure to such crops as could not receive it without hazard or positive injury. The principles of rotation will teach him how to obtain the largest interest on his capital. Science will show him that the culmiferous and legumenous plants should succeed each other alternately, and that the period of rotation should extend over six or seven years. Practice on the farm will prove the value of the theory of rotation.

Supply of complementary elements.

A knowledge of the particular substances which a crop absorbs from the soil, and of the elements needed by the crop which is to follow, will enable the farmer to form a good system of rotation—such a system as may be suited to the exigencies of the time, climate, and nature of the land. Knowing the composition and capabilities of the soil, he can apply such manures as will be most beneficial. By burning some of the plants which he intends to sow, so that he may examine their ashes, and by analyzing a portion of the soil in which he would expect them to grow, the farmer may judge by the component ingredients, and the peculiar habits of the plant, whether the crop would be productive. Having ascertained the component elements of the soil, and of the projected crop, and knowing what ingredients will be supplied by the atmosphere, he can apply that kind of manure which contains the proper supply of nourishment— the same or complementary elements. Children can be easily led to understand that if grasses, vegetables, etc., cannot find in the soil such substances as they need for support, the crop must necessarily be a failure in proportion to the deficiency in the requisite amount of food. The farmer can supply some of these substances, and atmospheric influences will furnish the remainder. The pupils will not find it difficult to remember that plants take in their food in a fluid form, and cannot under any circumstances absorb or assimilate substances in a solid state. Hence, a manure may contain the necessary ingredients, and remain useless through improper application. Plants cannot avail themselves of the nourishing properties of manures unless the latter are soluble in water. Solution must precede absorption.

Absorption and assimilation.

When the pupils have been well grounded in the foregoing facts, their attention should be directed to the great difference which exists between the respective grasses, so far as their nourishing properties are concerned—this fact being exemplified by reference to certain fields in the immediate vicinity. They may be led to perceive that some grasses possess more of the elements of which bone and sinew is made, than others—that the grass in one field gives the cows a large flow of milk and a certain quality of butter—that the grasses in another field have a tendency to fatten the

Utility of agricultural chemistry to the stock-raiser.

cows, etc.; so that chemistry is useful even to the stock-raiser; for it instructs him as to the particular kind of food —grass, hay, etc.—which should be furnished to certain kinds of cattle, or to cattle intended for certain uses. It also enables him to fix the amount of exercise, and to prescribe the quality of the accommodation or shelter necessary for their comfort and his profit.

Influences of light, heat, etc.

A series of well-arranged, well-connected lessons should be given on light, heat, cold, moisture, etc., and their influences on vegetation. If passably posted in the laws of absorption and radiation, the pupils will easily perceive that the degree of warmth, or amount of heat, which a soil obtains from the sun, depends upon its chemical composition and power of retention, and that this heat will materially affect vegetation. The temperature of a dry soil, for instance, may be 90° or 100°, when that of the air is only 60° or 70°; and the temperature of a wet soil is alway 10° or 15° below the temperature of a dry soil. Wet soils are favourable to evaporation. They thus lose much of their natural heat, and are, therefore, called cold soils. Hence the necessity of correcting this defect by draining. We might enlarge on this subject, but think enough has been said to show the utility and necessity of a knowledge of agricultural chemistry, as well as the advantages to be gained by placing it on the programme of school studies.

CHAPTER XVII.

NATURAL PHILOSOPHY.

Elements of Natural Philosophy to be taught at Public Schools.

No intelligent person will question the utility and importance of acquiring a knowledge of natural philosophy, or chemical physics; and but few will deny that the foundation of this knowledge should be laid at the public school.

We would like to dwell on this subject and, if possible, to give a few examples of how lessons in philosophy should be given in the school room ; but want of space prevents us from indulging ourselves in this respect. However, we will take the liberty of advancing a few hints as to the manner in which the respective branches should be introduced to the notice of children.

The teacher may commence his lessons in natural philo- First lessons in Natural sophy by a few simple experiments, illustrating the action Philosophy. of attraction of gravity, cohesion, capillary attraction, etc. He may then direct attention to the pressure of the atmosphere, and its effects in the economy of nature. Should he not be able to procure orthodox apparatus, his ingenuity will, in some cases, enable him to provide passable substitutes. A large basin will do service as a pneumatic trough, and a large drinking glass will suit, in some experiments, as well as a receiver. Both together will enable him to illustrate several important lessons, especially such as relate to the pressure of the atmosphere, etc. For instance, let him fill the basin with water and, inverting the glass, place its mouth horizontal to the surface. Inviting one of the pupils to press it downwards gradually until it is submerged, let the teacher call attention to the fact, that as the glass descends, the air confined therein occupies less and less space. He must then lead them to discover, by a series of logical well-arranged questions (based on facts within their comprehension), why the glass presses upwards against the boy's hand ?—why the surrounding water does not fill the submerged glass, no matter how great the pressure ?—why the air in the glass expands or contracts in proportion to the depth of the submergence ? From this, and kindred experiments, the pupils Subject to be taught by may be led to form correct ideas of the compressibility, elas- simple prac- tical experi- ticity, impenetrability, and other properties of the atmos- ments. phere. This experiment will also enable them to comprehend the philosophical principles involved in the construction

of the diving bell. Let the teacher now fill the glass with
water, cover its mouth with a sheet of paper, and then suddenly inverting it (mouth downwards), explain why the
water and paper remain suspended. They will thus be led
to see that the atmosphere presses equally in all directions—
that its upward pressure is sufficient to counterbalance gravity. Submerging the glass, and allowing it to fill with
water, let him invert it and raise it out of the water until
its mouth nearly reaches the surface. Let him then call
attention to the facts that the column of water in the glass
is supported—that it would be supported were the column
thirty-three feet high ; and why ?—that the same pressure
would support only thirty inches of mercury, and why?
—that the height of the column varies as the density or
specific gravity of the liquid—that the atmospheric pressure is about 15lbs to the square inch, etc.

The pupils to conduct the experiments under the teacher's guidance. Handing one of the pupils the barrel of a quill, or some
similar tube open at both ends, the teacher may direct him
to put one extremity in his mouth and the other in the water, (or in milk,) and try whether he can thereby help himself to a drink. The teacher may then direct attention to
the fact that the liquid rose in the tube as the "air was
sucked out ;" and why ?—that the liquid will not rise if a
hole be bored in the tube above the water; and why?—that
it will rise if this hole be submerged, etc. The pupils may
then receive a few special lessons on "the barometer and its
variations," "the common pump, and its construction, etc.
In explaining the philosophy of the latter, special attention
must be paid to the use of valves, the action of the piston,
its tendency to create a vacuum, the limit to which water
can be raised by the common pump, etc.; the pupils in all
cases conducting the experiments under the teacher's guidance.

By *actual* experiment, the pupils may then be led to perceive that air has weight—that it expands by heat—that
the lower strata are more dense than the upper, and have

to sustain a greater pressure—that the lighter bodies always rise above and rest on the heavier; each body taking its place in the order of sequence according to its relative specific gravity, as cream on milk, for instance, a cork on water, etc., and hence that smoke ascends, and a balloon rises above the clouds. Their attention may then be directed to the principles of rarefaction—why there is always a draught up the chimney, a current of air from the door to the fire?—why a current enters a room near the threshhold of the door, whilst another leaves the room at the top of the door, as may be proved by holding a lighted candle to these places—why the one current is cold and the other warm? —why the janitor raises one part of the school windows, whilst he lowers the other, when desirous of ventilating the rooms, etc.? The teacher may now direct attention to the philosophy of winds, their velocity, cause, and consequences —the different kinds of winds, and their uses in the economy of nature. Attention may then be directed to the nature and velocity of light and sound—their utility in calculating distances, as in the cases of thunder, lightning, cannon shots, etc. (light travelling at the rate of about 192,000 miles per second, and sound travelling 1,142 feet in the same time). They may then introduce a few simple experiments, showing that the speed of sound varies as the density of the media through which it passes—that it is about four times quicker in water, and twenty times quicker in solids, than in air. Why the Indians apply their ears to the ground when calculating their distance from foes on the march?—why boys apply their ears to the rails of a railroad when they wish to discover whether there is an approaching engine on the line. After the pupils have been well grounded on the preceding subjects, they should receive a series of lessons on the principles of radiation, reflection, refraction, absorption, evaporation, electricity, magnetism, etc., and then the laws relating to them should be committed to memory.

A series of practical experiments with suggestions.

17

Effects of Heat.

By a series of judicious experiments and well-arranged questions, the pupils may be led to discover that heat expands all bodies, and is present in all matter—that the increase of volume at a given temperature varies in different bodies—that air and gases expand most, fluids next, and then solids, examples being mentioned in each case—that conterminous bodies have a tendency to equalize their heat, or to assume an equal temperature—that air, gas, and porous bodies are bad conductors, and that metals and solids generally are good ones—and that the hair or fur of animals and plumage of birds vary with the climate, etc.

Construction of Thermometer.

The principles on which the thermometer is constructed may now be explained—the nature and use of that instrument—why the tube is of a narrow and smooth bore—how it is graduated—how the freezing and boiling points are determined—the best thermometer for warm countries—the best for polar regions, and why ?—and how we may ascertain the relative quantity of heat in different bodies, etc.

Properties of Water.

The pupils should receive a series of lessons on the nature and properties of water in its respective forms, during which their attention should be directed to the temperature at which it becomes ice, and whether it then expands or contracts in volume—why it should not be left in pipes in frosty weather—effects of its expansion on agriculture. When water becomes vapour or steam—how one cubic inch of water becomes 1728 cubic inches of steam—utility in the arts, etc.—how soluble salts and difference of pressure retard the boiling of water. How the formation of vapour absorbs heat and thus produces cold—evaporation and distillation.

When the text book should be introduced.

In this manner, or in a manner somewhat similar to this, the teacher should, from time to time, guide the pupils through a regular course of lessons on the philosophy of common things, making each as interesting as possible; asking for examples and giving illustrations; enlisting the active co-operation of the children so that he may be able to turn every available circumstance to good account. After receiving, *viva voce*, such lessons as we have alluded to, the pupils should refer to the text books, and supplement their knowledge by a careful study of the subject as given therein; or, at the close of the *viva voce* series, they may be required to take a regular course through the text book. The teacher's lessons will have enabled them to thoroughly comprehend the author's meaning in "all cases of doubt or difficulty," so that their studies, instead of being dull, will be considered interesting and agreeable.

CHAPTER XVIII.

MECHANICS.

The teacher may introduce his lessons on this branch of Natural Philosophy by asking the pupils for information as to the manner in which certain familiar tools, or simple machines, are used in every-day life—how a spade, hay fork, fishing rod, etc., are used—how a large stone may be moved with a walking stick—how water is taken from a draw-well by means of the wheel and axle—how casks are placed on or taken off a waggon by means of the inclined plane, etc.? He may then explain, or give a series of lessons illustrating what we mean by, such terms as force, motion, centre of gravity, momentum of forces, etc., and require the definitions to be entered in the pupils' note books, and committed to memory. Directing attention to the manœuvres of John and James, while balancing each other on a plank placed over a log of wood, to how they adapt the length of the arms to their respective weights, etc., he may lead the pupils

Introductory lessons on Mechanics.

to deduce the laws which regulate the power and action of
the lever. Taking a rod of any length (say 30 inches), and
assuming that the power multiplied by the units of distance
through which it moves is equal to the weight multiplied
by the units of distance through which it moves, he may, by
placing the fulcrum at different distances, show that the
equilibrium is not deranged, and hence that the assumption
is true in every case, and of universal application. The
pupils may thus be led to discover and enunciate the principle of virtual velocities or equality of moments.

Directing the pupils' attention to a chart (or to models)
of the six mechanical powers, the teacher, after giving the
name of each, should point out the fact that they may be
all referred back to two, namely, to the lever and the inclined plane. He may then lead them to observe that to
understand the power of a machine we must consider four
things, viz.—the force or power which acts, the resistance
to be overcome, the fulcrum or centre of motion, and the
respective velocities of the power and weight. The pupils
should then receive a lesson on each of the mechanical powers and their varieties. The art of illustrating is one of the
great secrets of successful teaching, and for this reason appropriate illustrations should precede or accompany the
enunciation of every mechanical principle. If the lessons on
the simple machines be properly delivered and efficiently
illustrated, the pupils, at the close of each lesson, should
clearly comprehend the principle involved, and be able to
form a rule, or to construct a formula, for its application.
[The following, with similar rules and formulæ for the
remaining powers, founded on the principle of the equality
of moments, may be deduced from such lessons and made
the bases of many useful and practical problems. As the
product of the extremes is equal to the product of the means,
a simple arithmetical operation will enable us to find a
mean or extreme when three of the terms are given.]

Marginal notes:

"Virtual velocities."

The mechanical powers.

Formulæ, and practical hints on the application of each power.

The Lever.—The power is to the weight as the weight arm is to the power arm:—Thus, P : W : : W's arm : P's arm.

Single Cord Pulley.—The power is to the weight as 1 is to twice the number of movable Pulleys:—Thus, P : W : : 1 : $2n$.

Pulley with Fixed Separate Cords.—The power is to the weight as 1 is to 2 raised to the power indicated by the number of movable pulleys:—Thus, P : W : : 1 : 2^n.

When the Cord passes over a Fixed Pulley attached to a Beam.—The power is to the weight as 1 to 3 raised to the power indicated by the number of movable pulleys:—Thus, P : W : : 1 : 3^n.

The Wedge.—The power is to the weight as one half the width of the back to the length:—Thus, P : W : : $\frac{1}{2}$ B : L.

The Wheel and the Pinion.—The power is to the weight as the continued product of the leaves is to the continued product of the teeth:—Thus, P : W : : $l \times l'$: $t \times t'$.

The Differential Screw.—The power is to the weight as the difference in pitch of the two screws is to the length of lever multiplied by 2 multiplied by 3.1416:—Thus, P : W : : Diff. : $l \times 2 \times 3.1416$.

The Endless Screw.—The power is to the weight as the radius of the axle is to the product of the number of teeth in wheel, multiplied by the length of the winch:—Thus, P : W : : r : $t \times l$.

During the progress of the series of lessons on the mechanical powers—in fact during the delivery of all lessons—the teacher may occasionally vary the exercise by some interesting observations of a simple kind, always encouraging the pupils to give him the result of their own thoughts, and also to mention such illustrations of the subject as may occur to them. If giving a lesson on the lever, for instance, he might ask, in connection with some of the examples mentioned by the pupils, Why hollow tubes are stronger than solid ones? Should they fail to reply, he may then state the reason, or reserve "the difficulty" to form the subject of some succeeding lessons. Then again he may ask, Why it is easier to break à ruler flatways than edgeways?—Why the joists of a house are made thin and laid edgeways in their respective places? Being thus brought face to face with another principle of nature, they may be led to perceive that in such cases *the strength of the material is equal to the breadth multiplied by the depth squared, divided by the length*:—Thus, $S = b \times d^2 \div l$. Or thus—$l : b : : d^2 : S$.

Hydrosta-tics and Dy-namics. The pupils may then receive some lessons on the principles of liquid pressure, the hydrostatic press, hydrostatic bellows, hydrostatic paradox, specific gravity, etc., after which their attention may be directed to the study of Dynamics. By a series of practical lessons, judiciously and logically arranged, the pupils should be led to discover (1) that when the velocities of moving bodies are equal, their momenta are proportional to their masses; (2) that when the masses of two moving bodies are equal, their momenta are proportional to their velocities; and (3), that when neither the masses nor velocities of two bodies are equal, their momenta are in proportion to the products of their weights by their velocities.[*]

Attention should also be directed to the facts that one of the bodies being stationary at the moment of impact, the velocity of the united mass $(v) = \dfrac{M \times V}{M + m}$ (V and v representing the respective velocities; M and m the masses of the respective bodies,

That when the two bodies are moving in the same direction, the velocity of the united mass $= \dfrac{(M \times V) + (m \times V)}{M + m}$.

Philosophy of falling bodies. That when the bodies are moving in different directions, the velocity of the united mass $= \dfrac{(M \times V) \sim (m \times v)}{M + m}$.

The pupils' attention may then be directed to the nature and effects of gravity with respect to falling bodies. They

[*] Dr. J. H. Sangster.

must be led to understand that it acts separately, equally, and continuously, on every particle of matter without reference to the nature of the body; and that all bodies falling freely, move through equal spaces in the same time; that gravity never ceases to act; that the falling body gains a new impulse and a consequent increase of velocity each moment of its descent, and that its final velocity is the sum of all the increments of velocity thus communicated; that the velocity at the end of the second moment of descent is twice that acquired at the end of the first; and that its velocity at the end of the third moment is three times that which it had at the end of the first, and so on. The pupils may be then informed that a falling body acquires a velocity of about 32 feet per second at the end of the first moment of descent; that the average speed being the arithmetical mean between its initial and terminal velocities, the descent in the first second must have been 16 feet. The following formulæ may then be constructed, each forming the basis and summary of a lesson :—

The space through which a body falls during any second of its descent $= 2$ (sec.-1) $\times 16$.

The final velocity at the end of any second $=$ Second $\times 2$ $\times 16$.

The whole descent in given number of seconds $=$ Seconds $\times 16$: (or $s = \frac{1}{2} gt^2$).

When a body descends with initial force, space travelled in given time $= V \times t + 16 \times t^2$: (or $s = vt + \frac{1}{2} gt^2$).

When a body ascends with initial force, space travelled in given time $= V \times t - 16 \times t^2$: (or $s = vt - \frac{1}{2} gt^2$).

When a body descends with initial force, the final velocity $= V + t \times 32$: (or $v = V + tg$).

When a body ascends with initial force, the final velocity $= V - t \times 32$: (or $v = V - tg$).

The foregoing, and Hydro-dynamics, will afford materials for many useful and interesting lessons of a practical nature. Sundry observations.

In a work of this description it would be impossible for us to do more than hint at such lessons; but even a young and inexperienced teacher would have but little difficulty in filling up the meagre outlines here presented. The teacher who would succeed in his profession must remember that *one of the great secrets of success is the power to make study attractive by practically illustrating what is taught*. Children can, and will, learn any subject, however difficult, if the teacher can only make it sufficiently interesting. In studying these things, or in directing others how to study them, prudence will not permit us to fetter mind by rules too rigid or too numerous. Curiosity, amusement, and natural tastes may be allowed to direct the student in certain exceptional cases in the higher institutions of learning, and we are of opinion that, within certain limits, a similar indulgence might be extended to the pupils of the *higher classes* in public schools. This principle is recognized in the Cornell University, (Ithaca,) and with marked advantage. The studies of pupils may be as wide as their condition in life and mental calibre will permit; but it is not advisable that their attention should be directed to the acquisition of a large number of subjects at the same time. Better at first to concentrate their attention on a few, and then gradually keep adding to the number as they grow in mental strength.

The manner in which we would have other subjects introduced may be inferred from the suggestions advanced in the foregoing pages. Further digression is unnecessary. We will therefore proceed to discuss other matters, hoping the preceding sketches may not be wholly profitless nor altogether uninteresting.

CHAPTER XIX.

PUBLIC EXAMINATIONS.

Public examinations at certain intervals—twice a year at least, four times at most—are very useful and desirable, if they be conducted so as to test the efficiency and accuracy of the instruction given, as well as the general progress of the youthful students. In fact they are commendable when they exhibit the school as it really is, and pernicious when they represent it in false colours or under false lights. These periodical examinations should certainly be held; but it must be borne in mind that they will do more harm than good should the pupils be led to act the hypocrite in order that they may win the applause and admiration of the spectators. No particular lessons should be appointed for these examinations; no special preparation should be made for them; nor should the examiners, beforehand, apprise the pupils of the nature of the questions they intend to ask. On these occasions the school should exhibit a true picture, a faithful photograph, of the real progress made since the last " periodical examination." These rules are frequently infringed, in fact we are well aware that they are seldom, if ever, observed. Their violation affords a cloak for much deception; but in such cases the people seem to enjoy and encourage the deceit " by bestowing liberal encomiums on the deceivers." However, the most intelligent minds, and the most discriminative audiences are liable to be deceived by appearances. No experienced teacher will deny that public periodical examinations are unreliable in their results, and therefore, unsatisfactory tests of the real progress of a school or any section thereof; nor do they afford sufficient data whereby to judge of the teacher's professional capacity, attainments or success. A teacher not possessing a high

Public examinations desirable at certain intervals.

The school to be exhibited as it is.

Results unreliable.

character, but favoured with a certain amount of self-assurance and "business tact," can very easily exhibit his school in such a light as to astonish spectators by its *apparent* efficiency, and thus command their favourable commendations.[*] A man who is dishonest and hypocritical can exhibit an inferior school in such a way as to induce visitors to believe it to be in a much more healthy condition as regards efficiency, than another school, which may be far superior to it but which is governed by an honest conscientious teacher. It follows therefore that on such occasions we should not place too much reliance on apparent success, as it is often the mere counterfeit of merit.

A superior private school.

Some years ago while engaged as editor of a paper in a large provincial town in Ireland, we received a communication from the Superioress of one of the local educational institutions requesting "the favour of our presence and assistance at an examination of the pupils in attendance at her school." Knowing from our official connections that this lady and her staff of sister teachers had earned the gratitude and esteem of people of "all denominations," by the affectionate interest they had taken in the educational welfare of the young, irrespective of creed, class, or condition, we gladly availed ourselves of her kind invitation. Next day we duly reported our arrival and were cordially received by the Superioress and Chaplain, and conducted through the several departments of the institution, the nature and the objects of the various arrangements being explained to us in due order. The walls of one room were decorated with specimens of the pupils' handwriting, drawing, and fancy work of different kinds. The schools were graded in much the same manner as corresponding institutions in this country—the Public School System being taken as a basis. The discipline in all the divisions or departments was perfect; and the Calisthenical exercises excelled anything

---

[*] David Page.

of the kind we have ever seen. We were proud to notice that neither the sisters nor pupils were ashamed to learn, or afraid to sing, good patriotic, freedom-loving songs; and, while devotedly attached to the land of their birth, we found that they not only "feared God" but "honoured the King." The examination in English history brought out the many laudable features in Queen Victoria's life; and at its close the young ladies (by request) sung the National Anthem with all the power, sympathy, and pathos, so characteristic of Celtic hearts. In fact their rendering of the music was so expressive as to incite the enthusiasm and command the encomiums of the oldest and highest ecclesiastics present. We could not help thinking, during the proceedings, how sadly we Protestants misunderstand our fellow citizens of the Catholic faith, and how much we might learn from them in matters of devotion, discipline, and patriotism, were we so disposed.

We must add, however, that notwithstanding the excellency of the discipline, and the apparent efficiency of the pupils, we were not quite satisfied as to the intrinsic superiority of the system of teaching as indicated by the mode of examination. We never heard better answering; still we think the result was unreliable. The pupils answered the questions addressed to them, clearly, pointedly, deliberately; but nevertheless, the answers were more "racy" than appeared natural, and more verbose than necessary—too formal and too exhaustive. The questions were given *viva voce* from a MS. volume on the examiner's desk; and we occasionally noticed, by certain changes in some child's face, and certain hesitations in her manner, that the intellectual energies were not looking for ideas but for half-forgotten modes of expressions. We therefore inferred one, or both, of two things—the pupils had been specially prepared for examination, or they were answering by rote. The good sisters told us during another visit some days afterwards,

Excellency of discipline and arrangements.

that the latter was the case, and that they always insisted
on accurate acquisition of the text by rote. The Memory
System never appeared to more advantage than under the
skilful management of these kind, patient, and indefatig-
able ladies. Their success was apparently greater than any
ordinary teachers could have commanded with all the newest
(and now more approved) modes of instruction ; yet we
could not recommend its unrestricted use in Public Schools.
Peculiar circumstances may make it popular and successful
in some places, subject to conditions mentioned on p. 222 ;
but the results will always be unreliable, and, more or less,
unsatisfactory, if pupils be examined through the medium of
formal stereotyped questions, copied directly from text books
or selected from recent catechetical acquisitions. Examinations should exhibit what pupils *really* know ; not what we
think they ought to know, or would wish them to know.

Defect of the
system.

The committal to memory of the words of text books,
and certain stereotyped dialogues, was once a very popular
mode of instruction ; but its fallacy has been long apparent.
Prussia, Switzerland, and Ireland were the first countries to
adopt an intellectual method of instruction and acquisition,
whereby the respective ideas concerning a subject are imprinted on the mind, the pupil being then permitted to express them in his own words—the best which nature can
suggest. We advocate the use of memory, though opposed
to its abuse, or special cultivation at the *expense* of higher
and more useful faculties. Under certain circumstances it
may be prudent to have certain subjects, or portions of subjects, committed to memory (see p. 222) : but the acquisition of whole text-books *verbatim*, especially those portions
required for examination, is an abuse of the faculty. The
examination alluded to was one of the best memory exercises
we ever witnessed, and the most likely to impress a visitor
with the absolute perfection of the system of teaching adopted.
Still it was far from being an infallible exponent of real edu-

cational progress—far from being reliable as a test of the right development of true mental power. It merely showed what could be accomplished by the persistent and judicious training of a single faculty.

"The rote system," with its unhealthy mode of recitation and "memory" examinations, is what prevails in many parts of the States. It looks well outwardly, but inwardly it is unsound. It prefers accuracy of expression to crude evidences of native intelligence. It deceives a non-professional visitor by inducing him to accept "accurate memory answers" as expressions of individual thought. Visitors who cannot look beneath the surface are apt to give credit for real progress when the efficiency is only apparent; and they often withhold commendations which have been richly deserved, because of their inability to measure aright the quality or quantity of intellectual work. Pupils are frequently "crammed" specially for such exhibitions. Even in this Canada of ours, instances have often come to our knowledge of public school pupils having been favoured beforehand with a list of questions they were to be asked on examination day, or the *number* of certain propositions to be solved on that occasion. This was in "the good old days," when teaching was a refuge for the outcasts of all other professions —an asylum for men who had little or no professional conscience. In the case above alluded to, the visitors might deceive themselves, and probably did; but the teachers —highly educated, accomplished, and religious ladies—were entirely above suspicion. As we ascertained during succeeding visits, the examination exercises differed very slightly from those pursued on ordinary occasions. The teachers believed that the acquisition of the text by rote was the best system of teaching, and adopted it accordingly. It was the system that was at fault and not the teachers. They acted conscientiously and in good faith—just as our fellow-labourers, its patrons, do to the south of the line.

The Memory System.

The system
of the
future.

There is, however, no method of instruction, or examination, so bad that it does not contain some good, and none so good that it does not admit of much improvement. In truth, the art of teaching (in all its branches) is yet in embryo. The system of the future has yet to be developed. It must be founded on practical experiment, and its philosophy interpreted by liberal-minded, generous-hearted men and women, whose souls are radiant with the light of science and full of sympathy with child-nature. As a necessary preliminary to this state of things, "the greatest liberality, in religious matters, should be shown in our public schools, and the greatest care taken in the preparation and right interpretation of our text-books. Nothing offensive to any class of citizens, should be tolerated or allowed in institutions supported by general taxation."* To effect these laudable objects, teachers must be persons of truly Catholic and unsectarian minds—free from all kinds of religious bigotry, prejudice, or intolerance, receiving the opinions and expressed feelings of others with all the courtesy and respectful consideration so characteristic of true Christian hearts; being always ready, like the bee, to extract honey from every opening flower.

When examinations re-
flect credit
on the
teacher and
the taught.

Public examinations, however, when conducted properly, are very useful and desirable, inasmuch as they cause the people to take a greater interest in educational matters than they otherwise would do. When conducted, not for show or applause, but so as to test the quality and quantity of the instruction given, and the cultivation and refinement developed by the same during the respective terms, the teacher and the taught are exhibited in their true light, and intelligent, well-educated men can form a correct estimate of the efficiency of the school. Under such circumstances, should the examination be a success, parents and guardians may justly be delighted with the efforts of their children,

* Rev. Dr. Ryerson.

while the latter, incited to renewed exertions, will in future be proud and happy when succeeding examinations afford them opportunities of acquitting themselves to the satisfaction of their friends. Parents and pupils will feel deeply grateful to the esteemed teacher, and he—whilst remembering that good men need no commendation for doing their duty—will feel happy to receive their encomiums, knowing that they speak the words of sincerity and truth.

Two public examinations each year, are quite sufficient— one at midsummer, and one at Christmas; nevertheless we are inclined to believe that it would be advisable to hold two minor examinations between these intervals. According to this arrangement there would be four examinations in the year—two public and official, and two of a "more quiet" and less pretentious nature—and the intervals between each would be of moderate length, so that the minds of the pupils while pursuing their studies, may be fixed on each subject with a view to its retention and possible use on examination day, as well as on the more laudable object of their own permanent personal improvement. The near approach of "the quarterly test days" will be a great incentive to study, and cannot fail to incite them to increased exertion and more accurate attention. On the other hand, more than one general examination each quarter would be objectionable, as they would interfere too much with the regular course of study. *Quarterly Examinations.*

At the half-yearly examinations, rewards or prizes (if any) should be distributed to the successful candidates, and those found duly qualified should be promoted to the next higher classes, the announcement of their promotion being made in presence of the audience. Parents or guardians, if not present, should be officially informed of the promotion of their children. On these occasions the pupils should be required to pass through a written (or printed) and oral examination. The examining committee should comprise the In- *Parents to be apprized of the promotion of their children.*

spector of Schools, the Head Master, and the Chairman of the School Board. It will be the duty of this committee to prepare questions and examine answers; after which they should make out an official report, carefully noting each pupil's standing in the respective subjects. Some member of the committee should copy same into the General Report Book, whilst another should prepare a "Roll of Honour," showing each pupil's order of merit; or absolute and relative rank.

Periodical evening examinations.

In many of the great schools in Europe an evening examination, partaking of the nature of a "celebration," is held once or twice a year for the gratification of parents and friends. This laudable custom is adopted by the principals of public schools in many of the more important French, English, and Irish cities. Part of the half-yearly examinations are held in the evening so as to suit the convenience of parents and other friends whose business avocations would not permit them to attend during the day. Recently the practice seems to have commanded general favour in many parts of Ontario and New York. These evening examinations are usually diversified by dialogues, recitations, and music. They are generally interesting, and afford an agreeable treat to parents and guardians. We therefore venture to hope that they will, in time, become a universal institution. There can be no possible objection to such popular entertainments provided they do not interfere with the regular course of study by inordinately engrossing the minds of the children. They have been very favourably received wherever adopted. Parents and pupils welcome their advent with much enthusiasm, being always willing and ready to do whatever they can to promote efficiency, and thus ensure the success of the enterprise.

Official books.

We may here be permitted to observe that it is the duty of the teacher to keep the daily, weekly, monthly, quarterly, and yearly registers of the school in a neat and proper manner. These registers are indispensable books in all well-regulated schools. "In them," as an eminent educator well observes, "the patrons and friends of the school have a tolerable record of their labours ; and by means of them the teacher can at any time exhibit the proficiency of every scholar who has attended the school." It is therefore a matter of the greatest importance that they should be accurately and neatly kept. In addition to the foregoing, each school should have a Visitor's Journal. It should be placed on a suitable desk in some convenient and conspicuous spot. On visiting days this book should be kept open, and visitors should be requested (by a notice attached) to insert in same any remarks suggested by their visit. On examination days the visitors may be formally, but cordially, invited to record therein their individual impressions of the proceedings.

18

PART IV.

CHAPTER XX.

CONCLUDING REMARKS.

Teachers'
intercourse
—its char-
acteristics.

The social and official intercourse of teachers should be free from any traits of character inimical to true friendship and genuine refinement. Its leading characteristics should be personal esteem, professional respect, and a delicate regard for the rights and feelings of others. Candid without rudeness, earnest without positiveness, mutual confidence and reciprocal kindness should daily cement their friendship. The younger "craftsmen" should look up to the older and more experienced with feelings of respect and devotion; likewise the Assistants to the Principal; and the latter should be always ready to sacrifice his own interests or convenience to promote the welfare of his colleagues or official inferiors. It behoves him to regard their welfare as inseperable from his own. It is his duty to prescribe their duties, and superintend the performance of their work; but whilst zealously guarding his own prerogatives and the public interests, he should carefully protect the rights and privileges of his colleagues, and on "no account wrong them or see them wronged." He should judge with caution, admonish with friendship, and, if necessary, reprehend with courtesy and candour. He should neither palliate nor aggravate their negligence or other short comings. First to advise or suggest, last to censure or condemn, he should strive to anticipate and remove the cause of what he could not approve. He may thus prevent what would require much pains to cure.

His hand given to his colleagues, like theirs to him, should be the sacred pledge of truth, confidence, and fidelity.

Teachers of Division should devote themselves to their respective duties without envy or jealousy, each preferring the other—the younger giving precedence to the more experienced. Nothing looks so bad in the eyes of the world, and nothing has such a deleterious effect on the school as dissensions amongst the teachers. Should such a malady exist to any extent it would not be amiss if the principal were to note its working in his private diary, with its probable cause and ultimate effects. Should his influence, judgment, and executive tact fail to restore the harmony and concord necessary to unity of action, the evil may be regarded as chronic, and he will then be justified in seeking exterior advice as to its removal. Better that one or more teachers be requested to resign than that the school should permanently suffer. Such cases of internal dissensions are, we believe, extremely rare. No such episode has ever fallen within our own experience; but we have observed evidences of their existence in more than one instance during our official visitations. True teachers never quarrel. Labouring in the same school, they have an identity of hopes, interests, and aspirations which effectually prevent (or should prevent) professional suspicion and social strife; whilst those labouring in isolated fields have, nevertheless, a community of feeling which binds them together in a common apostleship of peace and good will. Rejoicing with each other in prosperity, and sympathizing with each other in all trials, difficulties, and adversities, true teachers never ignore the claims of duty, or fail to strengthen the bonds of fraternal affection and christian charity. Being always actuated by a right spirit, their professional career becomes a living example of professional harmony, unity, and zeal; hence the alacrity, honesty, and cheerfulness with which they obey the respective commands of their superior officers.

To avoid dissensions.

To cultivate
a fraternal
disposition.

Teachers in the same school should regulate their intercourse—social and official—by the chivalrous sentiments ever present in true christian hearts, so that a sort of masonic atmosphere may pervade the scene of their united labours. All should stand together to form "a rampart of mutual defence and safety, supporting each other in all just and laudable efforts." They should protect a fellow-teacher's character in his absence as if he were present. "They should not revile him themselves, nor knowingly suffer others to do so, if in their power to prevent it." On the contrary, they should decline fellowship with his detractors, and "boldly repel the slanderers of his good name."

Absence of
professional
enthusiasm.

It has often been remarked to the writer that "lady teachers are generally deficient in that professional enthusiasm" which we regard as essential to success. But after a varied and prolonged experience in the Public and Collegiate Schools of this and other countries, during which we have had daily —we might say hourly—opportunities of studying the excellencies, deficiencies, and relative merits of our colleagues, we feel bound to say that some of the best, most enthusiastic, and accomplished teachers we have ever known were ladies; and some of the most indifferent and incompetent were men. In truth, professional apathy is common to both sexes, and not the peculiar property of either. Our own observations would lead us to infer that professional enthusiasm—like professional conscience—depends on age, education, and experience, irrespective of sex.

Its cause.

Young women, it is said, are always expecting to change their names, and leave the profession; young men are usually expecting to get a more lucrative appointment in some other calling; and hence both sexes neglect professional cultivation, and look on their position as a mere temporary arrangement which will secure them the necessaries of life until the advent of better times. Such temporary teachers can have no abiding love for children, no real regard for the profession—no correct sense of its importance, no just idea of its many responsibilities, and therefore no professional conscience. They probably have had no professional training, and do not feel the want of any. Possibly they have got legal certificates authorizing them to teach, and think that sufficient. What care they for professional devotion? What need for study—particularly for dry uninteresting professional study? " And even if there were need it would not be worth while; for in a month, or a year or two at most, they will leave the irksome profession, with all its troubles and annoyances."*

Such, we are told, are some of the favourite modes of expression adopted by young teachers to excuse their want of enthusiasm. Now all this must be changed. Of course it would not be desirable, or indeed possible, to prevent young women getting married; but we think it very desirable and very necessary, to prevent young men or young women leaving the profession for more lucrative appointments. It should be done : and the only way to do it is to make the teacher's profession as lucrative as any other, and to refrain from employing unskilled labour no matter how well recommended. If teachers be deficient in energy and zeal (and doubtless some of them are), then, in most cases, the people are to blame. They offer insufficient salaries (or wages as some call them), and, to keep up the supply of indifferent " educators," they —through their officials—grant certificates to unqualified persons. What right, we would ask, have any board, or body of men, to furnish young and inexperienced persons with diplomas, giving them the name and status of teachers, until they have supplied practical proof of their *professional* skill and enthusiasm, and of their desire and intention

margin note: How to remove the evil.

* In discussing the effect of their profession upon teachers, the San Francisco *Bulletin* says:—"Too many queer persons—eccentric, singular, and naturally small and pedantic—enter upon the business of instruction. On all such persons teaching seems to have an unfavourable effect, because it brings out those undesirable traits very prominently. Whenever teachers have striven to be something more than machines, and have endeavoured to balance any unfavourable tendencies by wide reading, high culture, and high aims, in nearly all such instances, so far from experiencing any ill effects, they have been made better by their vocation. The man or the woman who is not the better for teaching, and fails to develop what is best in the pupil, is unworthy of that vocation."

to devote their lives to their calling ? Third-class certificates, as granted in this country, are evidences of mere literary attainments ; and as such qualifications, without practical professional skill, cannot make a teacher, we are of opinion that the basis on which they are awarded is unsound, and needs alteration. The certificate of a physician testifying to the physical strength of a navvy does not qualify such an individual to set up as a surgeon ; much less does the certificate of a county, or other board, testifying to the scholastic acquirements of a candidate, qualify him, or her, to set up as a teacher. No certificate or diploma can make a teacher—a fact which no intelligent board will deny : yet strange to say these very gentlemen, though admitting the truth of our assertion, will next moment grant *Teachers' Certificates* to persons who never taught a day in their lives—even to mere boys and girls of sixteen.

Apprentice-ship to the profession.

Now, we maintain in the interests of the public, of the profession, and of the candidates themselves, that a certificate should not be awarded to any applicant until he, or she, has given proof of his, or her, professional fitness and natural, or acquired, skill in teaching. As in England, Ireland, and part of Germany, no person should receive a certificate of any class or grade, no matter how high his literary qualifications, until he has served a certain apprentice-ship (one year at least) to the profession in the capacity of pupil-teacher, student-teacher, or monitor, under the auspices of a legally-qualified Public School Master or Mistress ; or until he had attended a Normal School one or more sessions. The standard of qualifications now required for Third Class, should be raised to the Second, and subsequent promotion to the Second or First Class should depend more on length of service and professional success than on mere literary attainments. The principles and practice of education should be the most prominent subject on the programme of examination for certificates of all grades, instead of being the lowest and least important, as it is now considered even by the Government officials themselves—receiving (as it does) only half the number of marks awarded to other individual subjects. Such a fact is, in itself, sufficient to make teachers careless of progress in their art. As an illustration of its effects we may mention that not many years ago we were present at a large Convention of Teachers, in which a majority declined to listen to a lecture on "Method," proposed to be given by a gentleman from New York, who was well introduced— alleging (1) that the lecture was out of order, not being mentioned on the programme ; and (2) that a prolongation of the session would cause them personal inconvenience ! There were only five ladies present, and we were glad to notice that four of them voted with the minority. Since then, we were present at a teachers' meeting where a proposal to make "The best modes of discipline, and most approved methods of Teaching a standing subject of discussion," was voted down by the younger members of the profession.

These and similar facts which have come under our notice from time to time, would seem to indicate a dearth of professional enthusiasm sufficient, in itself, to prevent general advancement in the science of teaching. As Archbishop Whately well observes, "Such a dearth fills the heart of the inexperienced with a false pride, and impels them to believe that improvement is unnecessary." Regular apprenticeship to the profession, as in England, more extensive Normal School training, and greater restriction and discrimination in the granting of certificates are the best, and only real remedies for the evils arising from such professional apathy and official carelessness. The more a person knows, the greater his consciousness of his own ignorance— the greater his humility, and the more intense his desire to learn ; and *vice versa*. *The best remedies.*

As teachers advance in life they generally learn to love their calling and to identify themselves with its interests, so that their zeal becomes more ardent, and their efficiency *Advantages of experience.*

more certain than during their younger and less experienced years. Successful and continued practice increases their knowledge of human nature, enlarges their sympathies, invigorates their enthusiasm, and imparts a lasting impulse to their professional devotion ; and, not infrequently, transforms the indifferent recruit into a gallant, self-sacrificing " veteran."

The best use of wealth. When a community recognizes its greatest benefactors and most useful citizens in the persons of its teachers, and is not only willing but anxious to devote its resources to their proper remuneration, (and the consequent elevation and diffusion of education,) then will it have laid the foundation of lasting prosperity and true greatness. Wealth is best expended when used in relieving men of vigorous intellect and generous disposition from the ordinary cares of existence, thus enabling them to devote their lives with ardour and enthusiasm to the study of nature and science, so that with the professional light obtained they may be the better able to cultivate the heart, conscience, and mental energies of the rising generation. It can command the services, and enlist the sympathies of the most generous and highly-cultivated spirits of the age, by inducing them to seek commissions in the grand army of educators. The influence of wealth and of liberal national appropriations, operating in harmony with the intelligence and profound sympathies of such teachers, cannot fail to elevate the social status, whilst promoting the happiness and material comforts, of the masses. Well-paid, accomplished educators will elevate the art of teaching, and gradually invigorate the dormant intellectual energies of their respective communities; so that the people will not only have a better comprehension of the dignity of human nature but be better instructed in the laws, harmonies, and duties of life—more especially that portion of it which relates to the mental, moral, and physical education of children.

It has been said that, under the regulations of the new $\quad$ No excuse for want of text-books. school law, pupils in the higher classes have so many studies and require so many books that parents, when poor, cannot afford to send them to school in consequence of the necessary expense, nor to keep them at home in consequence of the penalties attached to the Compulsory Act. The new subjects of study are necessary if we would keep up with the progressive spirit and industrial progress of the times ; and if parents are too poor to provide good and sufficient text-books, the law authorizes trustees to supply them at the public expense. There is therefore no just ground for complaint, and no excuse for ignorance—no palliation for negligence. Every parent, or guardian, in the land can supply his child with all necessary text-books at his own or the public expense.

Want of books may retard but cannot stop the progress $\quad$ The great requisite. of education—a large supply is desirable, but not essential. Pestallozzi and others have taught successfully without any books, and but little apparatus. In most cases, chalk and black boards may be made to supply their place. The great requisite in the public schools is a class of teachers well acquainted with the philosophy of mind ; active, intelligent men and women who understand child-nature, and are always ready and anxious to avail themselves of every opportunity to develop mental growth, generous sentiments, and correct moral principles—teachers who will devote their lives to their profession with that energy and enthusiasm which always command success. The impulse imparted to education by the teaching of such officials cannot fail to invigorate, elevate, and regenerate society, and thus introduce a higher, holier, and more fraternal civilization than any known hitherto. The ever-increasing number of Normal Schools and Teachers' Institutes is an evidence of the national anxiety to produce and train such officials. To be successful the people must supplement the Normal Schools and

Institutes with better pay, higher social consideration, and greater permanency of engagements. As Channing truly remarks, "If it be the people's desire to secure and retain the services of such an order of teachers (as those under consideration), social circles must be re-arranged, so as to allow the educators of youth to take precedence of the moneyed and money-making classes; and, in point of rank, the woman of fashion must fall behind the female teacher. Education must be recognized by the community as its highest interest and duty, and parents must sacrifice pleasure and ostentation to the acquisition of the best possible aids and guides for their children." We must not be understood to imply by the foregoing remarks that a sufficiency of good text-books and apparatus are not desirable; or that teachers should ever become pompous, flashy, individuals, like certain fashionable folks outside the respective circles of our acquaintance—quite the reverse. We would advocate a sufficiency in the one case, and the judicious exercise of reason, taste, and judgment, in the other.

The laws of life and order of mental evolution.   Our ideas of education should not be of the aimless, confusing, cramming, or chaotic character. The nature and order of mental evolution or development, and the probable effects of certain modes of treatment, should be constant themes of professional study. Without a clear and intelligent knowledge of the general principles of mental phenomena, with their causes and consequences, we will fail to understand the laws which guide the evolution of intelligence, and cannot therefore properly regulate the process of education, or supply the necessary means to secure each special end. Moreover, in our ignorance, we will be in constant danger of thwarting children in their pursuit of happiness, thereby diminishing their enjoyments, with no other result than that of making them miserable, fretful, peevish, and ill-natured. We must remember that the intellectual action which a child likes at any particular age is just the action it needs, and therefore the most healthful and suitable for the requirements of its organization. As a learned writer remarks, "The rise of an appetite for any kind of knowledge implies that the unfolding mind has become fit to assimilate it, and needs it for the purposes of growth ; on the other hand, the disgust felt towards any kind of knowledge is a sign either that it is prematurely presented, or that it is presented in an indigestible form." We should reasonably indulge the child's love of variety, and combine improvement with the gratification of his curiosity. Unwise prohibitions, like unsuitable regulations, may undermine his mental or physical constitution, and gradually produce permanent disease, premature decay, or untimely death. It is cruel carelessness, therefore, on the part of those having the guidance and control of the young, to neglect the study of the laws of life, and those mental and vital processes, which are influenced or affected by rules, regulations, or example. "At present, and in the remotest future, it must be of incalculable importance for the regulation of conduct that men should understand the science of life, physical, mental, and social ; and that they should understand all other sciences as the key to the science of life........True education is practicable only to the true philosopher."*

If teachers would command success in their vocation, they must learn to understand the laws of mental activity viewed in connection with nature, instinct, and the various analogies of life ; they must be able to resolve intellectual phenomena into its primary elements, and from this analysis to deduce such facts as will enable them to think out methods of their own for dealing with the opening mind of childhood. The teacher's profession can never attain its true position until the majority of its exponents acquire such a knowledge of mental philosophy as will enable them to base

Teachers to study the science of Mind.

Conditions of professional success.

---

*Herbert Spencer.

every portion of their art upon its corresponding science, and to refer every manifestation or expression, mental or physical, to its native source. Once possessed of this knowledge, due development or repression of the mental and physical powers will be a mere matter of time and patience.

How to secure it.

It is essentially necessary that teachers, like other skilled workmen, should study the philosophy of their art. For this reason they should pursue a regular course of reading. When opportunities offer they should daily question Nature, in the school-room or nursery, as to the truth of the theories advanced in the works of their more experienced brethren. Should the student-teacher find it impracticable at all times to command such an excellent studio as either of those mentioned, he may nevertheless test the truth of such theories by looking inwards on himself. No work on education, and no study of other people's characteristics, can teach us so much of the science of our art as the revelation of human nature in our own hearts. The secret workings of the soul, the silent operations of our varied intelligence, the recollections of our own personal history in all the stages of its development, our mental struggles, our sorrows, our joys, and the spontaneous thoughts, longings, and aspirations which fill our minds from day to day—with all their mutations of ardent feeling and strength of purpose—compose a volume of priceless value, and form, in themselves, a fountain of truth, on whose eternal principles every true teacher must ultimately repose his art.

Nature's book on teaching.

The teacher's personal experience, and Nature's light in his own bosom, are the best books on teaching, and the first, as well as the last, which should engage his attention. His chief objects during his professional career should be, (1) to think strongly and actively, so that he may create a desire for study; (2) to form good and worthy designs; (3) to conceive and impart correct if not great ideas, so that while diffusing knowledge, he may communicate sound guiding principles. Such ideas and designs are often received by outward impressions, and often by direct inspiration; but are more frequently the result of the inward workings of mind on ideas already acquired. If we would be good and skilful teachers we must look inwards, and obtain a correct and more extensive knowledge of Nature's workings in ourselves; otherwise our teaching will lose half its influence, our lives lack half their usefulness, and our example never be a worthy beacon light to others. In studying self, and the principles and laws of our own being, we study nature, history, philosophy, and art. By retaining a consciousness of what passes (or has passed) in our own minds, under certain conditions, we can comprehend the effect of like conditions on other minds. The ideas derived from the study of our own nature will enable us to understand other natures; hence, *the key to successful teaching is the study of one's self.* The light gained by intelligent observation and the study of ourselves, supplemented by such as we may be able to obtain in the works of others, will not only increase our present happiness and enable us to serve our generation more efficiently, but it will open to us a source of perpetual enjoyment, entirely independent of the changes peculiar to time and circumstances. " Happy are they whose amusement is knowledge, and whose supreme delight is the cultivation of mind. Wherever they chance to roam the means of employment are still with them. That weary listlessless which renders life insupportable to the indolent and voluptuous is unknown to those who can employ themselves in study."*

The key to successful teaching.

We are inclined to believe that in matters of school government sufficient attention has not been given to the doctrine of natural consequences or relative re-actions, although the events of every-day life constantly proclaim their general operation and inevitable results—mentally, physically, and politically. We will find, should we question nature, that every action is followed by a corresponding re-action,

The doctrine of natural re-actions considered.

* Archbishop Fenelon.

and that the latter is the unavoidable consequence of the former. Natural re-actions are proportionate to the degree of transgression, other things being equal. "They are constant, direct, unhesitating, and not to be escaped." As Spencer observes—"No threats; but a silent, rigorous performance. If a child runs a pin into its finger, pain follows· If it does it again, there is the same result; and so on perpetually. In all its dealings with surrounding inorganic nature it finds this unswerving persistence, which listens to no excuse, and from which there is no appeal: and very soon recognizing this stern though beneficent discipline, it becomes extremely careful not to transgress.. ...It is the function of parents to see that their children habitually experience the true consequences of their personal conduct—the natural re-actions; neither warding them off, nor intensifying them, nor putting artificial consequences in their place." These natural re-actions have a tendency to develop caution, reflection, and other powers essential to self-guidance, and are, therefore, the best and most efficient physical and mental monitors. The great object of family or school discipline should be the production of reliant self-governing beings, and not the manufacture of slaves to be governed by others. For this and other reasons, too numerous to mention, parents and teachers, while prompt in sympathy, should, as a rule, let children experience the natural consequences of their own conduct and actions. Except in extreme cases, children may be governed efficiently and to advantage by means of the minor punishments and the penalties incident to natural re-actions. But to be truly salutary, instructive, or efficient the latter should be inflicted by nature herself, the teacher merely acting as proxy to direct or apply her manifestations. Artificial consequences, such as temporary displeasure, may justly accompany, though not be the substitute for, natural penalties. The expression of parental or tutorial feeling in such cases should assimilate as much as possible to the reaction of nature. By due observance of the doctrine of natural consequences, circumstances may be so guided as always to ensure the infliction of the right penalty by the operation of the right agent—the natural laws which regulate and govern things. An irregular, vacillating infliction of pains and penalties—too severe at one time, too merciful or moderate at another—promotes transgression instead of decreasing it. Hence the absolute necessity of being consistent in our administration, and free from the temporary, or traditional, impulses so characteristic of parental government even in this enlightened age and country. The difficulties appertaining to the right education and government of children will be reduced to a minimum when they discover that certain consequences will inevitably follow certain acts, and that the only way to avoid the former is to abstain from indulgence in the latter.

The American and Canadian people have many advantages over their European brethren in the matter of popular education. In the Old World popular education has never had a good start or a fair chance of due development. It is different in these countries of the Western World. The English-speaking States of North America are blessed with the best and most comprehensive school systems in the world. Each commonwealth recognizes its children as its most valuable property and, as a matter of course, makes State provision for their free education. Every resident has the privilege of attending the public schools, and most of the universities, irrespective of his creed, class, condition, or nationality. The law invests him with an inherent right to attend these national institutions, and thereby relieves him of any embarrassments arising from personal obligations· His thanks are due to the Commonwealth of which he is himself a part. All the States of the Union, and all the Provinces of Canada, recognize the right of the people to a good sound education, and, by the operation of compulsory Acts are about to compel the rising generation to avail them-

Provision for public education.

selves of the educational advantages provided for their benefit. The States have, from time to time, set apart one-sixth of their public lands (eighty millions of acres) to form a perpetual fund for general education. In addition to the proceeds of these lands a direct supplementary tax is raised annually for school purposes by the different municipalities, districts, or school sections.

Public School Boards.

The public schools in Ontario are maintained partly by Government grants based on the average daily attendance, and partly on direct local taxation. Public School Boards are the most powerful local corporations in the Province. They can erect and furnish schools, hire and dismiss teachers, and pay what salaries they choose. Their respective municipal councils are compelled by law to furnish them with whatever sums they desire for school purposes. In an economical point of view they seldom, if ever, abuse the immense power with which they are invested. On the contrary they are generally accused of being " mean and miserly in money matters."* So far as our own personal experience extends we must, in justice, say that we invariably found the members of the respective School Boards with which we have been connected, to be generous, liberal, and high-minded men according to their ideas of right and wrong ; but we have reason to believe that some of our fellow-labourers in other localities have not been so fortunate in their official connections. It is true that in consequence of a dearth of candidates of the right stamp* in rural sections, and a disinclination for office in cities and towns, men of limited, un-

---

* SCHOOL TRUSTEES.—The editor of *The Globe*, writing on the 5th January, 1875, says : " We are sorry to say that, in general, there is not that amount of care shown in the selection of school trustees which the interests of education require. We hold that among all our local officials, there are none who can influence the community for good or for evil to such an extent as those who have the management of our public schools. The powers of these officials are very extensive, and their duties are both numerous and important. They can tax to any extent. Whether willing or not, city and town councils must comply with their demands, and provide the necessary funds. They have the choice of all the teachers, and the building and equipping of the different school-rooms are entirely in their hands. We have only to make this statement to show that school trustees ought to be persons of more than ordinary intelligence, and of high moral character. It is of far more importance to have reliable school trustees than to have superior city or town councillors. By all means let us have the best for both, but if there are degrees of

sympathetic and prejudiced views sometimes find a seat at the Board. As the late Bishop of Illinois† observes, in speaking of the Western States, "It occasionally happens that a man of obtuse principles, and little chivalrous feeling, finds a seat amongst the worthy and enlightened friends of education—a man who, perhaps, in the plenitude of his rare intelligence, gives expression to his temporary authority by undermining the influence of, and fostering conspiracies against, school officers—a man who occasionally exercises factious opposition towards some teacher who may be of too sterling a character to flatter his weaknesses, or whose position he may covet for a relative." We believe, however, that in "this Canada of ours" the majority of trustees are straightforward honest men—lovers of justice and fair play, as they understand them. Hence, as corporate bodies, their offences are "sins of omission" rather than "sins of commission"—a failure to use their power rather than an abuse of it. It is often said (and apparently with some reason) that, as a rule, they are not sufficiently intelligent to be generous in the use of their authority—that they are negligent in the provision of suitable school accommodation, and so dull in their appreciation of education as to be incapable of paying good salaries to teachers. In truth, if the teachers be paid badly the fault must be referred to the local trustees, not to the State or Provincial Government. The Government, in this respect, has done its duty; it only remains for the people to do theirs (through their school trustees), in a generous and intelligent spirit, in accordance with the national will.

The Governments of Canada and the neighbouring States, Europe and America in proportion to population, have made almost as liberal a compared. provision for the education of the people as European nations

---

both, let those who are preferable be taken for the trusteeship. Yet, in a vast number of cases, it is exactly the reverse. It seems to be thought that any one can do for a school trustee, and instead of the office being sought by respectable and trustworthy men, it too often goes a begging, and is all but forced upon individuals totally unsuitable, both in character and intelligence."

† Right Rev. Dr. Whitehouse.

make for their fleets and armies, and their efforts have been nobly seconded by the more intelligent and enlightened sections of the community. The most prominent buildings in a European landscape are the castles of the aristocracy; the most striking buildings in European cities are prisons and pauper houses; but in American scenes the most imposing edifices are public schools and collegiate halls. Every American and Canadian is comparatively well acquainted with the history and politics of his country, and with the individual merits of the more prominent public men—whether they be writers, statesmen, teachers, farmers or inventors. As a necessary consequence he possesses a certain energy of will, tenacity of purpose, and intelligent reliance on self, seldom, if ever, found in ordinary European populations. America, in the diffusion of education and amalgamation of her heterogeneous people, is performing a noble work —difficult and gigantic. Her educational labours would be comparatively easy and light were it not for the presence of an ever-increasing foreign element. Year after year tens of thousands of Europeans, fresh from the bondage of serfdom, land upon her hospitable shores, bringing with them all the prejudices, poverty and ignorance so characteristic of antiquated *régimes* and Old World institutions. What does Columbia—the land of Washington and Cartier—do with these hardy "outcasts"—aliens in race and language perhaps? She gives them a cordial greeting—a hearty welcome —sends them out to the Great West—presents them with a little estate—and, if they so desire, adopts them as her own children, giving them all the advantages and privileges enjoyed by her first-born—the sons of the soil. Nor is this all. She establishes public schools to educate them—" to teach them the love of country, a reverence for law and order, and a preference of honour, not only to pleasure but to life."*

---

* Archbisiop Fenelou.

The majority of our eminent men are persons who have Higher education. graduated in the trying school of Experience—men who have never obtained a college diploma, not being able in early life to command the necessary capital. They are emigrants or the sons of emigrants, and have ensured their personal success by the force of their innate abilities. Such success is the best of all degrees, and can only be obtained in the University of Practical Life. The universities of Europe are aristocratic guilds, and may justly be regarded as the private academies of the rich. Universities on this continent belong to the people, and, like the public schools, are open to the penniless child of the friendless widow as well as to the aspiring son of the ambitious statesman. There is no national institution of learning amongst us which a poor boy may not attend, if he can command sufficient funds to pay his board; and there is no degree which he may not attain, if possessed of the necessary mental capacity. Weal this doubtless a great convenience, but time and mental ability are the only "necessary requisites." In Europe, education, like wealth, is generally confined to a class. In America, both are widely (though not yet sufficiently) diffused amongst the masses. Our institutions, however, have a mighty reflex influence on European countries, and, whilst breaking down social barriers and removing the prejudices of caste, are causing society to "level up." Those in authority are beginning to feel that the welfare and stability of nations and governments depend on the elevation, education, and consequent prosperity of the working classes. Hence the tendency of the mother countries to copy our laws and institutions.

The English-speaking States of North America have Popular education. made gigantic strides in material wealth during the present century; but public education, with its corps of faithful teachers, was (and is) the pioneer of their prosperity. Foreign nations are becoming electrified by our example. Our

wonderful progress has aroused them from the lethargy of
ages, and foreign statesmen—conscious of the dangers which
would threaten the peace, welfare, and stability of a nation
inspired by bigotry and ruled by ignorance or prejudice—are
desirous of having their people thoroughly educated ; but the
people themselves have not yet responded with the energy
which might have been expected.   The fact is, they have been
so long in darkness that their mental eyes cannot bear the
light.   This transition stage will soon pass away, and then
the light of knowledge will shine on their hearts and fertilize
their minds.   Public education, aided by the benign influences
of *real* Christianity, will enlighten the conscience, quicken
generous sentiment, and develop every power of the human
being—mental, moral, physical.   Whilst imparting courage,
strength, and stability, it will make each individual the centre
of a cheerful and radiant social circle, investing all his actions
with a genial grace, finally impelling him to love and cultivate all that is lofty, perfect, and beautiful in human character.   The intelligence and patriotism arising from such
culture cannot fail to promote the public welfare and secure
the national honour.   Mental and social elevation arises
chiefly from the promptings of a good and generous heart, and
from the continued activity of the intellectual forces exerted
in the acquisition of knowledge.   It is, therefore, the result
of the combined action of natural impulse and mental power.
The right cultivation of these promptings, or impulses, and
the proper development and judicious guidance of these
intellectual energies, comprise all the duties of the teacher,
and convey all we mean by education.   Such an education
must elevate each citizen intellectually, morally, socially.
Without it, no man can elevate himself or others ; so that
from the first to the last hour of life, he must remain oblivious of one of the greatest sources of happiness, and fail in
one of the most important objects of existence—that of being
a fountain of light and joy to "those who sit in darkness."

This is what every citizen should strive to be—each in his respective sphere of usefulness.*

The right education of the young is the best guarantee of the welfare of all classes in the future. But manhood, and even age, should not be forgotten. Philosophers and statesmen, while attending to the interests of the child, should not overlook the welfare of the adult. They are indebted to the present, as well as to the future. To discharge this debt in a wise and patriotic manner they must create facilities for the education of adults by establishing "Night Schools," and making arrangements for the delivery of periodical courses of lectures on technical subjects—Natural Philosophy, Mechanical Arts, etc. In such a population as

Provision for adult education.

---

* We have stated elsewhere that good home government was the essential basis of good school government, and that the children of amiable, high-minded, and intelligent parents generally inherited, more or less, these noble characteristics. In referring to these matters, Herbert Spencer justly remarks that it is very erroneous for teachers and others to ascribe all the faults and difficulties to the children and none to the parents; or to assume, like certain governments, that "the virtues are with the rulers and the vices with the ruled." "So far is this from the truth," says he, "that we do not hesitate to affirm that to parental misconduct is traceable a great part of the domestic (and school room) disorders commonly ascribed to children. . . . The truth is, that the difficulties of moral education are necessarily of dual origin—and necessarily result from the combined faults of parents and children. If hereditary transmission is a law of nature, as every naturalist knows it to be, and as our daily remarks and current proverbs admit it to be; then on the average of cases the defects of children mirror the defects of their parents. . . . The most glaring defect in our programmes of education is entirely overlooked. . . . Though some care is taken to fit youth of both sexes for society and citizenship, no care whatever is taken to fit them for the still more important position they will ultimately have to fill—the position of parents. . . . While many years are spent by a boy in gaining knowledge of which the chief value is, that it constitutes what some call 'the education of a gentleman;' and while many years are spent by a girl in those decorative acquirements which fit her for evening parties; not an hour is spent by either of them in preparation for that gravest of all responsibilities—the management of a family. . . . Not only is the need for such self-instruction unrecognized, but the complexity of the subject renders it the one of all others in which self-instruction is least likely to succeed. No rational plea can be put forward for leaving the Art of Education out of our *curriculum.* Whether as bearing upon the happiness of parents themselves, or whether as affecting the characters and lives of their children and remote descendants, we must admit that a knowledge of the right methods of juvenile culture, physical, intellectual and moral, is a knowledge second to none in importance. This topic should occupy the highest and last place in the course of instruction passed through by each man and woman. As physical maturity is marked by the ability to produce offspring, so mental maturity is marked by the ability to train those offspring in a proper manner. The subject which involves all other subjects, and therefore the subject in which the education of everyone should culminate is, the Theory and Practice of Education." Few will read these remarks without admitting the existence of the evils alluded to—evils which are more general than is commonly believed. It behoves every good and patriotic citizen to assist in removing such glaring defects. This can be done only by the creation of a higher intelligence, by the more general diffusion of education amongst all classes, ages, and conditions of men.—G. V. L.

ours, composed as it is of a large foreign adult element, anxious for and needing improvement, there should be suitable and comfortable provision made in cities and towns for the accommodation of all who may desire instruction in the Public School subjects. These students should, when practicable, be placed in charge of the local Public School teachers, the salaries of these officials being supplemented in proportion to their increased duties and responsibilities. Night Schools should be established during the winter months, for the benefit of young men—labourers, clerks, artisans, and all others, irrespective of age or condition, who might be willing to conform to the rules and regulations necessary for the successful government of such institutions. Night schools have been established, by the bounty of wealthy citizens, in many parts of England, France, and Ireland, and are the source of many blessings to the adult population in their immediate vicinity. It remains for some of our American commonwealths to make them State institutions, and thus give them a legal or recognized existence on this Continent. Night schools should be merely supplementary to, not rivals or substitutes for, day schools. Both institutions should, of course, be carried on in the same building and under the management of the same School Boards.

Influences of age on education. None are too old to learn; yet it cannot be denied that the influence of long established habits will, in some cases, make the minds of old people impervious to impressions which would have been happily received in younger years. "After a certain age (writes the amiable Archbishop Fenelon) men lose their pliancy, and become fixed in their habits, which have grown old with them and become, as it were, a part of their constitution." Much, however, as we admire the precepts of the good prelate of Cambray, we cannot concur with him (and other worthies) in believing that old men may become conscious of the existence of objectionable or injurious habits, and even sigh over their presence, earnestly desiring their removal, and yet not have sufficient fortitude, or energy of will, to resist and overcome such infirmities; nor can we believe that "the faults of age are hopeless," or that "youth is the only season in which nature can be corrected."* Without referring to history, many of us could adduce instances from personal observation which would prove the contrary. All men, of all ages, are capable of improvement; but "in youth," as the royal teacher well observes, "the power of correction is unlimited." In some respects people advanced in life are more susceptible of improvement than the young; but manhood and age have a multitude of cares which are apt to wage war for the dominion of the mind. The child, be he ever so ignorant, is, therefore, the more hopeful subject, and, on the whole, will probably be the more successful student.

Free libraries, cabinets of natural history, fine arts collections, and museums of the industrial arts, should be established in connection with the Public School system in towns. Similar institutions should be established at central places in the country, the adjoining townships combining to share the expense and advantages of same. These institutions might embrace the following departments :—

Supplements to the Public School system.

1st. A free reading-room, open to all who will conform to to a few simple regulations. Also an elevating resort, in the shape of an attractive, neatly-furnished room, where young men could meet to exchange opinions on current events and other topics.

---

* More than 150 years have elapsed since the good and amiable Fenelon put the foregoing words to the account of Mentor. But the world has changed since then, and our increasing knowledge of human nature has kept pace with the lapse of time. Fenelon's own life and example affords many proofs that old men may break old habits and form new ones—that they may learn to the latest hour of their lives—that they may rise superior to Fortune, and derive pleasure and profit in the evening of their days, not only from their own continued culture, but from their labours as practical educators. We append the passage alluded to in the foregoing :—" La vieillesse n'a plus rien de souple, la longue habitude la tient comme enchainée ; ell n'a plus de ressource contre ses defauts. Semblables aux arbres dont le tronc rude et noueux s'est durci par le nombre des annees, et ne peut plus se redresser, les hommes à un certain age ne peuvent presque plus se plier eux-memes contre certaines habitudes qui ont vieilli avec eux, et qui sont entrees jusques dans la moëlle de leurs os. Souvent ils les connaissent, mais trop tard ; ils gemissent en vain ; la tendre jeunesse est le seul age on l'homme peut encore tout sur lui-meme pour se corriger."—*Les Aventures De Telemaque.*

2nd. A free public library for the use of members.

3rd. A free course of lectures on literary and historical subjects to be delivered each session by men of acknowledged ability, as orators, teachers, and philanthropists.

4th. A popular course of lectures upon scientific subjects.

5th. A literary society affording opportunities for mental improvement, and general culture in writing and speaking.

6th. A gymnasium where persons of leisure may find pleasant and profitable recreation in physical exercise.

By these and similar means the people will be refined, educated, and ennobled. As they grow in intelligence they will acquire a more philosophical knowledge of their various callings; the forces of nature will be more fully subdued to man's use; the cost of production will be lessened, and labour economised to the highest degree. The people can then acquit themselves to greater personal advantage, and therefore command higher wages. Their duties will be discharged with greater avidity—more facility and less labour—because the light of science will guide their least as well as greatest efforts. Under such arrangements the toils of daily life will become potent instruments of self culture, mighty levers of elevation to the human race, because labour will thenceforth be applied with intelligence and "practical ease," being the mere physical expression of the knowledge and power stored up in the workman's mind. To effect this object, "labour and refreshment"—physical toil and mental education—must succeed each other at regular intervals; and life be so diversified in its aims, aspirations, and employments, as to call forth all the latent energies of the body and soul, inspiring the love of truth and imparting a sense of pleasure to its acquisition. The knowledge arising from the prosecution of original enquiry and the cultivation of scientific habits cannot fail to lessen labour and increase production, whilst elevating the people and increasing the comforts of life.

Nature never intended that the advantages of life should be monopolized by one class, caste, or order of men, as is generally the case in Europe. She is no respector of castes or classes, and doubtless intended that the trials and blessings of life should be the common property of all. The tendency of the present age is to ignore all distinctions not arising from personal worth—to rebel against any claims to superiority based on the merits of ancestors, or on the power of ill-gotten wealth. It has often been a matter of surprise to us that Christianity, and kindred influences, have not long ago succeeded in establishing reciprocal charity and an identity of interests amongst all classes, in these highly-favoured countries. However, the prejudices and delusions inherited from former ages are gradually evaporating; and although the present hour is not so full of light as we could wish, we have reason to hope for a bright to-morrow. On this continent, where the civilization of the East and West have met together, and the children of the Orient and Occident "have kissed each other," the people think, speak, and act for themselves, and enjoy the comforts as well as the toils of life. Yet even here there is room for much improvement. The people need more discrimination, more judgment, more education—in a word, more *real* Christianity. The age of intellectual enquiry has dawned upon the world. Men now ask for reasons for what they are required to do, suffer, or believe. They are no longer content to be "like dumb driven cattle." They are "up and doing." Henceforth they will and must think for themselves. It therefore behoves wise legislators and prudent teachers to lead them to think justly, strongly, impartially, and at the same time inspire them with the love of truth and justice—the first principles of Science and Religion. The affections, feelings, and enlightened opinions of the people—arising from rational conviction and the teachings of eternal truth—are now the only real basis of stability in human institutions. In every

Sorrows and joys of life, the common property of all.

The age of intellect.

civilized land the pomps and vanities of physical force are paling before the mighty energies and pulsations of the human mind, directed as they are by popular education and Divine intuition. No social or political ordinance can possibly survive the sweeping changes of the present and future ages, unless it has its foundation in the human heart; hence the advisability, if not necessity, of studying more accurately the principles of those laws or natural forces which control human action.

Growth of mind.

The mental energies of an educated people grow larger and stronger in the presence of danger—and in times of doubt, difficulty, or uncertainty—so that no obstacle, royal or democratic, can enervate their intelligence, or permanently withstand their onward march. If it be true (and it is) that the mind makes the man, it is equally true that mind makes the nation. In truth, it is the highest, greatest, and most god-like force in the universe; yet it can never attain its full development in the human being without the fostering aid of generous, sympathetic, and intelligent instruction. As education and civilization advance, the volume of mind—increased by ever-increasing rills and streams from the fountains of thought—will make the nations illustrious, and attain such an irresistible sweep as to overwhelm all opposing obstacles. The force of mind will increase from age to age until all other powers and forces are subject to it. Enlightened public opinion, even now, causes men to acknowledge it as intrinsically glorious —one of the noblest emanations from the Creator. Great thoughts are the characteristics of great minds. Once kindled, they transform the hearts of men into living fires, whence proceed those mental sparks, or ideal germs, which time and circumstances develop into great deeds. It may be regarded as an axiom in international politics, that the more intelligent and energetic races of men are endowed with the greatest mind—national and individual—and they are sure, therefore, sooner or later, to subdue their neighbours, mentally, morally, or physically. It is unnecessary to quote examples to sustain this statement: the history of man, from the first page to the last, emphatically confirms its truth. When this greatness of mind and activity of will are widely diffused amongst a people, their nation, in a certain sense, becomes omnipotent and immortal. Such were Greece and Rome in the past, and such may our own country be in the future.

It should be the ambition of all good citizens to assist in the creation and general development of such an intellectual greatness, of such moral and physical excellence, as will secure individual freedom and well-being, whilst perpetuating the unity and omnipotency of a strong, healthy, national will. The absence of such an ambition, or the neglect to cultivate it, indicates a want of real patriotism and vital religious sentiment. Influenced by the presence of such noble aspirations, true teachers express *in actions* the love they feel for their country and their God. They seek the higher truths through the medium of the lower—the spiritual and mental through the temporal and tangible. They zealously study the manifestations of nature, life and thought, and thus approach nearer to the Divinity, whilst obtaining a key to the right interpretation of individual and national existence, past, present, and to come. As patriotic men they must cordially and generously share their superior lights with less-favoured citizens; and further, they must aim at the correction or gradual development of public opinion, so that the national voice may ultimately do honor to vigour of *physique* as well as to vigour of mind. They must also remember that no nation can be justly regarded as educated until the great majority of its people are made fully conscious of the fact, that voluntary breaches of the laws of health or bodily development are criminal offences, injurious to the family or the community—physical sins for

Important public duties.

which nature will, sooner or later, inexorably demand satisfaction. The moral and vital energies necessary for the right conception and accomplishment of such worthy designs must be infused into the people by the more general diffusion of science and the more liberal encouragement of physical training; and our legislators must be inspired by the conviction that the intelligence of a community depends more on the high average of education, as distributed amongst the many, than on vast stores of knowledge monopolized by a few: nor must it be forgotten that the god-like principles and noble ideas inspired by knowledge are of more importance than knowledge itself— being, as they are, the true source of magnanimity and mental energy. In an age and country like ours, the great object of the philanthropist, legislator, and patriot should be the creation and accumulation of such powers and influences as may be necessary to awake, and educate aright, the slumbering energies and latent capacities of all classes and all ages; and this object will be best accomplished by making a more liberal national (and local) provision for public education, so that men and women of large and enlightened minds may be employed, at good salaries, to take charge of the Nation's schools, and thus send streams of light and mental life into every homestead in the land.

Conclusion. In conclusion we would say that teachers owe it to themselves, and to their profession, to avoid and rise above the din and conflict of professional, political, and sectarian strife —to lay broad and deep the foundations of intelligence, truth, and fraternity—so that, with Divine favour, they may be the better able to secure, diffuse, and perpetuate the many blessings, public and private, which flow from the judicious development of a free and comprehensive system of education such as that which has made this Province the light and life of our New Dominion.

APPENDIX.

NOTICE TO PARENTS AND GUARDIANS.*

The Report (see p. 296) which is prepared with great care and accuracy, furnishes each parent or guardian with a minute and exact statement of his son's (or ward's) progress and standing in every subject of study. Strict attention to the following particulars is requested:

1. No one but the parent or guardian should sign the Report. Should circumstances prevent due attention to this point, special arrangements should be previously made with the Principal.

2. The pupil's progress, as manifested by each Report, should be minutely observed, to see whether he is getting up or down in his Form (or Class), whether his averages are becoming lower or higher, and whether his demerit marks and detentions (if he has any) are increasing or decreasing. Sixty demerit marks will cause the suspension or dismissal of the pupil; but as soon as any pupil has twenty-five demerit marks recorded against him, the Principal will notify the parent or guardian of the fact, and the pupil will take home a daily report, to be signed by the parent or guardian, and returned to the Principal.

---

* The following pages (293 to 298 inclusive) have been selected from papers kindly furnished us by the Principal of the Upper Canada College, George R. R. Cockburn, Esq., M.A., to whom we are also indebted for many valuable suggestions contained in the foregoing work. The selections alluded to furnish a sample of one of the most perfect systems of Registration of Merit to be found in any school on this continent. They will richly repay patient perusal, and we can say, from practical experience, that teachers who may introduce such a Record of Progress into their schools, will reap an abundant harvest. No other system can surpass it as a medium of stirring up mind or exciting scholastic enthusiasm.—G. V. L.

3. Whenever the Report is unsatisfactory in any of these particulars, the parent ought to call immediately at the College (or School) and enquire into the matter, as prompt attention to this particular may often save the pupil being dismissed, or suspended, or put back a whole session.

4. No pupil is advanced with his Form (or Class) at the end of the session, who, in the written and oral examinations upon the studies of the Form (or Class) fails to obtain in each subject the " Minimum Value for Promotion," (see p. 297). * * * No pupil, on completing the course, will obtain a *Certificate of Distinction*, who fails to obtain honors in every subject, and First Class honors in Classics and Mathematics.

5. Parents and guardians are respectfully informed that their sons or wards have certain lessons prescribed for every evening, and they are particularly requested to allow no arrangements to interfere with the due preparation of them. From one to three hours are required for that purpose, according to the Form and ability of the pupil. * * *

6. Writing and Book-keeping are marked according to an average, ranking from 1 to 6 and 1 to 10 respectively, and those averages are determined by the attention shown and progress made by the pupil.

UPPER CANADA COLLEGE.

DAILY REGISTER OF PROGRESS* of Third Form, for Month of May, 1875.

SUBJECT—ARITHMETIC.

Register No.	NAMES.	3	5	7	10	12	14	17	19	21	24	26	28	Total	Average Rank.	Absolute Rank.	No. times head.	No. times absent.
38	Wilton, George	†a	1	1	1	1	2	1	1	1	:	1	1	1¹⁰⁄₁₀	1.10	1	9	:
26	Percy, Wm	1	2	2	2	2	3	3	4	3	:	3	3	2¹³⁄₁₁	2.54	2	1	:
27	Tilney, Robert	3	6	7	7	7	1	2	2	2	:	2	2	4⁴⁄₁₁	3.72	4	1	:
32	St. George, Edwin	2	3	3	3	3	4	4	3	4	:	5	4	3¹⁹⁄₁₁	3.45	3	:	:
31	Mostyn, Gerald	4	4	4	4	+Ex.	6	7	a	7	:	a	5	4¹⁄₉	5.12	5	:	2
35	Brougham, Henry	10	5	5	5	4	5	8	6	7	:	7	8	7¹⁷⁄₁₁	6.36	6	:	:

* Full explanations of the manner of keeping this Record of Merit will be found on pages 143-146.
† a means absent without leave.
‡ Ex. means excused, or absent with leave.   G. V. L.

UPPER CANADA COLLEGE.

SUMMARY OF PUPIL'S REPORT FOR THE MONTH OF MAY, 1875.

Absolute Rank.	SUBJECTS.	Average Rank.	No. of times head.	Lessons lost by absence.	APPLICATION AND PROGRESS.	Masters' initials.	Principal's remarks.
							Head of Form.
4 sq.	Scripture	5.00	....	....	Satisfactory	M. B.	Wilton, G.
13 sq.	Shakespeare	14.16	....	....	Has an average taste for higher literature.	G. R. R. C.	
1	Arithmetic	1.10	9	....		A. B.	
4	Algebra	5.67	....	....	Very satisfactory indeed		
4 sq.	Geometry	5.09	3	....			
8	Natural Philosophy	8.22	....	....			
2	English Composition		....	....	Very fair; bad spelling	J. M.	
6	English Grammar, Reading, &c.	6.05	3	....		J. M.	
6	Modern History and Literature.	6.92	1	....	Very fair		
1	Modern Geography	2.20	2	....	Most satisfactory		
6	Chemistry	7.00	....	....	Very satisfactory	M. B.	
13	Physiology	12.66	....	....	Very fair		
6	French	7.33	....	....	Very satisfactory	M. Br.	
7	German	8.16	....	....	Only fair		
	Writing	....	....	....			
4	Book-keeping	2.20	....	....	Good	C. J. T.	

RESIDENT SCHOOL-HOUSE REPORT.

			Times late.	APPLICATION.
Sum of averages	96.98			
* Demerit Marks	1		*Times detained	
Sum of Averages (after adding Demerit Marks)	96.98		2	CONDUCT.
† Average Rank	6.06		....	

He Ranks No. 4 in a form of 23 Pupils.

I have carefully examined the above Report, and compared it with the preceding, and the notice to Parents and Guardians on pages 293-294.

..............*Guardian.*

* Many Pupils pass through College without ever incurring a Demerit Mark or being once Detained.

† The Average Rank is found by dividing the Sum of Averages, after adding the Demerit Marks (if any), by the number of subjects in which the Pupil is absolutely ranked.

UPPER CANADA COLLEGE.

RESULTS FOR THE SESSION.

EXAMINATION MARKS ACCORDED TO GEORGE WILTON.

SUBJECTS. (Third Form.)	Maximum Value.	Minimum Value for Promotion.	Value actually obtained.		Remarks on 1st Examination.	Remarks on 2nd Examination.
			1st Examin.	2nd Examin.		
Shakspeare	75	50	45	69		
Latin Grammar	50	25	46	49		
Arithmetic	150	65	100	125		
Algebra	125	55	97	100		
Geometry	125	50	104	110		
Natural Philosophy...	75	35	61	60		
English Composition..	50	25	29	40		
English Grammar	50	25	37	35		
English Dictation, &c.	50	30	29 abs	45		
Mod. Hist. & Literature	100	60	70	85		
Modern Geography....	75	40	66	70		
Chemistry............	75	35	56	65		
Physiology	75	35	55	60		
Fr. Trans., Reading, &c	100	45	88	85		
French Grammar	50	25	33	40		
German	100	45	67	90		
Book-keeping	75	35	53	70		
Total value actually obtained			1,038	1,180 1,038		
Average of Average Ranks ...		6.15 2.21		2,218*		
Session Average Rank		3.94				

Session Absolute Rank, 4, in a Form of 23 Pupils.

1st Ex., 8 abs.

2nd Ex........

For careless Penmanship and bad Spelling in each Subject, five per cent. of the "*value actually obtained*" will be deducted.

---

* I have filled up the 1st and 2nd Examination Columns merely to illustrate the manner of working.   To find the Session Average, by which the Session Absolute Rank is settled, and Prizes, &c., distributed, add the 1st and 2nd Examination totals together, then divide by 1,000, and subtract quotient (2.21) from the Average of Average Ranks (6.15).

UPPER CANADA COLLEGE.

Report ending..............of..............Form VI.

RESULTS FOR THE SESSION.

EXAMINATION MARKS.*

SUBJECTS.	Maximum Value.	Minimum Value for First Class.	Minimum Value for Second Class.	Minimum Value for Third Class.	Value actually obtained. 1st Examination.	2nd Examination.	Remarks on 1st Examination.	Remarks on 2nd Examination.
Latin	200	150	120	100				
Latin Grammar	75	56	45	37				
Latin Composition	75	56	45	37				
Greek	150	112	90	75				
Greek Grammar	75	56	45	37				
Antiq. Anct. His. & Geog	65	48	39	32				
English	125	93	75	62				
English Composition..	60	45	36	30				
Modern History & Geog	75	56	45	37				
Arithmetic	125	93	75	62				
Algebra	150	112	90	75				
Geometry	150	112	90	75				
Mensuration and Trig..	100	75	60	50				
Chemistry & Physiology	75	56	45	37				
French	100	75	60	50				
French Grammar	60	45	36	30				
Total value actually obtained								
Average of Average Ranks.....								
Session Average Rank........								

Session Absolute Rank......in a Form of......Pupils.

Please to examine carefully the above Report, compare it with the preceding (if any), and the notice to Parents and Guardians on page ——

N.B.—This Report to be carefully preserved by the Parent or Guardian. The duplicate is kept by the Pupil.

1st Ex....................

2nd Ex....................

Pupils answering three-fourths of *Maximum Value* of any Subject, are entitled to First Class Honours in that Subject, while those who answer two-thirds secure Second Class Honours. Those answering one-half of the Maximum Value are placed in the Third Class.

---

* Teachers will easily perceive, by above Report of Examination Marks, how they might prepare similar programmes, embracing the Public School Subjects.

G. V. L.

CLIFTON PUBLIC SCHOOL.

DAILY RECORD OF PROGRESS of 2nd Division, for Month of April, 1875.

SUBJECTS—GEOGRAPHY AND GRAMMAR.

Geography on Tuesdays and Thursdays; Grammar on Mondays, Wednesdays, and Fridays.

Register No.	Names of Pupils.	M.	T.	W.	Th.	F.	M.	T.	W.	Th.	F.	M.	T.	W.	Th.	F.	M.	T.	W.	Th.	F.	Total.	Order of merit.	Remarks
	Date..	5	6	7	8	9	12	13	14	15	16	19	20	21	22	23	26	27	28	29	30			
350	G. Coulthurst	3	1	5	3	1	1	3	3	1	5	3	5	1	3	5	3	5	1	3	3	58	3	
341	A. Mitchel	1	3	3	5	1	3	1	3	5	1	5	3	1	3	5	3	3	5	3	3	60	1	abs. 1
352	R. Lawrence	1	3	5	3	3	1	1	1	3	5	3	3	3	a	9	1	3	3	1	5	59	2	
353	S. Wagstaff	5	3	3	3	3	5	3	3	3	3	1	3	5	5	a	a	8	3	5	1	57	4	abs. 1
354	R. McGarr	1	3	3	1	3	3	5	3	1	3	5	3	5	3	3	3	1	a	3	3	55	5	abs. 1
355	W. McMurray	1	3	1	1	1	3	a	3	3	1	3	3	5	3	1	5	3	5	3	5	54	6	
356	C. Groom	3	1	1	3	1	5	3	1	1	1	3	1	a	3	5	3	5	3	3	3	50	7	abs. 2

NOTE.—The system, of which the above is a specimen (see pages 146-148), is more simple than that of the Upper Canada College, and may therefore be regarded as more suitable for the generality of Common Schools. But it makes no provision for ascertaining the *Average* and *Absolute* Ranks, the "No. times head," or the "No. times absent"—essential elements in any system which aims at giving the *true* standing in scholarship of each pupil. In the above sample we have suggested an improvement which, to some extent, obviates the defects of the system while retaining its simplicity—namely, the addition of the columns headed "Order of merit," and "Remarks," in the latter of which the letters "abs" indicate absent. These columns are not used in the American system. The "Order of merit" column corresponds with that headed "Absolute Rank" in the Upper Canada College system; but instead of being indicated through the medium of "Average Rank," it is assumed to be shown by the number of marks obtained by the pupil as exhibited in "the Total." In this system, 5 marks are awarded for a Perfect Recitation, 3 for a Good Recitation, and 1 for Middling (see page 148). In the Clifton Schools the numbers 2 and 4 are omitted in this system, so that the degree of merit may be more characteristic, and the method of recording it more simple. If the intermediate numbers were used, it would sometimes be a matter of some difficulty to remember the various shades of merit until the close of the lesson—the time when they should be recorded. G. V. L.

CLIFTON PUBLIC SCHOOL.

RECORD OF PROGRESS of 1st Division (Fifth Class), for Week ending 25th June, 1875.

PUPILS' NAMES	Register No.	MONDAY					TUESDAY					WEDNESDAY					THURSDAY					FRIDAY					SUMMARY				
Subjects		P.	G.	AE	R.	Dp	Sp.	Ch.	A.	B.	Dp	Gr.	R.	A.	H.	Dp	Sp.	G.	A.	B.	Dp	Gr.	NP	H.	C.	Dp	Total	Average Rank	Absolute Rank	Failed in Recitat'n	No. times Absent
L. Wallace..	342	5	3	3	5	5	5	3	3	5	5	5	3	5	5	5	5	5	3	5	5	0	5	5	3	5	108	4.41	1 Eq	1	
L. Butters..	343	3	5	3	5	5	5	5	5	3	5	3	5	5	5	5	0	5	5	3	5	5	5	5	5	5	107	4.41	1 Eq	1	
M. McKerley	348	5	1	3	3	5	5	5	3	5	5	5	5	3	5	5	5	0	3	5	5	5	5	0	3	5	99	4.30	2	2	
L. Redpath..	344	1	5	6	1	5	3	5	5	3	5	3	3	5	5	5	5	5	3	0	5	0	5	3	5	5	96	3.95	3	2	
A. Butters..	357	3	5	3	5	5	5	1	1	3	5	5	3	3	5	5	3	3	5	3	5	3	0	3	5	5	93	3.91	4	1	
N. Preston..	360	3	3	1	5	5	3	3	3	0	5	3	3	3	5	5	5	3	3	3	5	5	0	a	a	a	75	3.40	5	1	3

NOTE.—The Record system, of which the above is a sample, is chiefly our own invention. It imposes less labour on the teacher than either of the foregoing methods, and may therefore be preferred in those schools where the attendance is large in proportion to the number of teachers. It combines most (if not all) the advantages of the preceding methods, and has but one disadvantage—namely, that its tendency is to exhibit merit in the aggregate of subjects rather than in each individual subject. This, however, may be considered an advantage by some, as it simplifies the teacher's work without affecting the pupil's general standing. In this system the slip (or slips) to the left, on which the pupils' names are to be written, is not attached to "the rest of the sheet", except at the top. Hence, when a leaf is filled up with merit marks, another can be turned over and filled up in like manner, without imposing the necessity of re-writing the pupils' names. In fact by this system, the names, once written, will do for the whole year, and for all subjects. The pupils' register numbers should be placed on the Record sheet to the right of the slip, so that the latter, if considered desirable, might be dispensed with, without inconvenience. The space allotted to each day is divided into five or more equal portions, at the head of which the teacher (before recording the results of a recitation) will write the subject or its initial letter.* The numbers 5, 3 and 1 are used, as in the preceding system, to indicate the respective degrees of merit. At the end of the week the total marks obtained are added together and divided by the number of lessons received. The result gives the Average Rank of each pupil for the week. This Average Rank indicates the Absolute Rank. The succeeding columns to the right indicate respectively the number of lessons in which the pupil failed, and the number which he did not attend. We may here observe that, unless the teacher wishes to keep a Record which will indicate the slightest relative difference in merit, he may take it for granted (as in the preceding system, page 299) that the *Total* (without division) will sufficiently indicate the Absolute Rank or individual order of merit. To find the monthly, or quarterly, order of merit, add the weekly Absolute Ranks together and divide the amount by the number of weeks. In a short time we purpose to publish a *Recitation Record*, or *Daily Register of Progress*, for use in public schools. It will be based on the preceding principles, and will contain all the more recent improvements, whilst imposing the least possible amount of work on the teacher.　G. V. L.

* Thus as above :— P.—Physiology. A.—Arithmetic or Algebra. Dp.—Deportment. Ch.—Chemistry. Gr.—Grammar. N.P.—Natural Philosophy.
G.—Geography. R.—Reading; E.—Euclid. Sp.—Spelling. B.—Botany. H.—History. C.—Composition.

CLIFTON PUBLIC SCHOOL.

FIFTH CLASS.

Report of...............................*for the term of 4 weeks*
ending..............*187*

	Possible.	Obtained
	MERIT MARKS.	
SUBJECTS OF STUDY, ETC.	Possible.	Obtained
Deportment	100	......
Spelling, Dictation, and Derivation....	40	......
Reading	40	......
Geography and use of Globes..........	40	......
Writing and Book-keeping............	60	......
Arithmetic—Mental and Written......	80	......
Natural History	20	......
Composition	40	......
Grammar and Analysis	60	......
History—Ancient and Modern	40	......
Algebra	30	......
Drawing and Mapping................	40	......
Botany and Chemistry	40	......
Natural Philosophy	20	......
Geometry and Mensuration	50	......
Reviews	..	......

Days absent......... Times late.........
Ranks........in a class of.............pupils.

Left margin: " As Sands make the Mountains, so Moments make the Year."

Right margin: "Act well your Part, there all the Honour lies." "No Pains, no Gains."

Parents are requested to examine, sign, and return this Report, and to visit the School as often as convenient.

.... *Parent or Guardian.*

.... *Head Master.*

TIME TABLES.

In pages 100–103 of this work, we pointed out the absolute necessity of a good "Working Time Table." We believe that the construction of such a plan of work is no small test of a teacher's administrative ability, especially when there is a great inequality between the number of classes and the number of teachers. Such a duty is a matter of more than ordinary difficulty to young teachers who have had little or no professional experience, or Normal School Training. We therefore append a few specimens, which may be of some assistance. In the construction of a Time Table, teachers must necessarily be governed by circumstances—by the number of pupils, teachers, studies, classes and class-rooms. They should not be too hasty in changing, or prescribing a plan of work ; but once fixed or adopted, it should be scrupulously followed. Let the teacher first prepare, and work for a week or two by, a *trial* Time Table in which due provision is made for the more essential subjects. He may, in the meantime, distribute the less important subjects according to their relative value and the time at his disposal, making sure that, while each class (or section) is reciting, the others are engaged in the work of preparation. He will thus provide suitable work for all classes at all times during school hours. The following Tables are copies of those in use at a Canadian Public School, in which there is a registered attendance of 360 pupils, and an average of 230. This institution may be regarded as a fair average specimen of the Graded School. It has five class rooms ; but only four teachers—a head master and three lady assistants. The pupils are graded, according to their attainments, into four divisions, each division being subdivided into two sections.

In rural districts, schools cannot, of course, be graded in this manner; still the following tables may afford such suggestions as will materially aid the young teacher in the construction of a plan of study suitable to the attainments, requirements, &c., of his pupils, and the peculiar circumstances of his locality.

A GRADED PUBLIC SCHOOL OF FOUR DIVISIONS.

TIME TABLE—Fourth or Primary Division.

Hours.	Length of Time.	Subjects.
9.00 to 9.10	10	Opening Exercises.
9.10— 9.45	35	Tablet Lessons (1st Sec.)
9.45—10.00	15	Singing, &c.
10.00—10.30	30	Tablet Lessons (2nd Sec.)
10.30—10.50	20	Intermission.
10.50—11.20	30	Arithmetic (Mental).
11.20—11.30	10	Calisthenical Exercises.
11.30—12.00	30	Reading and Spelling (1st Sec.)
12.00— 1.00	60	Intermission.
1.00— 1.40	40	Tablet Lessons (2nd Sec.)
1.40— 2.00	20	Writing on Slates or Black Board.
2.00— 2.10	10	Calisthenical Exercises.
2.10— 2.30	20	Arithmetic (on Slates or Black Board.)
2.30— 2.50	20	Intermission.
2.50— 3.20	30	Object Lesson.
3.10— 3.20	10	Singing.
3.20— 3.50	30	Reading and Spelling (1st Sec.)
3.50— 4.00	10	Closing Exercises.

A GRADED PUBLIC SCHOOL.

TIME TABLE—THIRD DIVISION (SECOND CLASS).

Div. of Time.	Min.	Monday.	Tuesday.	Wednesday.	Thursday.	Friday.
9.00 to 9.10	10	Opening Exercises.	Opening Exercises.	Opening Exercises.	Opening Exercises.	Opening Exercises.
9.10— 9.45	35	(1) Arithmetic.	(1) Arithmetic.	(1) Arithmetic	(1) Arithmetic.	(1) Arithmetic.
9.45—10.20	35	(2) Arithmetic.	(2) Arithmetic.	(2) Arithmetic.	(2) Arithmetic.	(2) Arithmetic.
10.20—10.30	10	Tables.	Tables.	Tables.	Tables.	Tables.
10.30—10.50	20	Intermission.	Intermission.	Intermission.	Intermission.	Intermission.
10.50—11.20	30	(1) Read. and Spell.	(1) Read. and Spell.	(1) Read. and Spell	(1) Read. and Spell.	(1) Read. and Spell.
11.20—11.30	10	Singing.	Calisthenics.	Singing.	Calisthenics.	Singing.
11.30—12.00	30	(2) Read. and Spell.	(2) Read. and Spell.	(2) Read. and Spell.	(2) Read. and Spell.	(2) Read. and Spell.
12.00— 1.00	60	Intermission.	Intermission.	Intermission.	Intermission.	Intermission.
1.00— 1.30	30	Geography.	Grammar.	Object Lesson.	Geography.	Grammar.
1.30— 2.00	30	(1) Read. and Spell.	(1) Read. and Spell	(1) Read. and Spell.	(1) Read. and Spell.	(1) Read. and Spell.
2.00— 2.30	30	(2) Read. and Spell.	(2) Read. and Spell.	(2) Read. and Spell.	(2) Read. and Spell.	(2) Read. and Spell.
2.30— 2.50	20	Intermission.	Intermission.	Intermission.	Intermission.	Intermission.
2.50— 3.30	40	Mental Arithmetic, &c.	Mental Arithmetic, Writing.	Mental Arithmetic, &c.	Mental Arithmetic, Writing.	Object Lesson.
3.30— 4.00	30	Writing.	Vocal Music.	Writing.	Vocal Music.	Dictation.

21

A GRADED PUBLIC SCHOOL.

TIME TABLE—Second Division (Third Class).

Time.	Min.	Monday.	Tuesday.	Wednesday.	Thursday.	Friday.
9.00 to 9.10	10	Opening Exercises.	Opening Exercises.	Opening Exercises.	Opening Exercises.	Opening Exercises.
9.10— 9.20	10	Tables.	Tables.	Tables.	Tables.	Tables.
9.20—10.00	40	(1) Arithmetic B. B.†	(1) Ment. Arithmetic.	(1) Arithmetic, B.B.	(1) Ment. Arithmetic.	(1) } Written
10.00—10.30	30	(2) Arithmetic B. B.	Dict. and Spell.	(2) Arithmetic, B. B.	Dict. and Spell.	(2) } Examination.
10.30—11.00	30	§				
11.00—11.30	30	(1) Geography.	(1) Grammar.	(1) Geography.	(1) Grammar.	(1) Composition.
11.30—12.00	30	(2) Grammar.	(2) Geography.	(2) Grammar.	(2) Geography.	(2) Grammar.
12.00— 1.00	60	¶				
1.00— 1.30	30	(1) Parsing, &c.	(1) Arithmetic.	(1) Parsing, &c.	(1) Arithmetic.	(1) Crit. Comp. ‡
1.30— 2.00	30	(2) Reading.	(2) Reading.	(2) Reading.	(2) Reading.	(2) Reading.
2.00— 2.30	30	(1) Reading.	(1) Reading.	(1) Reading.	(1) Reading.	(1) Reading.
2.30— 2.50	20	‖				
2.50— 3.30	40	{(2) Ment. Arithmetic. Writing.	{(2) Drawing. (1) Copy Prose.	{(2) Ment. Arithmetic. (1) Copy Poetry.	{(2) Map Drawing. Writing.	Spelling (General).
3.30— 4.00	30	Vocal Music.	Writing.	Writing.	Vocal Music.	Drawing.

† Black Board. § Intermission and Studies. ¶ Dinner Hour. ‡ Criticism of Compositions. ‖ Intermission.

A GRADED PUBLIC SCHOOL.

TIME TABLE—FIRST DIVISION (FOURTH AND FIFTH CLASSES).

Time.	Min.	Monday.	Tuesday.	Wednesday.	Thursday.	Friday.
9.00 to 9.15	15	Opening Exercises. ‖	Opening Exercises.	Opening Exercises.	Opening Exercises.	Opening Exercises.
9.15— 9.55	40	(5) H. Physiology.	(5) Dict. and Spell.	(5) Gram. and Anal.	(5) Dict. and Spell.	(5) Gram. and Anal.
9.55—10.30	35	(4) Grammar.	(4) Geography.	(4) Dict. and Spell.	(4) Grammar.	(4) Dict. and Spell.
10.30—10.50	20	*				
10.50—11.30	40	(5) Geography.	(5) Correspondence.	(5) Algebra or D. E. ‡	(5) { Geography and Use of Globes.	(5) Nat. Philosophy.
11.30—12.00	30	(4) A. Physiology.	{(4)(5)} ‡. E. Chemistry.	(4) Geography.	(4) Composition.	(4) Drawing.
12.00— 1.00	60	*				
1.00— 2.00	60	(5) { Arithmetic and (4) } Euclid.	Arith. Mensuration and Book-keeping.	Arithmetic and Euclid.	Arithmetic, Algebra and Book-keeping.	(5) Botany.
2.00— 2.30	30					(4) Reviews, &c.
2.30— 2.50	20	*				
2.50— 3.10	20	(4) Reading.	(5) Botany.	(4) Reading.	(5) Reading.	Crit. Composition.
3.10— 3.35	25	(5) History.	(4) History.	(5) History.	(4) History.	Readings and Recitations.
3.35— 3.55	20	Writing.	Writing, †	Writing.	Writing, †	§
3.55— 4.00	5	Closing Exercises.	Closing Exercises.	Closing Exercises.	Closing Exercises.	

* Intermissions. † Fifth Class, Drawing. § Military Drill alternate Fridays. ‡ Domestic Economy.

‖ Prescribed Prayers, and Readings from the Bible (without comment).